atara
press

There Goes a Mensch

ALEXANDER GRANACH

There Goes a Mensch
A Memoir

Atara Press

Original title:
There Goes an Actor

Published by Atara Press, Los Angeles
Library of Congress Control Number: 2011961416
Copyright © 2019 Atara Press and the Estates of Gad and Alexander Granach
No part of this work may be reproduced without publisher consent in writing
Photo permissions: Akademie der Künste, Alexander Granach Archive, Berlin
Originally published in 1945 as *There Goes an Actor* by Doubleday Doran, New York, and as *Da geht ein Mensch* by Neuer Verlag, Stockholm
Translated from the German by Willard Ropes Trask
Leopold Lindtberg permissions: Susanna Lindtberg
Lindtberg translation by David Edward Lane
Text set in Linotype Janson 11 pt.

ISBN-13: 978-0-9822251-5-8

Paper sourced from environmentally aware forest product companies. Editions printed in the United Kingdom, United States, and Germany

Contents

Leopold Lindtberg on Alexander Granach..............................ix
1. *I Bear the Name of a Friendly Man*..................................1
2. *How I Came into This World on a Rainy Night*.................8
3. *How I Was Exorcised of a Little Toothless Goblin*............13
4. *My Big Brothers, or One Is Missing*..............................17
5. *Mama Dreams*..23
6. *Two Families – Four Friendships*..................................28
7. *The First Victim*..35
8. *He Could Not Read the Bible. But Neither Had He Heard the Sermon of the Village Priest*......................40
9. *We Go Out into the Wide World, but It Wears the Same Face*..45
10. *The Village Spits Us Out*..48
11. *The County Seat Horodenka – Fierce Competition*..........55
12. *My Rabbi-Teacher, Schimshale from Milnitz, for Whom You Would Do Absolutely Anything*................63
13. *Perhaps My First Part*..73
14. *Moische, Does One Smash Windows?*..............................82
15. *Our Family Grows Smaller, Our Poverty Greater*...........86
16. *My Brother Schmiel, with the Rich Imagination, Comes Home* 92
17. *Everyone Fights with the Weapons He Has*....................98
18. *People and the Awakening of Love in Horodenka*..........104
19. *Away from Home It Is Cold – but Instructive*................106

20. Curiosity..127
21. It Is Good to Have a Big Brother When You Are Far
    from Home..136
22. Malka..146
23. The Theater..155
24. A Dog, a Cart, and a Woman......................170
25. First Steps in Berlin.................................191
26. The Word...203
27. There Is Something in a Name..................217
28. And the Crooked Shall Be Straight.............231
29. Alas for a Beautiful World!.......................246
30. Almost a Stranger in My Native Land.........255
31. The Prospect for the Common Man............267
32. Let People See What People Are Like!........277
33. "We'll March Right into Sunny Italy!".........287
34. Roads Always Lead Somewhere..................295
35. Life Comes to Meet You Halfway................315
36. A Promise That I Shall Always Keep...........333
37. "Home, Home – There's Where a Welcome Waits You!" 345
38. A Man Is Not a Tree..................................358
39. Interrupted Rehearsals.............................368
40. Shylock..376

Timeline...383
A Note on the Translator.................................384
Further Readings & Resources.........................385

Leopold Lindtberg on Alexander Granach

Granach's lovely autobiographical book is entitled, in English, *There Goes an Actor*. The German title is *Da geht ein Mensch*. Both titles are actually correct. Indeed, it takes the two together to best express the spirit and intent of his book. Alex – as his countless friends called him – loved and idolized the theater with a level of passion as if he were completely possessed by it. Yet he could also allow himself to become fully absorbed in almost anything to do with the human condition that he happened to stumble upon.

He was the warmest and most generous friend one could possibly imagine. Among his circle could be counted actors – mostly young and hungry – writers, celebrities and *schnorrers* alike, but also ordinary respectable people, craftsmen and laborers, taxi drivers, and girls of every stripe and social status. Perhaps surprisingly, he actually spoke about the theater much less than other actors. One would frequently find him in the company of people from his homeland, speaking in Yiddish, Ukrainian, and occasionally Russian, amongst themselves.

His countrymen called him the "King of the Eastern Jews." Sometimes he had a bit of the air of a Tatar horseman chief about him. Only with more bourgeois types did he not keep company so fondly. Indeed, he was seen as an iconoclast, and it was a role he relished. He often ran around Berlin in character, whichever one it was he was playing at the time – with a shaven head when performing as the convict Karl Thomas, or as Lenin, or with hair dyed flaming red as Red Adams in Upton Sinclair's *Singing Jailbirds*. In reality, he bore a resemblance to the world chess champion, Boris Spassky.

Granach was medium height, broad shouldered, stocky, very agile, strong as a bear and fierce, but through and through good natured, and endlessly tender and considerate towards the weak and less fortunate. Only when things turned anti-Semitic could he become a threat to someone. He once sent a stagehand, a very Prussian type, to the hospital. At home he liked to go around unclothed, would stand on his head, and in the kitchen, when he was preparing his ever popular and always imaginative, transformative stew of leftovers, he wore an apron in front and left a fantastically harry backside open.

The last time I saw him, it was in Zurich. He had returned from Kiev wearing high boots and was delivering his final performances in German with a German ensemble, as Macbeth at the *Schauspielhaus*, and as the blacksmith in Gerhart Hauptmann's *The Weavers*. He was stupendous. The reunion of our old Berlin group – Kaiser, Steckel, Ginsberg, Horwitz, Teo Otto, and myself – was a celebration. Of his experiences in Russia, he spoke half with great admiration and half with skepticism. He was treated as a prominent guest while there and shown around extensively. He was deeply impressed by the large-scale industrial projects and the new housing and cultural centers of the Soviet Union. While still in Kiev, he wanted to send a telegram to Stalin to express his enthusiasm and addressed it to "Comrade Joseph Vissarionovich Stalin." However, at the post office he was told that any telegram to the Great Leader of the Soviet People had to be addressed with all his titles. That was a bit too much for him, and he forewent the idea.

I came to New York in the spring of 1945 and learned Granach had passed away after an appendix removal surgery, suffering a sudden blocked artery afterwards, all just a few days before. He was fifty-four years old and his film career in the US was solidly underway. His passing was swift and painless.

– Leopold Lindtberg, April 1971

There Goes a Mensch

1

I Bear the Name of a Friendly Man

The earth in East Galicia is black and juicy and always looks half asleep, like a sleek good-natured cow standing still to be milked. Thankfully and a thousand times over, the earth of East Galicia gives back whatever it receives, and you do not need to bribe it with manure or chemicals.

The earth of East Galicia is prodigal and rich. It spouts forth black oil, and bears golden tobacco, and grain as heavy as lead, and old dreamy woods, and rivers, and lakes, and, above all, handsome, healthy men: Ukrainians, Poles, Jews. The three all look alike, despite their different manners and customs.

The men of East Galicia are slow and good-natured, a little lazy, and fruitful like their mother earth. Wherever you look, you see children, like litters of little kittens. Children in the farmyards, children with the animals, children in the fields, children in the barns, children in the stables, children! – as if they grew on trees every spring like cherries.

When spring comes to a Galician village, there are calves and foals and suckling pigs, and lambs and chicks and ducklings and those small whimpering human creatures: children.

The village in which I was born is called Wierzbowce in Polish, Werbowitz in Yiddish, and Werbiwci in Ukrainian. It is near Seroka. Seroka is near Czerniatyn. Czerniatyn is near

Horodenka. Horodenka is near Gwozdziez. Gwozdziez near Kolomea. Kolomea near Stanislau. Stanislau near Lemberg. Lemberg became famous in the world through the Hollywood picture, *Hotel Stadt Lemberg.*

My parents lived in the village of Werbiwci and already had eight children. Life was hard, especially for my mama. She was everything to my father: wife, sweetheart, she gave birth to a child every year, kept the house, cooked and baked, did the washing, waited on customers in the shop, dug in the garden, where she raised, not flowers, but potatoes and cabbages and onions and cucumbers. And every other minute a brat would come running up and pull at her skirt and demand food.

It is true that the older children helped her take care of the little ones – kept them busy, carried them around, fed them, washed them, dressed them, undressed them, put them to bed, and even spanked them. But all the burden fell on her, my little mama: she was here, there, and everywhere all day long. She got up with the chickens and was the last to fall into bed – oh, so tired! The whole household of ten souls was in her hands, and the chief worry was always: not enough to eat.

We baked bread of the cheapest, blackest, coarsest flour, but it tasted good to us even without butter. Yes, onions and garlic were kept hidden, because onions and garlic made us want to eat more. The newly baked bread was kept hidden too, not because it might spoil our little stomachs, but because fresh bread went down faster; and we never got to see it until it was several days old. We cooked huge pots of potatoes, we baked corn bread, we cooked polenta with bean soup – the polenta was always cut with a string – we cooked cabbage and carrots, and rice with peas, and often made dumplings with buckwheat, and even *piroushki* stuffed with potato, and we ate everything clean like locusts.

At the same time our childhood had wealth of adventure and play that we would not have exchanged for the prettiest, richest and gayest and best-equipped of nurseries. We dug in the garden, built houses out of straw and clay, wagons out of old chairs, sleds out of kindling, and the young of the neighbors' livestock had to join in. Calves and foals, even the ducks and hens, were harnessed to our wagons. We made lanterns out of pumpkins; the dogs had to take part in everything. Only the cats and geese were left out. The cats disappeared and the geese bit – the silly geese!

Whether the animals enjoyed it as much as we did, I do not know – we certainly were happy. The older children acted like grownups, but when no one was looking, they joined in too. Father especially enjoyed taking part in our games more than anyone else. But Mother – poor Mama! – was generally tired and cross. When we bothered her she struck out, distributing cuffs and shoves and pinches, and even kicked us when we got in her way. Poor little Mama! Things were hard for her. For the grown children loved Father much better. Though Father worked hard all day long too, somehow he always had time for us. Especially on Sabbath morning – then most of us would creep into his bed and we were allowed to ride on him and braid his beard into funny pigtails. And he answered the little ones' questions as if they were grown-up, and had a wise word for everyone, always something different. Yes, Father knew how to treat us. He took us seriously.

So we grew to have a deep admiration for our father, and, because he was learned, knew the Talmud, could quote the whole Bible from memory and read and write – even Polish! – our neighbors and the peasants of the village revered him too. But in us, his children, there developed a blind love and veneration for him – and almost the opposite for our mother. Poor little Mama! She was very unhappy, mother and wife, sweetheart and housemaid, childbearer and nurse, poor thing, poor little thing! And she was only a child herself, an innocent, unsuspecting child, with no freedom and no joys; all that she knew was work and duties, duties and work.

One day she broke down, overwhelmed by weariness, and could not go on. She went to bed in the middle of the day and lay there weeping and shrieking and wanted either to die or be divorced.

When such things happened a poor relative of ours always came out from town – old Isaiah Berkowitz. He was even poorer than we were, and he came often to the village and spent a week or two in turn with each of the four Jewish families. He cleared up misunderstandings and quarrels, talked with the teacher, examined the children, scolded the men, advised the women, and everyone listened to him, everyone liked him, especially the Ukrainian peasants. Wherever he stayed, in the evening that house was full. The old peasants flooded him with questions, and he had an answer for everything, with a parable and a lively illustration.

He was in his seventies, short, and peasant-like. His face, tanned like leather by wind and rain, was almost smooth; there were only little white tufts of wiry hair on his upper lip, under his chin, and between his cheekbones and his ears. He dressed partly like a Ukrainian peasant, with a fur cap, summer and winter, for hot weather and cold. He had large, wise, kindly eyes, and the peasants called him "Shaiko Rozum" – that is, "Isaiah Wisdom."

He would often even pray and sing Hebrew psalms in Ukrainian, for he held that God understood all languages, if only those who prayed and sang were honest with Him. And he, Shaiko Rozum, was honest with everyone. He spoke his mind to the rich and the respected, but always good-naturedly, with a joke and an anecdote. And another thing – he never had any money, and never touched any. Yet he loved eating and drinking, and on Friday evening or the Sabbath, when he had had a few glasses, he sang Yiddish and Ukrainian melodies, and told folk tales that were mixtures of Yiddish and Slavish legends with parables and instances and wise sayings.

So that was old Shaiko Rozum, who came to us now.

He sat down by Mother's bed like a doctor and sent everyone out, and listened to her and talked to her for a long time. Father waited outside, embarrassed, and began one piece of work after another. He milked the cow, winnowed grain, chopped straw, prepared the calf's food – as he always did; that day he even cooked. We children were always happy when Father cooked; he always did on High Holidays and when poor Mama brought forth a child; and our good Mama brought one forth every year.

Shaiko Rozum came out of the room, started to reason with Father, and together they went for a walk in the fields. The little ones were shouting and running about in the next-door neighbor's garden with the next-door neighbor's children; the grown children kept on with their work. The two men returned, serious and silent.

That day everyone went to bed early, and the next morning the horse was harnessed and Mother and Father and old Shaiko Rozum set off for the town. The older children looked after the house, the little ones disappeared with a troop of neighbors' children to rob someone's orchard, and no one knew what was going to happen.

The wise white horse, who was like a member of the family, something like a big brother, had been fed oats that morning, and he pulled with a will, strong and brisk as if he wanted to say, "Yes, if you give me oats, I'll show you what I can do!"

The three sat together on one rather narrow seat of straw and blankets. Father drove, and no one spoke.

Old Shaiko began to tell a story, about *his* uncle who had once gone to the rabbi with *his* wife for a divorce, and this is what happened:

"When my uncle and his wife came to the rabbi's house to be divorced, there was a neighbor standing by the door, and he took my uncle aside and said, 'Well, Chaim, you must be glad you're going to get rid of that old shrew at last.' But Uncle Chaim looked at his neighbor and said, 'Who gave you the right to speak like that about my wife?' And when the rabbi had divorced them and my uncle stepped out of the house, the same neighbor came up to him and said, 'I congratulate you on getting rid of that old witch. You must be very happy!'

Upon which my uncle turned to him and said, You should be ashamed of yourself, neighbor, to say such a thing to me about a strange woman,' and left him standing there."

After that they drove on in silence for a while; then, in the distance, they saw a shining brown carriage drawn by four horses approaching at a gallop. Shaiko made Father stop. There were a coachman and a footman on the box, and in the carriage sat the Polish landowner, Podbielsky, and his wife, both wrapped in a green velvet carriage robe. Old Shaiko said, "Look well at those two."

The carriage was coming nearer and nearer, the landowner and his wife were in high spirits, laughing and joking so loudly that you could hear their words, and when the two Jews greeted them, baring their heads, the landowner merely answered by putting his finger for an instant to his hat. When they had driven by, Shaiko Rozum turned to Father and began:

"Did you hear how happy they were? Did you see how he looked at her and flattered her, and how she laughed? What do you think, Aaron: is she more to him in his house, at his table, in his bed? She has borne him two children and has cooks and servants and coachmen and nurses and governesses. And yours has borne you, God be thanked, already eight children, and is to you wife and cook and nurse and governess and maid and washerwoman – everything, everything. But he laughs with his wife and flatters her and makes her gay, while you, Aaron, are driving to town, to the rabbi, to be divorced!"

Father murmured, embarrassed: "Don't twist things around, Shaiko Rozum. It is not I who is going to town to get a divorce, it is my wife, and it isn't my fault, either, that he is a landowner and I only a poor man."

And the woman, my mother, had tears running down her cheeks, and was already much lighter of heart, and said: "Well, I don't insist on being divorced, either, and I never reproached no one for being rich or poor."

"Yes, yes," said old Shaiko Rozum, "we must go home first anyhow, to ask the children which of them want to go with their mother and which with their father."

But the woman's face, on which the tears had not yet dried, was already smiling, and she said softly: "Go home, yes. But nobody is going to be asked, and nobody should know nothing."

Father turned the wagon around, and Shaiko said, "Come, Aaron, drive home quickly, for at home it is always best."

But Father said: "No. See the inn over there to the left? We're going to stop there first."

So they drove over to the inn. Shaiko Rozum crawled down from the wagon first, then Father lifted little Mama down from the seat of straw, and now her cheeks were glowing. And for the first time that day they looked into each other's eyes, and they stood there together quite still, and he said:

"You belong to me. You are not my maid, you are not my washerwoman, you are not my cook, and you are no one's governess. But you are mine, the mother of my children, my sister, my child, and my friend, for all eternity, amen."

And, embarrassed and smiling, they came into the inn, and sat down at the table with old Shaiko, and drank vodka and ate hard-boiled eggs with white rolls, just like rich people; old Shaiko drank and smiled across the table at them. Then they bought more rolls and pretzels to take home to the children.

And just nine months later I came into the world.

And during those nine months old Shaiko came to visit us several times, and then he died, the good man.

So I was given his name, and my father often used to say to me, "My son, you bear the name of a friendly man."

2

How I Came into This World on a Rainy Night

In our village of Werbiwci there were about a hundred and fifty Ukrainian families and four Jewish families. All made their living by tilling the soil. The Jews kept little shops besides, and one of them rented the village inn from the landowner.

There were two hills in the village: On one stood the little wooden church with the dome like an onion; and on the other lay the landowner's estate. The little huts of the village had thatched roofs, browned and blackened by chimney smoke; the rain came down the chimney, and you could always tell by the smell of the smoke whether your neighbors were cooking meat. The landowners' stables and barns and servants' quarters had thatched roofs too. There was only one house that was white and had a flower bed; and its roof was laid with wooden shingles. To us, it was something foreign – that house belonged to the Polish landowner.

Between the landowner and the village there was a wall. A strange world. He and his wife and his children, and even his servants, did not mix with the people of the village. They spoke a different language too: Polish. The landowner's clothes were different, his children's clothes were different, they talked differently and ate differently. I still remember how little Nikola, my foster brother who was the same age as I, came running one day and said, "Oh, Mama, Mama, white rolls and butter taste wonderful!"

"How did you find that out?" asked his mother.

"I've been watching the landowner's children eat them."

We children of the village, Jewish and Ukrainian, seldom had an opportunity to encounter the landowner's children, and when we saw them drive by in their carriage, they were always shining clean, with their hair carefully curled. They wore rubbers when it rained, and even in summer they wore gloves. They looked down at us crossly and haughtily and stupidly. Just as their father looked down on the village.

From the landowner's house a close-set avenue of poplars, led to the highroad, for the village lay a few miles to one side. The village inn was kept by Elikune. Then there was old David Berkowitz, and my uncle Leiser, and we, the Aaron Granachs, who had little houses, gardens, a few acres of land, domestic animals, and small shops. We stocked our shops with everything from the town that the village needed: horseshoes, nails, dyed wool, thread, herrings, needles, petroleum, rolls, lubricating oil, work clothes, pepper, salt, candles, rolls of bright cloth, honey, sour pickles, and many other things. But we also dealt in eggs and grain and cattle which we raised.

The house we lived in consisted of a stable, a barn, and there was a dung heap, a garden, and two rooms. In both rooms there were a great many sleeping places. In summer most of us children slept in the barn and even in the stable. In winter both rooms were packed full, and often when the frost began to paint its flower pictures on the windows, a young calf or foal had to spend the night with us – a great amusement for us little ones. In one of the rooms was the stove, with an oven, and a place for cooking in front; the shop counter was installed in another corner. Beyond the empty doorframe was the other room, the good one. In there were two beds, a table with benches, and pictures on the walls. One was of the Jewish baron, Hirsch, clean-shaven except for a twirled mustache, with a stiff white shirt front, a stand-up collar, and a black cravat. Another represented Aaron, the High Priest, with twelve jeweled tablets across his chest, on which were engraved the twelve names of Jacob's twelve sons, from whom we are descended. He stood before a seven-branched candlestick, had a long snow-white beard, and was dressed in bright colors like a girl. Another picture showed Moses with a long staff, leading us by the nose from somewhere to somewhere else.

In one of the two beds a small, vigorous woman was lying now and writhing with pain: she was expecting her ninth child. Her husband, a tall, broad-shouldered man with kindly dark eyes and a long brownish black beard, was standing behind the counter in the outer room. The room was packed full of peasants. They were drinking hot tea with *prekuska*, which means they bit crunchingly into large lumps of sugar, while they sucked up the hot tea loudly and thoughtfully, smoked their pipes, spat on the floor at intervals, and talked slowly and inquisitively about politics and harvests, prices and the Bible. Others came and went, bought a candle or a herring, petroleum or a braided roll, matches or honey, salt or a horseshoe, a whip or a laxative, and paid sometimes in fresh-laid eggs, sometimes in grain, or linseed oil, or flour, or they "put it on the books" until their hens laid again or till the next calf or the next harvest. They would bargain a little, and they went to all three shops, doing business with the one who offered the most for their produce.

The groans from the other room now grew louder. The older peasants looked at each other in silence; one of them winked; others smiled a little slyly. They understood that the Aarons were about to multiply. And one after the other, they rose and went out, with a "good night" to Aaron in which there was already a little note of congratulation or a little note of condolence. For a new member of the family always meant: another hand to help, or another mouth to feed.

Only three young *parobki*, as the village lads who had just reached manhood were called, sat without moving, asked the Jew unimportant casual questions, made jokes, enjoyed the man's embarrassment, enjoyed the woman's groaning, and made no move to go.

The midwife came – an old crone who was part witch, part doctor, and part fortune teller. She did everything in the village. She brought children into the world, told girls who their husbands would be, advised unfruitful wives how to conceive, and made salves and remedies for the old peasants' sundry ills. What she did was not always successful, but she also knew how to cast spells and how to make curses, and she always reeked of vodka, so she was an authority before whom the village trembled.

As she entered the house, she snapped her fingers, and that meant, "A glass of vodka." For she never opened her mouth until she had been given a tea glass full. She drank, then said: "Good evening."

She looked around and told the lads to leave the house. But they got their tobacco out of their wide leather belts and rolled themselves cigarettes, and paid no attention to the old crone. She made a fire, put water on to boil, spat three times on both doorsills, and placing herself in a threatening posture before the lads, once again told them to leave the house. They laughed, took their shepherd's pipes out of their shirts and piped a folk song with an air of complete casualness. The old witch emptied her glass of vodka and began making signs in the air, threatening and cursing; she made a triple cross over the room and cried, "Quick, quick, good children, quick, you miserable lads, quick, take yourselves out of here or you'll sit there all the rest of your lives, as lame and stiff as a cow flop in winter!"

In the next room a human being was groaning because another human being was about to come into the world. The lads laughed and said that the witch's curses must have taken effect quickly, because they were stiff and lame and frozen already and could no longer get up from where they were sitting.

But now the four grown sons of the house came home from the weekly market; a scuffle, half play, half earnest, ensued, the lads were put out, the old crone threw hot water at them, and the door of the house was bolted. The woman groaned, the witch drank her second glass of vodka; those in the room heard the three lads playing a mocking song on their shepherd's pipes. Then a convulsion shook the woman's body: a small something appeared and whimpered.

The peasant lads outside greeted their newly arrived fellow man by smashing a windowpane and disappeared.

The men plugged the broken window with pillows and rags. The new boy creature seemed suddenly to suffer a shock; it began to wriggle, its small, delicate limbs writhed in a cramp.

The old crone was already drinking her third glass of vodka; the men sat in the other room and smoked in silence. The sons looked at their father almost reproachfully, and the father was embarrassed.

Then the old crone bathed the little one while cramps were twisting its tiny body from one side to the other and the mother was weeping desperately. The witch comforted her and said it was nothing to worry about, it was only a little third-class toothless goblin that had gotten into the baby; it could not be the big devil himself, because at this time of the year he was in a black nothingness at the other end of the world, where he was so tormented by a clever little pink angel, and in such terrible straits that he would stay there sweating blood and water for the next three months, and certainly could have no influence here.

And she could – here the witch drank her fourth tea glass full of vodka – yes, she easily could, in the next three or four months, drive the little toothless goblin out of the baby, but, of course, only if the mother would promise to keep quiet and tell no one and do just what the witch would tell her. The mother promised to obey.

And the little something was I, who came into the world on that rainy April night.

3

How I Was Exorcised of a Little Toothless Goblin

On that rainy April night, then, I came into the world. And brought still more anxiety into an already anxious existence. And brought still more disorder into a disorderly life.

Mama got up from her bed a week after I was born. The youngest boy, Schabse, who was just one year old, suddenly was grown-up and was no longer the baby; the baby was I. And what a baby! A little something, forever throwing its arms and legs about and crying day and night.

The old witch-midwife would always appear when my father and my big brothers were not there, bringing directions for exorcising me of the little toothless goblin. These she imparted to poor, worried, frightened Mama, who kept her promise to tell no one anything about the cure. So no one knew what the witch prescribed and no one knew what my mother paid her, not even Mama herself. For the witch took whatever she wanted from the shop: salt, kerosene, honey, herrings, braided rolls, spades, nails, and once even a saw and an ax. These she sold, much cheaper than we could, to our rich neighbor, Jus Fedorkiw, and thus turned it all into schnapps.

She was very careful not to encounter Father or my older brother; of my eldest brother she was especially afraid. He once came in when my mother was giving her a tea glass full of schnapps; he emptied the glass on the floor and forbade Mama once and for all to give her any. Whereupon she threatened to bewitch his calf. My brother immediately declared before witnesses that he held her responsible for the health of his calf, and if anything happened to it, if it showed even the slightest signs of diarrhea, he would have her taken away by the police. From then on she worried more about the health of his calf than he did.

My cure began with the old midwife digging around in our garden – no one knew for what, but one night, before the men returned from the market in town, she placed the infant in its swaddling clothes in a tub of water and put the tub into a hole in the garden and covered it over. Mama stood beside her with a lighted candle. The other children were crying with terror in the house. And the old woman muttered and spat and performed her hocus-pocus, saying:

"Listen, listen, wife of Aaron – as the grass grows, he will live, live and overcome the evil one!" And now she opened the pit and took the tub and baby into the house. And the next morning the high grass was to have grown over this place again.

But the baby was still plagued with cramps, and in the morning he vomited too. Then the old woman ordered that when the baby was restless at night, when the devil possessed him again, he was to be laid on the ground beside the bed and Mama must wait quietly until the evil one took flight.

So one night Mama laid me on the earthen floor. But the baby, no doubt with the assistance of the toothless goblin, bellowed so loudly that the whole house woke. Father lit a candle, thought the baby had fallen out of bed, and put him back beside his mother, who gave the child her breast, and hungrily it drank in the milk and the warmth and was quiet.

Then came the third cure. It was Tuesday again; the men were in town at the market. The old woman came, bringing with her some dough she had prepared, heated the oven, and began to bake a roll shaped like a giant doughnut. When the roll was beginning to brown, the baby was fastened to the bread shovel and pushed in and out of the oven at intervals, thrice three times, nine times in all. When the baking was finished, Mother took the baby and the old woman the huge doughnut, and they passed the baby nine times through the hole in it, while the old woman muttered over and over:

> *"Little Shaiko through the roll,*
> *Little goblin in the roll,*
> *He who eats, let him not forget,*
> *That he the goblin too has et."*

Then the baby was given a bath and the old woman disappeared, carrying the roll away in a sack.

When the villagers were coming home from the fair that evening, rich Jus Fedorkiw's great black wolfhound, who had run ahead of his master, found the huge ring-roll hanging from the stone cross at the road junction. Hungry as usual, he jumped up and bit into it. But he did not eat much, because not only flour and water, but phosphorous and sulphur of nine times nine boxes of matches had been baked into it. The great black wolfhound howled suddenly as his ancestors, the wolves, had howled when they were near death. All the dogs in the village howled and barked with him; he rolled over and over, and tried to run, and fell, and whimpered pitifully, and came home, and a few hours later died a horrible death.

The village was electrified, panic-stricken. The next day the police took the old woman away.

My cure was thus forcibly interrupted. I was put to my mother's breast in normal fashion, and our neighbor's wife fed me too, because I was always terribly hungry. A year later Mother had another child, and now it was my turn to be suddenly grown-up and not the baby any more, and soon I was crawling around the courtyard and the garden with the other children and the animals, and I grew healthy and strong and became the wildest boy in the village, the best coaster and slider, best cartwheel-turner and tree-climber. For which reason I was always full of scratches, and my clothes were always torn, and I was always losing my little pants and the string that was meant to hold them up.

And when my beloved mama was very angry, she used to say, "I'm still not sure whether that little toothless goblin has ever left you."

4

My Big Brothers, or One Is Missing

My eldest brother was named Schachne Eber. He was big and strong, quiet and ambitious, and very industrious. No one ever saw him sitting around or hanging about gossiping. Even on the Sabbath and on holidays when work was forbidden, he had ways of keeping himself occupied. He went into the fields to look at the grain or inspect the cattle, or into the shop to count over and rearrange the wares in their boxes and chests. He was really the head of the house. Father treated him as if he, the father, were the younger brother, because Schachne Eber's judgment on everything was better.

Schachne Eber despised poverty. He always said that poor people were wrong in *first* having children and *then* looking for means to feed them; it ought to be the other way around. The rich have the money *first* and *then* the children. He was always looking for a chance to earn money, and he saved. For all that, he was good-natured, and he didn't like bossing people around or giving orders. He always said, "It takes less time to pitch in and do the work yourself than to order it done."

One market day my brother Schachne Eber brought a load of grain to Kolomea and delivered it at the grain merchant's; the merchant, Herr Brettler, was much impressed with the skill and ease with which my brother unloaded the sacks; and he gave him a job in his warehouse as a combination clerk and porter. He earned ten gulden a year, with board and lodging, and on market day he earned five kreuzer extra for each wagon he loaded or unloaded. After a year he came home, with new boots, a fine black hat, a silk kaftan, two white shirts made to measure, presents for the children, eight gulden he had saved, and something torn in his "insides." He was pale as a scholar and he coughed. But he bought a calf with his money, raised it, brought the heifer to a bull, she calved, he sold her, and in that way had more money, and a calf too, as the foundation of a little fortune. Now he was well off and respected, and admired by the younger children and by Father too.

He managed the affairs of the house and was looked upon as a sort of representative of Father's who had even greater powers than Father did. But he never abused his authority. His face, framed by soft down, wore a serious look now. Father often asked him for advice and many a time borrowed a gulden from him, or even two. He no longer ate our black bread; instead every week he brought home from market a big loaf of bread made of bolted rye and strewn with caraway seed. The loaf lay on the shelf, covered with a napkin, and none of us touched it. But when one of the youngsters ran an errand for him or took care of his calf or polished his new boots, he gave him a thick slice of the new, delicious bread. And he always came back from the market bringing bright-colored candies or a honey cake. Ah, that honey cake tasted so good that our mouths watered when we spoke of it, and when we ate it our eyes filled with tears!

After Brother Schachne Eber came the next oldest, Abraham. Abraham was about a year younger, but bigger, broader, stronger, and clumsy in thought and speech. Whenever he said something he was laughed at, which made him blush, and therefore he was called, "The Beet." To avoid this he used to speak very little. And as he observed that the less he spoke, the less people laughed at him, he became almost silent, and people almost stopped laughing at him. He was the strongest lad in the village, and did the heaviest work effortlessly, like an ox. But he suffered silently because people did not take him seriously when he spoke.

He was not ambitious or jealous of his older brother, but he wanted to earn money too. So he used to go to town to work as a porter; he would go away Monday and come back Friday; this went on for several months, and he saved some money which he put in a pot and buried somewhere in a garden. With this money he formed a partnership with the poorest peasant in the village, Ivan the Hunchback, and bought a sow.

The sow farrowed fourteen piglets. The village became suspicious and attacked the poor peasant; many were sure that he had stolen the sow somewhere, till he finally admitted the secret agreement – and then we were in disgrace. A Jew dealing in pigs – *kosher* people making money in unclean livestock! It was unheard of!

Abraham took back his money without any profit and withdrew from the partnership, but it did no good. He and the whole family had been laid open to shame and to scandal. Then he had an idea: he began to talk again – and behold, people began laughing once more. But that was easier for him to bear, yes, far pleasanter in fact, than to have everyone thinking of him and his shame in silence.

At this point my eldest brother jumped into the breach and sold his calf. He and Abraham formed a partnership and began to trade in horses so that the family's shame of dealing in pigs should be wiped away.

My third brother, Jankel, joined this new partnership too. Jankel had a sense of humor and was always making jokes – he could roll his eyes in all directions and look cross-eyed, he could bark like a dog and moo like a cow and cackle like a hen and bend his knee joints backward into half circles. He wore Ukrainian clothes because they were warmer in winter, cooler in summer, and cheaper the whole year round. He went about with the village lads, was as handsome as a picture, and the peasant girls were always running after him. He had no ambition, spent his time in the inn, and the innkeeper often treated him because Jankel kept the customers amused. Once, even, the landowner's steward had played cards with him. Otherwise there is not much to tell of Jankel, but all the more about my next younger brother, Schmiel.

Schmiel was slender and quick, had a head of curly black hair, and was certain that he was the cleverest of us all. He was ingenious, smart, enterprising, and pompous. He had two passions: he loved to invent fantastic stories and he loved horses. He spent his days wandering through the village from stable to stable, he knew every horse by name, and the villagers believed that the horses knew him and loved him as much as he loved them. When a horse was ill and the veterinary from the nearest town failed to cure him, Schmiel would always find further remedies. The veterinary hated him, and the peasants called him, "Schmilko Kon," which means "Schmiel of the Horses." It goes without saying that he entered the horse-trading partnership. But on the very first market day there was trouble between him and my eldest brother. The traders came home from market late that Tuesday night. The next morning Father and the neighbors looked at the string of young horses they had brought back, pronounced judgment, discussed prices, as they did after every market day. Then everyone went to see what others in the village had bought, and discussed what so and so had paid out or taken in for his cow, or his horse, or his calf, or his pig. And so Wednesday passed.

Then came Thursday and, as always, there was a great to-do; it was time to begin preparations for the Sabbath, and there was dough to be mixed for the everyday black bread and for the holiday white bread and corn bread. The women ran around breathless and excited, borrowing leaven from the neighbors or looking for wood or advice, everything at the last minute; it was utter confusion.

From Thursday to Friday they worked through the night, mixing dough, heating the oven, peeling potatoes, cooking various and sundry dishes. Then came the baking: black bread, white bread, corn bread, potato bread, called "Mandaburtschinik," which was devoured on Friday and tasted wonderful with butter or sour cream.

Friday everything was washed and polished and put away. The smaller children's heads were washed with kerosene and combed by the larger ones; kerosene is good against lice. The hut smelled of fresh-baked bread, roast meat, and kerosene all mixed together. Late in the afternoon things were at last ready for the *chollent* (a dish consisting of buckwheat, beans, and some meat) to be put into the oven, the oven was hermetically sealed and then oiled and cleaned. The earthen floor was whitewashed with a thin coat of lime, then a green stripe was painted around the wall just above the floor. The table was laid with a white cloth, and brass candlesticks placed on it and set; everyone had his place at the table by right of age and dignity.

The male members of the family had already gone to prayers. A sort of private temple was set up in the back of the inn. There were only four Jewish families in the village, but there were more than enough grown men to make a *minjin*, the ten required for a congregation. Meanwhile Mama blessed the candles, and mingled her prayers with private asides; every week she talked to God like a grown daughter to a father reminding him of his responsibilities and duties.

Then the male members of the family came home from the temple; wishes for a "Good Sabbath" were gaily and fervently exchanged. Father recited the kiddush over the raisin wine, tasted it and handed the glass to Mother; then it went around the table. Our sister helped Mother to serve, Father presided over the table, the smell of spiced fish tickled our noses, water was passed around for the washing of hands before the Sabbath bread. Everyone looked expectantly at Father, but Father did not begin; instead he looked down the left side of the table to the third place where a cover was untouched – one of the family was missing!

Then everyone saw it too. Father asked, "Where is Schmiel?"

Schachne Eber, the eldest, answered: "The last time I saw him was Tuesday at the market."

We realized then that none of us had seen him since Tuesday; but we had not noticed it till now, for it was only on Friday night and the Sabbath day that we all sat down at the table together. Mother was already crying, softly at first, and then louder; and when Mother cried, she cried for a number of reasons: "God, O God," she sobbed, "why am I punished more than all the other mothers in the world? The devil is in one of my sons, and another is going to the devil! For what sins do you punish me, O Lord?"

But Father said, "Wife, do you know what the greatest sin of all is? To break the holy Sabbath!"

And he began to sing in his warm bass-baritone, "*Schabbes sholem miwoirock* [Praised be the peace of the Sabbath]." And softly murmuring, the others joined in the chorus: "Praised be the peace of the Sabbath."

Then the food was served, and although everyone was hungry, they ate wearily, without appetite, and Mother kept biting her lips to keep from crying and surreptitiously wiped away tears with the back of her hand. And between the courses there was singing as always, gay, happy melodies; but that evening they sounded melancholy and heartbreaking, for everyone was thinking: "Where can Schmiel be?"

The first one had gone out into the wide world – how wide…how wide…is this world?

5

Mama Dreams

In our village the seasons came and went like human beings. Spring came like a visit from a dear, long-awaited friend – you knew very well what he looked like, but still, when he came, you were surprised. He was even pleasanter and friendlier and warmer than you had expected, and every day he brought forth new gifts. Somewhere in his trunk there was always another little offering, another present, till you were almost embarrassed to accept them.

First came the soft, yellow sunshine, then the paths and the roads dried out and were again passable, then golden green carpets spread over the meadows and fields, then the trees and the bushes put out tender delicate buds; and at last the spring was not a guest any more. You make friends with him as with a dear and familiar person; you become more and more intimate and warm and, without being aware of it, you had wandered together into the summer. There was a wedding, and a forming of goals, and a building of a life.

Then comes the ripening together, you develop and grow, happiness comes and success; then comes the harvest and wealth, everything is safely stored away. Autumn! The earth lies shorn and naked, she is ashamed to have given everything away. You begin to count and reckon and save. Then comes rain and wind and cold. You begin to put up storm windows, bundles of straw and cornstalks are piled around the walls of the house to make them tight. Then suddenly it is cold, the air is clean and clear, and one day you get up and everything is white. Snow white. Snow and frost, and everyone stays indoors, except those who have good shoes and can go sliding and coasting.

On such a winter's day we children were standing at the window with Mama; she kept wiping the frozen pane with her apron to make a place to see through, and we peered out at the hill opposite, where the little onion-domed wooden church stood; there was a procession of the people of the village, and they carried thick lighted candles, which the wind threatened to blow out; at the head of the procession was carried a large, metal cross bearing a carved wooden figure of a crucified man; then came little boys in white robes, singing, then the village priest, and behind him the whole village, all very festive – it was Christmas.

It was all more than strange to us. During the week everyone was friends, all helped one another and were helped; we had the same cares, the same needs, the same measles, the same chicken pox, the same medicine, we went bathing or sliding in the same brooks; but every Saturday we were reminded that we were Jews, and every Sunday they were reminded that they were Christians. The two ideas confronted each other like strangers, coldly and with hostility. When we celebrated a holiday, the other children told us the next day what their parents had told them, how unfortunate and stupid it was to be a Jew, who had no inkling of the blessings of salvation, or of the resurrection, and above all of the taste of pork. And when they had a holiday, we were told how terrible it was to be a "goy," who could never be with Moses and the Good Mother Rachel in heaven and could never taste leviathan. And who would think of comparing leviathan with pork?

So now Mama was standing at the window, making fun of the procession and of the priest and of the villagers. "Yes," she said, "our God, our great God, sits in heaven on a fiery throne and sent Moses down to divide the roaring sea for us and lead us out of a place that was worse, far worse, than it is here; and he led us into a promised land where milk and honey flowed in the streets and everyone could eat or drink as much as he wanted, and he gave us the Torah too and all the wisdom in the world. And they kiss images and pray to carved wood."

Then she began to tell us, little Mama, all sorts of things. There was nothing more to be seen outside the window, but Mama's tongue had been loosened. It was growing dark, and now she told us of ghosts and devils, of lost souls and goblins that filled the air, of the witches and specters that were abroad at such hours, and that we could never be pious enough, and that we must pray, pray with pure hearts to our God, the Lord of the world. For only He could lead us through such darkness.

And now it was really dark in the room, and we all had goose flesh, and the hair stood up on our scalps and prickled like needles, and little Mama herself did not dare to leave us to go light the lamp, and we nestled together and pressed against her like chicks around a hen.

Suddenly the door opened, creaking, and we jumped, and Mama cried: "Who's there?"

And Brother Jankel, who was always playing jokes, struck a match, rolled his eyes, and said in a hollow tone: "I am one from the beyond." Then he lit the lamp and laughed.

We were still frightened, and with our little fists we rubbed the sudden light out of our eyes. Mother was already scolding again; she kindled the fire, but none of us dared to go into the outer room to bring in water and wood, not even Mama. So Jankel went. Then the supper was cooked. That day we had polenta and bean soup.

Father and the older boys came home. Schachne Eber gave each of us some colored candies again. But our fright was still in our faces. Supper was eaten quickly and in silence, and we were all glad to get to bed and shut our eyes and stop thinking of all the ghostly tales that little Mama had told us.

Our evening prayers, which we usually mumbled sleepily and mechanically, were spoken that night with a fervor that we had never felt before. But it didn't help.

In the middle of the night we suddenly heard Mother calling loudly: "No, no, I will not let you have my child. Aaron, Aaron, look, there comes the other witch, down the chimney – see how she's crawling head first with her hands stretched out and her long black hair hanging down! Witches! Help! Aaron! Children! Get up! We are pious people! No, no! I will not let you have my child! Help! Help! Aaron! Aaron! There are two witches in our house!"

Meanwhile Father had gotten up and lighted the lamp; all the children were awake. Father put on his prayer shawl. Now we began to be really frightened. Mama was moaning unintelligible words; the little ones were crying loudly. Now Mother lay with her eyes open, clasping her youngest child to her heart, holding it with both hands as if someone were trying to take it from her; Father began to recite a Psalm: "*Aschrei huisch ascher loi ulach bazass reschoim* [Blessed is the man that walketh not in the counsel of the ungodly]," then he went to the doorframe and kissed the mezzuza and monotonously intoned a prayer chant: "Our house is blessed and clean, and the unclean have no right within it; our holy books protect us, and the mezzuzas at the door are our witnesses and our guardians."

Now we were trembling more than we had at Mother's outburst. For Father was the one toward whom we all turned, and since he was taking it so seriously, we felt especially frightened.

Suddenly the comical Jankel yawned and said quietly: "Father, wouldn't you like to roll yourself a cigarette? I made a bet today and won a package of 'Thirteens.'"

And our eldest brother, Schachne Eber, said: "Did you hear, he has a package of 'Thirteens.' Give me one too."

Father suddenly stopped praying, folded his prayer shawl, rolled a cigarette, and lit it at the lamp chimney. Jankel and Schachne Eber, the only ones who dared to smoke in Father's presence, rolled cigarettes too. They began to talk of everyday things: why Jus Fedorkiw wanted to sell his mare, and that the corn must be put in the barn, that the potatoes in the pit should have more straw or they would freeze, that the cow should be brought to a bull, and so on and so forth.

And Mother's dreams were forgotten, and the little ones were already snoring, and this time Father did not put the lamp quite out, but turned it low, and lay down to sleep. He called once or twice to Mother, but little Mama was already asleep; and Father said, as if he were speaking to himself: "Well, well, now God sends us dreams!...Good night!"

6

Two Families – Four Friendships

The next morning we were the talk of the village. The grownups went about their business. The children had only one pair of boots among them, and the right to wear the boots belonged to the one who was doing something useful for the household, such as hauling water on the hand sled to which a barrel was fastened, or bringing in wood for the stove, or running to the neighbors to borrow or return something. That day there was a struggle over the pair of boots, everyone wanted to haul water, everyone wanted to bring in wood or run an errand, everyone wanted to do everything. Everyone wanted to get out of the close, stuffy room as fast as possible that day, out into the ice-cold air; everyone wanted to see friends and to coast and slide, and hear the news, and above all to tell our sensation.

That day we searched everywhere for the last remnant of a scrap of leather; we tied together torn fragments of shoes, soles and uppers that had long parted company; everything that had ever been on a foot was patched together with straps and wire and rags. Anything to get out! Out of the room that no longer kept out witches and ghosts!

Each of us told his own version of our experience, painting it with our own colors, leaving out or adding parts, each according to his character or temperament. And we were a huge success.

The Jewish families said that this visitation was a warning that we were not pious enough, especially the children, who ran wild all day with the Ukrainian children and were not taught manners and their religion properly; and that everyone else should be warned as well. The Ukrainians, too, the men, women and young people who were gathered in the square in front of the inn before going to church, dressed in their white sheepskins and holiday clothes, saw God's warning finger in it, not without malicious satisfaction.

"A family with so many children, the Aarons," said Jusecha Fedorkiw, our friendly neighbor, "and unbelievers! And on our holidays there come warnings also to unbelievers who are not quite lost yet."

Later old Jus Fedorkiw came to visit us, accepted a glass of tea, and sat in silence. His bushy mustache hung solemnly over his mouth, his gray hair was uncombed, and his linen shirt was open so you could see his hairy chest.

For many years he and Father had been carrying on the same discussion, a discussion in installments. They always began where they had left off the time before. It was always: "Aaron, yesterday [or "the day before yesterday," or "last week"] you asserted such and such."

And the prompt answer would be: "Not I, Jusiu; I never assert anything. I only say that if anyone wanted to assert this or that, you could say..." and then they were at it.

And this discussion that went on for days, weeks, yes, even years, always dealt with the same question: *Why* God, Whom all people of all religions recognize as the final authority, and Who, as All Father, recognizes everything that lives, down to the earthworm – *why* had He not made *one* people, *one great people*, and, consequently, *one* religion?

And they talked of His omnipotence, the wonder of which was witnessed in the spring by every returning stork and by the tiniest field mouse; and He, who, if He wished, could shut up all the devils and all the goblins in a rat hole and leave them there to sweat – why had He created them, these ghosts and devils, who exist only to trouble us?

For the last few weeks their talk turned on the six days of creation, which filled them both with real, pious enthusiasm. He had merely said, "Let there be," and there was! Out of nothing, out of less than an empty pocket, for before a pocket can be empty there first has to be a pocket!

Only one modest little question troubled our friend Fedorkiw: the mouse has her hole, the stork his nest, the horse his stall, the dog his kennel, the lion his wilderness, the landowner his estate, we too have our houses and our chimney corners, *and God has His heaven* – and the most beautiful thing in the world is the deep, wise order – but God had not made heaven until the second day of creation! Where then had God lived before He made heaven?

These were very serious talks, not for an instant cynical or godless, for to disbelieve, even only to doubt, that would mean disbelieving or doubting that the dependable, solid earth could carry you, doubting that the sun would rise in the morning, doubting that after the iciest winter, spring would return, and doubting *that what had been sown in the fall would come up when the snow had melted away!*

That day they talked about the experience of the previous night. Father said that he intended to go to consult his wonder rabbi, who was a man of great wisdom. As far as he himself could understand, it was simply a warning, because the younger generation was becoming skeptical.

"I was coming home from Horodenka last week with your son, the student, and he was saying godless things about your own faith, and he did not bare his head when we came to the crucifix at the crossroads, nor did he cross himself."

"Yes, yes," said old Fedorkiw, "you are right again. My children don't cross themselves, and yours don't pray, and so we are sent signs and warnings."

The relations between the Fedorkiws and our household were very close. We lived in the same neighborhood, and

Father and Jus Fedorkiw were a pattern of friendship. Then, too, each of us found a playfellow of the same age in the other family. Mother and Jusecha gave birth to their children at about the same time, and the children crawled around in each other's houses, exchanged bits of food, and the infants sucked at both mothers' breasts.

The next friendship was between Ivan, the student, who went to school in Horodenka and my fourteen-year-old sister, Rachel. When Ivan came home from town, he always appeared at our house on some pretext or other, to buy something or to bring Father some message. But everyone knew that he really came to exchange tender glances or a few words with Rachel. Once I saw him secretly slip a thin book into her hand. Rachel always blushed when he came, and on the days when she expected him she always had a red or green ribbon in her hair, or wore her best apron, the one embroidered with flowers.

My older brothers soon noticed this and taunted her about her fondness for the "goy," Ivan, and threatened to thrash her. But they did not really dare to go that far, for she was the only girl in the family and Father pampered her, and she was very pretty.

She had deep black, flashing eyes, breasts like small hard apples, she was tall and slender, and had two long brown pigtails which came down to her behind. She liked to laugh long and loudly with her friends among the Ukrainian girls, who envied her for Ivan's favor.

She jeered at her brothers and said that they were only jealous because they were boorish and narrow-minded, while young Fedorkiw studied and read books and thought about everything differently even than his own brothers, who did not understand him either. And he knew more than the village schoolmaster and the priest, and even more than the Jews. He would bring her books that told of clever and handsome and brave men who always got into the most difficult situations and always found ways out. She certainly wasn't going to let her know-nothing brothers tell her with whom she could talk, with whom she could go walking.

But Ivan's friendship with Rachel did not suit his brothers either. They jeered at him and abused him because he went with the "Jew calf." They called him "The Gent" and "Ivan the Jew." But he was not even angry with them for this. He thought they were just like Aaron's boys, and one must be patient with them, because in time they would learn to understand things better, then they'd be sorry for their bad behavior and even apologize to him, their younger brother.

So these were three of the friendships between the two families: Father's with old Fedorkiw, Mother's with his wife, and sister Rachel's with the student Ivan.

But there was another Very Important Friendship between the two families. Among the Fedorkiws was a backward boy whom everyone called Bohugekowate, which means "Thank God." He was about twelve years old, heavy and squat, with a girlish face that was too big for his body and glassy calf's eyes. When you asked him a question, he babbled and smiled and looked you straight in the eye and answered, "Thank God, thank God, thank God!"

Stupid and malicious people would take advantage of this and play all sorts of jokes. They asked him questions like: "Are you going to marry the village priest soon?" and he answered, "Thank God, thank God." "Is your father going to die soon?" and he, "Thank God, thank God!" "Are your brothers going to kill you for Easter?" and he always answered with his candid calf's eyes, and his pleasant voice, "Thank God, thank God!"

People would play these jokes only when none of his brothers was present, for the Fedorkiw boys were feared in the whole village. Once they caught the village elder's son teasing "Thank God," and they thrashed him within an inch of his life.

Mother Fedorkiw and the old man and the sons loved "Thank God" tenderly and were always giving him something to nibble, and he ate and ate and grew fat like a little pig.

And in our family there was a boy of the same age, his foster brother, who one day fell out of our apple tree, head first, and lost his speech and hearing and began to grow lopsided; that is, he began to grow more on one side than on the other, so that in the course of time he had one shoulder, one hand, one leg, and one half of his face smaller than the other. He withdrew from the play of the other children, though Father had urged them to try to include him. He grew melancholy and he had large, brown eyes that pleaded, and everyone pitied him, and so he was nicknamed "Little Pity." And without anyone trying to bring it about, a tender friendship sprang up between "Thank God" and "Little Pity."

They were always together. They would sit for hours in silence, then they would touch and feel each other, and roll about, and even laugh sometimes, then sit still again. They shared everything they had, and "Little Pity" often came home in "Thank God's" shirt or "Thank God" in "Little Pity's" coat. One would often find them in the haystack or on the dunghill, with some of the animals. Sometimes they would hit each other slowly: one would receive a blow, grab himself where it hurt, wait, and then give the blow in return; or they bit each other's arms and ears and noses, but never maliciously – it seemed rather out of curiosity – and their faces were always friendly. But their favorite pastime was to stand at the well and look down at their reflections, making faces and laughing and spitting. Oh, how they loved to spit in the well!

So the two families were bound together by four friendships: the two old men, who had been carrying on the same conversation for twenty years; the two women who gave birth to their children at the same time, helped each other bring them up, and mothered them, and gave them suck; Ivan, the student, and my sister Rachel; and "Thank God" and "Little Pity." The little children played in both gardens, shared their food, and spoke the same language.

But among the grown sons, those between eighteen and thirty, there was rivalry. One could not call them enemies, but there was always friction, an inflammable substance that anything might set off.

On Sundays and holidays they would all be at the inn; first there would be a joke, then an insult, then someone would boast a little, others egged him on, two would start feeling each other's muscles, then they would be wrestling; for fun at first; one would break the rules, the first punch landed, then a kick, then one grabbed the other by the hair, and the fight was on. They were still laughing; then they got really heated; glasses and bottles, chairs and lamps and candles began to fly; the riot spread into the street. People came to watch; more and more joined in. The parties grew larger, two great bands were hammering at each other, blood flowed, women screamed.

The village elder appeared after an hour or so, and the prudent and the cautious began to soothe and parley and patch up a peace. And I soon they were all back in the inn, where they made up, drinking beer and schnapps and reviewing the various holds and punches with professional objectivity; and everyone was proud of his bruises and gouges and black eyes; and all felt great warmth for one another and were the best of friends and very drunk. And so they parted until on another Sunday or holiday *exactly the same thing happened in exactly the same way.*

7

The First Victim

It was the last of the holidays. The little church was packed, and the stout village priest, with his low forehead and wiry bristling hair, preached and preached. Everyone knew that he had gone to visit the landowner the day before and had been wined and dined and gone home loaded with presents; indeed, he repeated what he had been told there: that the Jewish banker, Herr Jungermann, wanted to attach the landowner's property. So he told how all the Jews ate white rolls and fish and plum jam on Friday evening. And after all it was the Jews who had crucified our Saviour. And yet there were people in the village who lived on friendly terms with them, who mingled with them and even nursed their children.

He did not mention the Fedorkiws by name, but everyone knew of whom he was speaking. In the little church stood the Fedorkiw boys listening now to these incitements and provocations, and they were already thinking of the various holds and punches that would be used in the fight which would *certainly* take place that day.

That same day we younger children were in heaven, for the frozen brook had been swept clean and was smooth as glass for sliding.

"Little Pity" was with us, and when the crowd of the young Fedorkiws appeared with their sled, "Thank God" was among them and left them to join "Little Pity," and no one noticed that the two went off together. They ran about in the snow and then went into our barn and crawled into the haystack where it was warm.

In front of the village inn it was very lively by now: people were coming from church; several went into the inn and had their first drink. The poor men stood outside and waited for the richer ones to invite them. The women stood together in groups. Some had already bought bottles, and the glass was making the rounds. They drank according to the old custom, kissing each other's hands; they were very friendly and with every glass became friendlier and warmer.

Ivan Fedorkiw, the student, was sitting in our house and talking very seriously to Father and Rachel. He said that, since the priest had stirred up the people that morning, Father must try to hold back his older sons; none of them must let himself be provoked into a quarrel that day. Then Ivan went home and talked to his father, and then the Fedorkiw boys came home, already a little tipsy, and Andry Fedorkiw asked his father how he had liked the sermon. Old Fedorkiw opened the Bible and showed his sons what the good God Himself had written there: "Thou shalt love thy neighbor as thyself." And the priest had spoken only of hatred and not a word about love and forgiveness. But then the dinner was served, and a big bottle made the rounds....

In our stable "Little Pity" and "Thank God" lay biting each other. They scratched each other's faces and rolled over and over, shrieking and laughing loudly, until someone heard them and separated them. "Little Pity" was brought into the house; he lay on the stove and giggled.

When "Thank God" came home, scratched and bleeding at the nose, Andry, the oldest son, held him up before his father and said: "There – you see how the Jews love their neighbors, Father! We'll settle this tonight."

The other brothers began to bring in sticks and to cut cudgels of them, but old Fedorkiw took one of the sticks and struck the table with it so hard that the splinters flew, and they all rose and looked at him for a few moments coldly and in silence. Then Ivan, the student, said, half to his father and half to his brothers: "Just because the landowner made a bad bargain with a rich banker, you and the Aaron boys have to beat each other to death!"

"That's what your Jew calf tells you, is it?" said Andry.

"No," said old Fedorkiw, "that's what our priest told us today."

And one after another the young men left the room and went to the inn, which was already packed. And the lamp was lighted, for it was getting dark.

And then old Fedorkiw went with Ivan, the student, to Aaron's house. Aaron made tea. Everyone sat in silence, and Ivan again tried to persuade the Aaron boys not to let themselves be provoked into a fight that night, just that one night when the whole village was aroused. Sister Rachel listened, her eyes fixed in rapture on her friend, who spoke so wisely; and the brothers saw that, and only that, and did not listen to what he was saying. Then Abraham went up to the student, and, without any prelude, in a harsh voice said, "Good night, Ivan." Ivan rose and went out.

There was an embarrassed silence. Rachel took her cloak and ran after her friend. After a while "Little Pity" crawled off the stove and followed his sister Rachel, whom he loved very much. Then old Aaron lit the lamp, and everyone noticed that night had fallen.

Outside, the clouds were driving past the moon, and "Little Pity" thought it was the moon that was driving so fast, and he forgot he was following his sister, who was now walking toward the poplar grove with Ivan.

"Little Pity" stood leaning against the wall of the house and staring at the flying moon. Meanwhile at the inn there was carousing and laughter. One of the Fedorkiw boys' friends who always drank with them and never paid took off his sheepskin and turned it wool side out and began to crawl on all fours, barking like a dog and growling like a bear, and everyone laughed. Then several others began to imitate him, and soon the inn seemed full of bears and wolves sitting there on their haunches. And someone proposed that they should crawl under the Jew's window and play a joke on him. They fortified themselves with another glass, then they all crawled out of the inn on all fours, barking and bellowing.

When they came to Aaron's house, "Little Pity" was still standing outside playing with the moonbeams, and he took fright at the barking and bellowing beasts and began to run. And they did not even see who it was that was running from them. And they ran after him, and he came to the well and ran around it. And they came nearer and nearer, laughing and bellowing drunkenly.

"Little Pity" stood still, and the beasts behind him stopped too, and his little sick heart beat wildly, and suddenly he saw the moon running too, and he tried to run in the opposite direction. But the beasts chasing him changed their direction too.

Twice at full speed around the well – and still they did not see whom they were chasing. He started to run the other way again, more and more desperate. The hunters were enjoying themselves immensely. This chase was repeated several times, always around the well: the stopping and the running, the running and the stopping, back and forth, back and forth.

Suddenly "Little Pity" caught hold of the well coping, and down there he saw another moon, and also the moon above him and beasts on either side. And then he shut his eyes and moons and beasts and the well spun around in his sick brain, and he jumped...

And round the well the Fedorkiws leaped and squatted on all fours, and after a while they noticed that their quarry had vanished. And they did not know how he had vanished, and they did not know whom they had been pursuing.

Disturbed by the noise, old Aaron and Fedorkiw came out of the house. Old Fedorkiw only said, "Those are my grown sons." They were standing there now, rather bashful and embarrassed; but no one saw the tender little hands that tried and tried to catch hold of the slippery, moss-covered stones – tried and failed.

Old Fedorkiw went home, and his sons went home. Ivan brought Rachel back.

All were in their warm houses, and if anyone had looked down into the well just then, he could have heard the last splashing of the water, he could have seen the last ripples spread out in rings the way they do when you throw a stone into a pool.

Then the water was quiet too. It had swallowed its first victim…

8

He Could Not Read the Bible. But Neither Had He Heard the Sermon of the Village Priest

The next morning the first neighbor who went for water found "Little Pity" in the well, a floating corpse. The village was instantly awake – and struck dumb. Everyone wore a face of stone. Soon there lay something in our room, bedded in straw on the earthen floor.

We, the youngest children, were taken to our uncle Leiser's. No one spoke to us, but the looks on their faces! Everyone looked at us so seriously and sadly; and the tears ran down our cheeks. We tried not to cry, and we huddled in a corner of Uncle Leiser's hut and sobbed. It was as if there were an empty place around our hearts, and our sobs came out of that emptiness.

Near the village on the road to town there was a small fenced field – the Jewish cemetery. There were only two graves there: that of Uncle Leiser's old father and Shaiko Wisdom. Now, close to Shaiko Wisdom, another grave was dug for "Little Pity."

At about noon we were told that we could take our last leave of our brother. The four oldest Jews took up the bier and carried it halfway; then they changed with Father and my three eldest brothers. Two women supported poor Mama, who, all that morning, had neither spoken nor shed a tear. Indeed, no one cried, but the little ones' teeth were chattering.

Now "Little Pity" in his burial clothes was lowered into the grave, and Mama suddenly muttered to the women who were attending her: "Look how fast it goes, how fast it goes, how fast it goes."

Suddenly Father threw the first handful of dirt on "Little Pity" and everyone did the same, and Father began to recite the Kaddish, the prayer for the dead. But he did not get far. After the first words of the prayer, he broke off and said, quite simply, as if he were sitting over a glass of tea: "My son, this is against the rules; it should not be the father who says Kaddish over his son. You should have said Kaddish for me." And the rest of the prayer was lost, for now everyone began to cry and sob aloud like a chorus, and the silence was broken by a storm of tears and lamentations.

In the village the people were gathered in groups before their houses talking. Suddenly little fat "Thank God" appeared, running breathlessly, stopping, looking, searching. He approached one of the groups; a woman broke into tears and said, "Poor boy, you have lost your best friend." And he only said, "Thank God, thank God!" and ran off.

After a while "Thank God" came running back again, and this time he went straight to Aaron's well and looked down and saw his own face in the water and threw chunks of bread to it. Then he stopped and ate, then threw more bread and peered into the well and smiled, and all the time he only kept on saying, "Thank God, thank God!"

Meanwhile a woman had told the Fedorkiw boys and they took their brother away from the well and began to board it over. One of them told him that his friend was not going to live in the well, but in the little cemetery where the two stones were.

When a friend goes to live in a new home, you bring him salt and bread, "Thank God" thought. So he ran home and took salt and a loaf of bread and set out again, running and running.

When he reached the edge of the village, the Jews and their children were returning from the burial; so he knew that they had been to see his friend in his new house; and as he ran past, he showed them the salt and the bread that he was taking to his friend. But no one noticed him, not even the children.

When he reached the cemetery, Uncle Leiser had just finished filling the grave; he looked at "Thank God" and said only, "Yes, 'Thank God,' there is his everlasting home, and your friend will stay there longer now than all our lives put together," and went away.

But "Thank God" knelt down by his friend's grave, took the bread and salt out of his bundle and put it on the mound, and waited for his friend to put out his hand and take the food into his new house.

But nothing happened. So "Thank God" buried the bread and salt in the grave and waited for a sign from his friend....

When one of the Aaron boys saw that the well had been boarded up, he took an ax and pliers and began to pull the boards away. The sons of both families were standing around the well; the Aarons pulled the boards off, and the Fedorkiws nailed them on again; and, tired and sad as they were, they began to tussle with each other and exchange halfhearted punches and try out a few holds. At any other time it would have been a real battle, but today the fighting looked like full men trying to eat. It simply didn't get going.

Then Rachel appeared in the distance with Ivan Fedorkiw, and Andry said, "There comes my dear learned brother, who soon will be going to pray with you Friday nights."

And Abraham said, "And our dear sister will soon be presenting your family with some little Ivans."

And Rachel cried, and Ivan, who was always so quiet, hit Abraham in the face with his fist, and Andry jumped between Abraham and Ivan and shouted: "This is my business! Out of the village, Jew Ivan!"

And Abraham turned to his sister: "And you, you goy's whore, can go with him!"

And suddenly all the hate and all the grief of the Aarons and the Fedorkiws was turned on the two of them. Several other people had come up, and Andry's wife, big fat Varvara, suddenly screamed: "We are Christians, and the Aarons are Jews, but those two are neither one nor the other. And they are to blame for everything that has gone wrong. Out with them, out of the village with them!"

And a real chase began through the gardens and lanes, and the snow began to fall, and it grew dark. But the chase went on.

And by "Little Pity's" grave "Thank God" sat shivering with cold, and he dug up the bread and the salt, and many things passed through his mind and through his heart: Cold – my friend is cold; so cold that he cannot take the bread and salt into his new house. He is cold, my friend – oh, my poor, poor friend, how cold you are!

And he took off his own sheepskin and spread it over the grave and tucked it in tenderly and carefully all around, and he grew numb with cold. But he smiled, and the snow fell in thick flakes, and he closed his eyes and thought: Thank God, thank God, thank God – now my friend will not be as cold as I am – thank God, thank God, thank God. And slowly he fell asleep…

And through the gardens and through the lanes Rachel and Ivan were hunted out of the village. And the two bands, satisfied now, went to the inn to celebrate their latest piece of heroism. And Rachel and Ivan thought it was all like the book he had given her, except that they couldn't talk to each other as beautifully as the two people in the book had talked. They could only weep, and they were tired.

And Rachel said, "I want to see 'Little Pity's' grave, and then we will go."

And they went to "Little Pity's" grave, and a something sat there, buried in the snow. And they recognized "Thank God," frozen stiff by his friend's grave.

And Ivan took his dead brother on his back and carried him home.

And it was already midnight, and the brothers were still at the inn. And old Fedorkiw had the sleigh harnessed, and

Rachel and Ivan were driven to the town. And suddenly the whole village was awake again, and dumb again.

And the next day "Thank God" was buried too, but without the priest. For old Fedorkiw said: "'Thank God' could not read the Bible, but neither did he hear the sermon of the village priest – so he loved his friend truly and tenderly. And surely, truth and tenderness are acceptable to God – even if little village priests could never understand that."

9

We Go Out into the Wide World, but It Wears the Same Face

There was a brook in our village, where we children paddled around in the summer and went sliding in the winter. My foster brother, Nikola, said that when we went to sleep at night, together with the horses and the cows and the sheep and all the birds, and someone lit all those millions of candles in the sky, the brook stopped too and rested from running all day.

We were curious to know when the brook went to sleep, but no matter how late we stayed up, or how early we rose, it was always moving.

But we were moving too. Every year another little mouth was added to the family. Father talked things over with my eldest brother and the other grown-up Jews in the village who came to sit and pray with us during the shivah days, the seven days of mourning, and who had at other times discussed the same problems with Father: "The children run wild here"; "You can't keep a teacher any more"; and "In the town at least you have a cheder and schools."

It was not yet a week since "Little Pity" was buried, and Father and Mother and the older children were still "sitting shivah," sitting on the floor or on a low stool in their stocking feet.

On the day of the funeral we had eaten nothing; on the second day, the youngest children were given slices of Schachne Eber's good light rye bread and an apple, and we choked it down tearfully, for we were thinking of "Little Pity" lying alone in the ground.

On the third day Aunt Feige, who was Uncle Leiser's wife and my mother's sister, came and cooked a wretched, watery bean soup. No one liked Aunt Feige, no one liked her food, no one wanted her sympathy. Not even then; and we ate only a little, silent and uncomfortable.

And Father read to us out of a holy book, about a very pious and God-fearing man, whom the Lord loved and who had great herds of sheep and kine and well brought up scholarly children. And suddenly everything went wrong with his affairs, and he became poor as a beggar; his cattle perished of the plague, his sons died in poverty, his houses and stables, barns and granaries burned down, and they weren't even insured; and on top of all that, God sent him the itch and scabs and a hideous leprosy.

Yet in the end it all turned out well, and the man recovered slowly and became even richer than before – what luck! So this should really be a comfort to us: after all, we had only lost a little brother; we were certainly poor, but we didn't have leprosy or scrabs or the itch, because our heads were washed with kerosene every week.

And that afternoon a man in city clothes came to our house and spoke in a very friendly manner and smiled. He counted the grownups and the children and wrote something in a little book with a silver pencil. He told us that a rich Herr Lifschitz had started a match factory in the town of Skolje, and Herr Lifschitz had sent him, the smiling man, to find families with many children and that he would even pay their transportation to Skolje. And instead of the children running senselessly and godlessly loose in the village, and going sliding and doing nothing but eat and grow up like savages, they could work in the factory, and earn money, and help their parents. The little ones could go to cheder and to school, and grow up properly. And was it not written: *"Meschane mokim, Meschane mazl* [Change your place and you change your luck]"?

Father talked it over with my brother Schachne Eber and agreed. As soon as the seven days' mourning was over, three wagons came. We loaded our worldly possessions into them, trunks and beds, chairs and tables, baskets and bundles. And some of us sat on the beds and some of us on the chairs and some of us lay bedded in hay and straw.

The neighbors and peasants saw us off, and only my eldest brother, Schachne Eber, stayed behind in the village in our house alone. We little ones acquired a new importance in our own eyes, and for the first time we felt a sort of pride, for now we were going out into the wide world.

And we traveled through fields and small towns, through forests and villages, and night came and we fell asleep, and when we little ones woke, we were in the wide world. But we could hardly believe our eyes: it was dark in the wide world, just like at home, and the next morning it grew light just like at home, and there was grain in the fields just like at home, and in the gardens there were potatoes – all in all, the earth wore the same face as it did at home.

And that was good: we did not have to feel that we were such strangers in the wide world.

10

The Village Spits Us Out

Skolje was a little town of Jews and Poles and Ukrainians. Father went to the factory, as did all the children over eight. It was a match factory, and it stank of sulphur and phosphorus. Some worked in the joinery, where the raw wood was put through various machines, emerging as matchsticks. Others worked at the frames in which a series of notched bars were set, one next to another, and in each notch was placed one of the finished matchsticks. Others lifted these frames and dipped the matchsticks in a yellow liquid; then they were pushed into the next room, where they were again dipped, this time into a green liquid. From there the frames made their way to the drying room, then to the packing room, where the little children just over eight years of age worked. Over and over again they grabbed handfuls of finished matches from the notched bars and packed them into the matchboxes.

After a few days, everything in our house stank of sulphur. Our food, our bread, our clothes, our wash – everything smelled musty and rotten and bittersweet. We became acquainted with our neighbors and people who, like ourselves, had come from the villages with their families, and they told us that the fumes of sulphur and phosphorus got into the bones and that after a time everyone who worked in the factory became knock-kneed. Father refused to be frightened or let himself be talked out of his intentions – he did not believe everything he was told.

My brother Schabse and I went to the cheder; he was six, and I was five, and we spoke Yiddish with a village accent, and we were nicknamed "The Dumbbells." The rabbi-teacher did not like us either. He pinched us secretly. I hated him, and every day there were scenes and I had to be taken to the cheder by force. We would rather run about in the nearby woods, where we found strawberries and blueberries, which tasted wonderful with bread.

Skolje was still East Galicia, but it was on the other side of Lemberg, on the Russian border – very far from home, according to the ideas of that time.

One morning a blindworm was discovered in the market place; the town was in an uproar; they hacked the little snake to bits with axes and spades, amid insane excitement, and wild rumors flew from mouth to mouth. On another day a rat sprang at a cat and the town became absolutely hysterical.

And one Saturday a hairy man came running out of the woods, barefoot, and went straight into the synagogue; the town rabbi came, the people waited outside. The rabbi remained for some time in the synagogue, alone with the hairy man. Then he came out and bade the people turn their backs, then the hairy man came out and disappeared. The rabbi was showered with questions, and he smiled and said that the really pious people didn't ask so many questions, and he sent them home to read Psalms. So Skolje lived from one excitement to the next.

We had a Polish neighbor who was called Dobusch, which was also the name of a legendary robber in the district. Neighbor Dobusch had a lot of children too, somewhat older than we. The first day they saw us, they called us names and shouted, "The Jews are here," and sang a mocking song:

"The Jew, the Jew, the mangy Jew!
I found his hat – and what did I do?

*I shit in it — and so would you.
Now he'll have to buy a new!"*

We were warned about Dobusch; he was strong and hot-tempered, and when he was drunk he always tried to pick a quarrel; he used to shout: "When I drink schnapps, I have to have a Jew for a *zakuska* [to eat after it]."

A disagreeable neighbor, with disagreeable children.

Winter came, and we began to take our sleds to the forest to coast and bring home wood. One day, as we were coming home, the Dobusch boys stopped us, upset our sleds, thrashed us, and ran away laughing. We were frightened and decided not to say anything at home, for we knew that our big brothers were only waiting for an excuse for a fight. But the Dobusch boys were proud of their deed and immediately informed the whole neighborhood, and old Dobusch stood outside of his house with his heroic sons, looking over at us and laughing and jeering.

It was Friday afternoon. Father came home from the steam bath, bringing with him, as usual, a square bottle of 98-proof vodka for the Sabbath. On the way the neighbors stopped him and told him what had happened to us.

Our father was a patriarch. He had brought us up strictly; we behaved ourselves and he seldom had to thrash us. We obeyed because we loved him; we obeyed our older brothers and sisters too. It was almost part of our religion, and we were very pious. When Father occasionally beat us, the pain did not make us cry; we accepted our beating in silence, and then went off into a corner and were unhappy only because he, whom we loved, could strike us. Once I was caught robbing an orchard. The keeper of the orchard beat me so that I had to crawl home on all fours like a dog. Father took me by the hand and led me to the keeper, confronted him, and in my presence gave him the same kind of a beating. What did it matter after that if Father beat me again at home and said that it was he who must punish me, not strangers!

Father with his sense of justice taught us a thousand unwritten laws.

So that Friday afternoon, as always, Father came home from the steam bath, stopping on the way to buy a square bottle of 98-proof vodka.

He asked us what had happened. We looked like whipped puppies, and we could not lie to him, but we understated it a little, thinking of the Dobusch legend. All this took place in front of our house.

Father, to our terror, went over to look for Dobusch, who had gone inside his house, and beat with fist on the window and called, "Hey, Dobusch, come out! Here's some vodka with a Jew for *zakuska*"

Dobusch appeared with an ax in his hands, but before he could make a move, he had the square bottle of 98-proof vodka in his face, and a punch and a kick in the belly, and Dobusch and his legend were lying in the dirt.

Father took the ax and came home, and funny Brother Jankel said, "Father, send him over the spiced fish too – because it won't taste good without vodka anyway!"

And Father gave Jankel some money and said, "Excuse me, Jankel, you must treat a good neighbor to a bottle once in a while." And Jankel went for more vodka.

No, it was not very pleasant in Skolje.

After a time, most of us began to look pale and to have pains in our joints, in the knee joints especially. And Abraham and Jankel began to show signs of becoming knock-kneed. Then one Saturday we had visitors. Our uncle Leiser came with a carter and two big vans. That evening everything was packed, quickly loaded on the carts, and we moved away.

The next morning the "smiling" agent caught up with us in the little town of Dolena, but now he was not smiling. With him were two gendarmes, who ordered Father to return to Skolje. Father refused and with the gendarmes he went to the mayor of Dolena, who said that as long as the "smiler" couldn't prove that we had robbed Herr Lifschitz or committed a slight murder, no one could stop us. For you can't do anything to a man who merely objects to seeing his children become cripples.

We returned to Werbiwci, where my eldest brother was staying alone in our house; and he and Father had a long talk.

The next day they both went to town to look at a bride for my brother. She was a poor relative of the rich Schloime Baer Offenberger. She was a very pretty, healthy girl with broad hips.

The betrothal ceremony took place at Herr Offenberger's. My brother was promised a dowry of one hundred and fifty gulden. This he offered to Father so that he could leave the village again and go to Horodenka, the county seat. A few months later the wedding was celebrated; we little ones stayed at home, and sweetmeats were brought back for us. We moved in with a neighbor temporarily leaving our house to the eldest brother.

He brought his young wife home. She did not like us at all, and the feeling was mutual, and even our brother became estranged from us.

Then one day we were loaded into two wagons again and left the village. On the way it started to rain; the wagons were open and everything was soaked through. Father said it was a good sign: "It has washed away all the evil of the past."

And when we reached Horodenka the sun was coming out. But as we entered the first street of the town a woman with two empty jugs crossed our path. Father called a halt, turned white, wiped the sweat from his brow and said, "Children, this is not good, but we can't go back again."

So we drove through a back street to a wretched little house which belonged to a poor tailor Chaim Karinik, from whom we had rented a room. There was no stable, and no haystack, and no dung heap, and no animals. We slept all over the place, packed tightly together, four of us on a small, narrow, benchbed, with one across the head and another across the foot, and others sleeping on the stove and on the floor.

In the very first days after our arrival typhus broke out in the town: on one house after another there appeared a black stripe drawn in coal which meant: TYPHUS! Soon there was one on our house, and the entire household lay ill with fever and chills. I did not know whether I was asleep or awake; I only saw great troops of enormous lice with green bellies and red backs, millions of them, a mountain of them, crawling over me and under me and back and forth, and I was paralyzed and couldn't move my limbs, and I was dumb and couldn't cry out, and then Jus Fedorkiw's black wolfhound appeared, and now he had a green belly and a red back too, and a fiery red smoking tongue hung out of his huge jaws, and he took my head in his jaws and twisted it back and forth, and still my head stayed fixed to my body and I shrieked and bellowed with all my strength, but no sound came out of my throat, and the green and red lice crawled over my legs and between my thighs and along my belly and my back and in my armpits and between my fingers and around my neck and over my eyes, and I tried to shake myself and scratch, and my limbs would not obey me, and I saw Father and my dear brother Leibzi coming on fresh from the steam bath, and I screamed and screamed and screamed, but my lips only moved and no sound came out; and they both looked at me kindly and smiled and thought I was only joking, and I could not make them understand. Then the whole mountain of lice reared up into a steep precipice, and I rolled down it, and then I was lying somewhere, and I opened my eyes timidly and wearily and my whole body was wet, and my brother Leibzi was lying on the stove with me, and Father bandaged my forehead with a handkerchief and slices of cool raw potato, and fat Dr. Kanafass held my hand in one of his, and in the other he had a watch as big as an onion, and he asked me something in Polish, and through his eyeglasses I saw two bloodshot eyes like those of Jus Fedorkiw's wolfhound, and he told me to put out my tongue, and I thought of the wolfhound's fiery tongue and wept, and I heard myself weeping, and Father heard me and spoke to me and fondled me, and soon I stopped crying, and I was so tired, and then I fell into a long restful sleep; then I woke up and was lying on the oven with Brother Leibzi, and there was a wooden trough full of bread and rolls on the oven too which the neighbors regularly put through the window, but we were not allowed to eat of it. That day I stole a small loaf of white bread, and my brother and I ate it in secret and it tasted good to us, so we took another. Now we had both a game and a wonderful secret: we stole and ate and ate and stole and thus secretly fed ourselves back to health. Therefore we were the first to get up and the first to leave our musty room and breathe clean air at last.

So the county seat Horodenka received us most unkindly; but the village had finally spit us out.

11

The County Seat Horodenka – Fierce Competition

The difference between the village of Werbiwci and the little town of Horodenka was greater than that between the town of Horodenka and any European capital, for Horodenka already had all the insecurity and drive and hurry and competition of a city, while Werbiwci was a quiet, stable, and peaceful village.

In the village men lived by the soil, and they were in contact with it. In Horodenka men lived by one another, next to one another, and yet there was no contact between them. In the village everything was orderly and good; everyone knew where his living came from, everyone knew what he had. People lived with their animals, with the soil, even with the seasons – lived on good terms with them. Misfortunes occurred: often a beast fell sick or a drought dried the soil, or suddenly in the middle of the spring hail came and blighted seed and bloom. Or in the summer, when the work in the field was at its height, a strange big-bellied cloud would appear from nowhere, stumble over a peaceful little native cloud, and pour itself out.

When such things happened, people were not merely unhappy, they got really angry. They looked up at the sky and raged and reviled the ridiculous spring that suddenly brought hail and blighted its own seeds and blooms. Or they made bitter fun of Mr. Summer whose clouds always rained at the wrong time and at the wrong place.

That is how it was in Werbiwci. There were poor and rich in the village too, and hail and drought and pestilence. But such things were everyone's concern, and people were close to one another and helped one another. But in Horodenka it was otherwise.

In the town men no longer lived by the soil, but by man. In the village people looked up at the sky and believed that everything was ordered there. In the town it was the Polish property owner Romaschkamm and the Jewish banker Jungermann, that people looked up to because they could make you prosper or ruin you. They had their managers, their agents, who gave out good positions by which people prospered, and on these prosperous ones lived others who were poor, and on them, the poorest of all.

In the village the men all wore the same linen shirts over the same linen breeches, the same sheepskin of better quality or worse. But in town everyone dressed differently. Some, especially the officials, wore short coats and patent-leather shoes and stiff collars and steep hats and gloves and drove around in carriages; while others went barefoot and in rags.

The town was built differently too. Our village was scattered and planless – a house, a garden, then at intervals in all directions other houses, other gardens, better houses or worse houses perhaps; but they all had the same thatched roofs. Horodenka was built in circles. The outermost circle was most like the village. There were many thatched roofs, though here already there were some that were tiled; here the Ukrainian population lived who sold their potatoes and onions and turnips and beans and green stuff and chickens and other produce at market every day.

Next came the middle circle; there you began to see villa-like houses with shingled roofs and flower gardens. There lived the higher officials of the county, the personnel of the courts and the board of assessors, and in the center, hedged in by these two circles, lived the Jews.

How did this center, the Jewish quarter of Horodenka, look? In the middle of it there was the great market place surrounded by public buildings. The post office was the biggest of them, but what took your eye was the neat Polish Catholic church with its onion-shaped dome and its clean, white plastered and painted walls; you could see where two bricks were missing in the belly of the dome, and there owls had made their nests.

The market place was cut in two by the main highway and again by a second highway, so that in front of the church there was a crossroad with four signboards. The road to the east led to the Dniester River by way of the town of Usciecka and on to the Russian border. The road to the west led to Kolomea and Stanislau, and on to Lemberg. The road to the south led to Zaleszczyki, the Galician Meran, and the road to the north led to Obertyn, the city of horse dealers and thieves. If you asked a man, "You're from Obertyn, aren't you?" the prompt answer always was, "You're a thief yourself!" And then all around lay the forty-eight villages belonging to the county of which Horodenka was the county seat.

The Jewish quarter was divided into two parts by the main highroad: the upper streets and the lower streets. The part of the town that contained the upper streets had a promenade framed in a wide avenue of chestnut trees, running from the courthouse, the first large building, toward the west down through the market place, past the church, then southward along the road that led to Zaleszczyki as far as the Baron Hirsch school. The upper streets were swept and sprinkled and cared for by town employees; but no one bothered about the lower streets.

And there was a big ditch in which people dumped their excrement and their garbage and their swill, and in the early morning you could see whole swarms of them with their bodies partly exposed doing the most private things. The lower streets were dirty and they stank, and when no rain or frost came to wash away the filth and clean the air, people were simply suffocated. The small wooden houses were set one against another in rows, for it was cheaper to build up against your neighbor's wall. One house pressed and leaned and supported itself against another like those frail, sickly beings who are afraid of being alone. In these houses lived poverty: cobblers, tailors, carpenters, barrel makers, masons, furriers, bakers, and different sorts of carters and porters – all industrious men who bustled around the whole day to earn a loaf of bread for five kreuzer so that their roomful of children would have something to eat.

They waited especially for Tuesday, the day of the market, on which the peasants and Jews from the forty-eight outlying villages came to town. Those Tuesdays, those market days, gave them their livelihood, and then what a scrambling and running and shoving and sweating – you would have thought the world was coming to an end! The most important part of it was the big cattle market outside the town. On market day stallions sniffed the air, recognizing their old brides or getting the scent of a yet unknown virgin, and all, mares and stallions, greeted each other with wild whinnies. The poor cows who hadn't been milked that day, so that their udders might look tight and full, mooed desperately for help. Sheep bleated their longing for green fields, but the loudest of all were the pigs: they screamed as if someone were cutting slices of ham out of their living fat rumps.

...Through all this dart the dealers with their brokers, sweating, bellowing, bargaining, looking angry, slapping their customers' hands, until finally they have brought the difference down to only three gulden – both parties have long been of one mind, the buyer has long since decided to take the horse, the cow, the pig, or the sheep at the dealer's price except for those last three gulden! Finally they meet each other halfway, each concedes one gulden, and with the remaining one they drink to the success of the deal and to the health of the animal.

In the town market place the transactions are smaller. Here the poor peasants display their chickens, their geese or ducks, their grain, their flax, their linen, their oil. Then they go to the shops and buy colored cloth, glass beads, wool to embroider their shirts, sugar, salt, pots, matches, herrings. The restaurants and saloons are packed with the men drinking vodka, beer, mead, rum, eating their bits of bacon or sausage. Many are gay, some drunk; everyone shoves, pushes and talks, his eyes wide open, timid, curious, searching – a child has got lost, a pickpocket is caught, a nervous horse has broken loose and galloped straight into the pottery market. Yelling and bellowing, pushing and pulling, hundreds of offers and bids being made at once. Merry-go-rounds luring and calling. And through it all goes poverty from the lower streets, looking for a chance to earn something. The carpenters offer their boxes and chests, the cobblers their boots and shoes, the furriers and tailors their scraps; in exchange they are offered grain, chickens, geese, ducks, eggs.

The women and the young people are the liveliest. The women offer white bread, rolls, cakes, cooked peas, beans, *piroushki* with various fillings: potato, cheese, meat, sweet cherries, sour cherries, blueberries. Everyone runs, bellows himself hoarse as he bids against the others. Competition and cursing and swindling for pennies....

We young children were the wildest of all, because it was fun for us to be there too, to belong to it, to be a part of the enormous congestion. We peddled kvass, which we carried in glass pitchers. It was a sort of apple cider sweetened and mixed according to a secret formula by Feivele Kvasnick, who cheated us. We bought his product because he was the only dealer in town and hated him and sang a mocking song about him:

> *"Your Feivele, our kvass,*
> *Twenty times come lick my arse!"*

We put ice in the kvass; it melted and the kvass got weaker, colder, and we called out our wares glowingly or entreatingly or threateningly:

> *"Fresh kvass gives might,*
> *Ice-cold and just right!"*

or:

> *"Buy kvass, buy!*
> *Drink it and feel spry."*

I was best with threats. I cried out shrilly:

> *"Kvass, kvass, ice-cold kvass!*
> *Drink my kvass and you'll be well.*
> *Pass it by*
> *And end in hell!"*

Many an old peasant woman, hearing me sing out my imprecation, only shook her head and crossed herself and bought a glass and gave me a heller extra and told me I mustn't swear. She was quite right; but I then I reflected that if I had not sworn, she would neither have bought my kvass nor given me an extra heller. Cursing brings the money in, I thought to myself, and went on crying out my threats and curses, and many a Tuesday I earned from thirty to forty kreuzer. This small fortune I always paid over to Father, who praised me for my industry and that made me proud and happy.

And my brother Schabse, who was about a year older than I, earned about one third of what I did, and he was envious and insecure. And I that made me even happier and surer of myself; and that was the beginning of a *rivalry*, of a *competition*, in the town.

On one such Tuesday my eldest brother Schachne Eber came in from the village, and toward evening he went with Father to the flour dealer, Scholem Luft, and paid him twenty-five gulden, and thus it was arranged that we should open a bakery: Herr Luft was to furnish us flour, giving us credit for another twenty-five gulden for which my brother made himself responsible. So one day we moved from the lower streets, rented Froim Gloger's bakery which was next to Herr Zulauf's property near the Baron Hirsch school – and all of a sudden we were something elegant! We baked black bread and white, and crescents and Vienna rolls, and since we had no steady clientele and all of us shared in the work, we sold everything cheaper than the other bakers, but we were our own best customers, for we could not resist temptation, and, despite strict orders to the contrary, each of us devoured from forty to fifty of the fresh, crisp crescents or Vienna rolls every day. Each of us felt sure that he was the only one who did it, and we all did it. The bakery did not prosper.

My brother Schabse and I went to the Baron Hirsch school, but at night we were awakened to twist crescents or shape Vienna rolls. Now something happened which was to have an important effect on both our lives. My brother was seven, I was six. But he was tall and thin, and I was stocky and strong. I had to look up to him, which annoyed me. When we were called, it took him a long time to awaken, but I jumped up like a weasel. He would resist and cry; I saw this and made myself out to be very alert and willing. That was the beginning and the foundation of my self-confidence. I was praised at his expense; he began to hate me, and I to enjoy his helplessness. He became less and less confident, I more and more so. It was the same thing at school, in the street, and at play. It had really begun with our kvass peddling. God forgive me, it was partly my fault.

And when I saw my brother thirty years later, I had a painful feeling. He had not changed at all. He had grown-up children who treated him as badly as we, his brothers and sisters, used to. He had the same red, weepy, reproachful eyes, and he spoke with the same slight, hesitant stutter, only now he wore a beard that looked as artificial as the beards they put on young supers in an opera chorus.

I had the feeling of having committed a delicate little murder. I took his self-reliance away from him and added it to mine. For we were already competitors; we were not in our village any more, but in the county seat Horodenka, where all the evil traits of city people were already at play: rivalry and greed. Because it is a far greater distance from the village of Werbiwci to the town of Horodenka than from the town of Horodenka to any great European capital.

12

My Rabbi-Teacher, Schitnshale from Milnitz, for Whom You Would Do Absolutely Anything

My experiences at the cheder in Skolje were soon forgotten for our rabbi-teacher, Schimshale from Milnitz, was a weary and peacable man. Not only did he never beat us, but he was grateful if we would let *him* alone. He used to say that he liked a fresh boy with a good head, who learned something, better than a "good," "well-behaved" boy whose head was empty. We often abused this tolerance of his and played little practical jokes on him.

Once we fastened his caftan to his chair, and once we tied his foot to the table leg with a piece of string. But he would only shake his head and smile wearily and kindly. Another time, when he fell asleep over his book with his head in his right arm on the table, as he often did, we fastened his beard to the table top with hot wax. When he woke he simply scraped the wax off the table and then pulled it out of his beard, bit by bit; he said nothing about it that day, nor did he show any other reaction.

A few days later, he simply said: "Children, recently someone played a trick with my beard. I said nothing, but it was not because I didn't mind. On the contrary, I was so unhappy that I simply could not say anything. You know that I have many cares and that I am very poor, but God has given me a beard just like the beards of people who are prosperous and have no cares, a beard like any other man's. So that my beard was a comfort to me in my troubles. But when you insult my beard, even to my face, you make me poorer than I already am – and none of you is the richer for it."

This happened on a Thursday. On Mondays and Thursdays it was his habit to fast, and so he spoke very softly on those days; and we looked at the floor in embarrassment that afternoon, and he sent us home an hour earlier.

But from that day on he was as sacred to us as the Torah itself. We never joked about our rabbi again and never again played a trick on him.

First he patiently taught us the letters of the Hebrew alphabet; they looked rather like little boxes and little tools, like little houses with doors and gates, or like cubes with little windows.

In Skolje those letters used to dance before my eyes, and I could not tell one from another, but here, under our patient, weary teacher, I soon had them sorted out, and it was even fun to distinguish between them, and soon I could put them together like little boxes, with the vowel signs under them, and read them; I could not understand them, because we spoke Yiddish and this was Hebrew. So we learned to pray without understanding what we prayed, and to sing without understanding what we sang.

And soon after, I began to learn the *Chumisch*, the five books of Moses. And there, translated with commentaries and interpretations, lay a whole wide world, a world that had once upon a time existed, in which humanity had once lived, and where heaven and God were so close that people like Moses and Abraham and Jacob and Mother Rachel and other notables went in and out to see Him as the prominent merchants and officials here in Horodenka went in and out to see Baron Romaschkamm or the banker, Jungermann. And when a boy began to study the *Chumisch*, there was always a celebration. And one Sabbath afternoon I was presented with a new suit; and a number of watches and watch chains, twenty, at least, were borrowed from our friends and relatives. And the watches and chains were hung on me and on another small boy, who was to act as the Questioner and Blesser. Then we both stood on top of a table, which was covered with a cloth, and the teacher and parents and relatives and neighbors were sitting and standing around the table in the narrow room, expectantly, with shining eyes; and then it began.

The other boy spread out his hands and said:

"*Hatienu es rojschchu, wej awirechechu* [Bow your head, that I may bless you]."

"*Ben Pojress Josseff ben Pojress Elihoju* [Joseph the Beautiful, Joseph the Charming], even as Joseph Hazadik found favor with God and men, so may you, *jingali* [little boy], find favor with God and men!"

And everyone cried in a chorus, "Amen, amen, amen!"

Then the Blesser questioned me, and I answered.

Questioner: "What are you studying, *jingali?*"

Jingali: "*Chumisch.*"

Questioner: "What does *Chumisch* mean?"

Jingali: "Five."

Questioner: "Five what? Five pretzels for a kreuzer?"

Jingali: "No, the five holy books in the holy Torah."

Questioner: "What book are you studying, *jingali?*"

Jingali: "*Wajikru.*"

Questioner: "What does *Wajikru* mean?"

Jingali: "'And he called.'"

Questioner: "Who called? The *shamas* called to the synagogue?"

Jingali: "No, God called to Moses to tell him the laws of the Sacrifice and the Sacrifice is holy, and I, little *jingali*, am holy, too, and that is why, luckily for me, the Rabbi teaches me *Wajikru.*"

Questioner: "Study, *jingali*, study! Show us what you know," and he winked at the others, who were smiling with pleasure and amusement.

Jingali: *"Wajikru* – 'And He called'; 'Moses' – a man named Moses – "

But I was not able to finish; everyone was congratulating, *"Mazltov, mazltov,"* and Father filled the glasses and Mother was weeping with joy and happiness and pride, and the other women were weeping with her. Everyone kissed me, much against my will, for I felt almost a grownup. I knew that everyone was looking at me, I avoided their eyes, and was sure that never before had so many people looked at me so hard, and that they were all there on my account, and around my heart I felt a sweetness far sweeter than the honey cake that I was eating....

Since the incident of the beard, we loved our haggard, wonderful Rabbi Schimshale. In winter, when we studied until nightfall and went home with lanterns, it was nicest, and we listened gladly while he explained and illustrated each sentence and sometimes even each word by telling whole stories. And he spoke of the holiness of the printed word and of the interpretation of words, and of what was between the words. It would begin like this: *"Szymon w'Levi achim* [Simon and Levi were brothers]...." And then he would start to tell us what kind of brothers they were, how strong and big and broad-shouldered, and he was named Levi because once, when he was pursuing the Philistines and was almost dead of thirst in the desert, lions fell on him, but he seized a lioness, picked her up by her nose and her tail, drank the milk from her teats, and flung her away. Simon could uproot mountains with his shoulders and scatter them about, burying his enemies. And they had a sister, a most beautiful sister. And the Philistines had one day fallen upon her while the brothers were away from home. Because the Philistines had defiled their sister, the two brothers went into the town of the Philistines and cut down all the men with their swords and burnt the city to ashes, and so revenged their sister's honor.

And then when we were studying *"Wej Ani* [And I, Jacob]," and we hung on our teacher's lips as he told us in simple Yiddish, such as the people in our street spoke, the story:

"*Wej Ani* [And I, Jacob], dying now in Egypt, tell you, my son Joseph, to carry me to Canaan after I am dead and to bury me there, though I did not do thus with your mother, Rachel. For I buried her on the road to Bethlehem and did not bring her into the town. And if you think: It rained, or the roads were heavy, I say to you, no. The road was as dry and as full of holes as a sieve. This was after I had served my time with Laban, first seven years for Leah and then seven years for your mother, Rachel, after which we set out. But Laban sent after us and caught us and said that we had stolen his idols. I was angry at his suspicion and I cried: 'Let whoever has stolen your idols die,' and look you, your mother, Rachel, had stolen the idols and she died, and I buried her there in the fields on the road to Bethlehem. Why? You will ask again, my son. I will tell you: I had a prophetic vision and I saw our people wandering in the wilderness, downcast and lonely and desperate; and they will come upon Mother Rachel's grave and seek comfort and weep and wail and cry, 'Mother Rachel, Mother Rachel, see what is happening to your children!' and Mother Rachel will go up to God and say to Him, 'Father in heaven, what are you doing to my children?' and God will answer, 'I am punishing them.' And Mother Rachel will say, 'Why are you punishing them?' And God will answer, 'I am punishing them because they danced before the golden calf!' Then Mother Rachel will say, 'Father in heaven, let me tell you a story:

"'When Jacob came to woo me, he was big and broad-shouldered and keen-eyed, and we found favor in each other's eyes and we liked each other as soon as we met by the well. But my father, Laban, was sly and cunning and crafty like a peasant and wanted first to get rid of Leah, who lisped and was little and ugly and pock-marked, and when it grew dark he called Jacob into the room and I had to hide under the bed and speak for Leah, so that Jacob would think that Leah was I and I was Leah, and he married her. And I loved Jacob with my whole heart and with everything that was mine, and yet

I was not *jealous* of poor Leah. I was only a creature of flesh and blood and I was not *jealous*. And You, *the great God, the Maker of all worlds, are jealous of a golden calf.*' And God will answer, 'Go, my daughter, Rachel, go and comfort your children and say to them that I will never forget them.'"

And about Moses he always had new explanations to give and new stories to tell. Once he asked us to drink nothing for half a day because of a very important story he had to tell us. We obeyed, and when he saw that some of us were beginning to have parched lips, he made us drink and said that a good story is not only to be heard with the ears and felt with the heart and understood with the mind: a good story can be tasted on the tongue, with hunger and thirst. He had told us not to drink that day, for example, so that from half a day of thirst we could understand how hard it was for Moses and the people to wander for forty years in the wilderness where there were no wells at all. And he began to tell about how Moses led the people through the wilderness for forty years:

"The people were worried and desperate and lost the strength of their belief in the promised land and grew fainthearted and quarrelsome and longed to be back in slavery, eating the food of slaves. And discipline was undermined, and Moses looked sadly up to heaven; and one day it thundered, and lightning flashed, and everyone knew that the Lord was calling Moses, and Moses disappeared and then came back and gathered all the people together and spoke: 'Thus spoke the Lord: Let each male, young and old, take a spade and dig himself a grave this day, and tonight let him lie down in it and not ask why or wherefore, for such is the will of the Lord.'

"And each of them, young and old, dug his own grave; and in the evening they lay down in their graves as the Lord, through Moses, had commanded.

"And when the sun came up the next morning, two thirds of the people lay dead in their graves, and only one third arose, and Moses said: 'Thus spoke the Lord: The fainthearted and the fearful, those of little faith and those who are afraid, shall lie in their graves, but the strong and the brave, the valiant and the fearless, the stouthearted and the believers shall be strengthened and restored and sent with new courage to journey on and enter the land of Canaan.'"

He was a tired man, our teacher, Schimshale from Milnitz, and only poor children studied with him. He had a houseful of children himself and was forever running around borrowing money and asking for credit. He got his bread from us as pay for his teaching, but it was never reckoned up. Father said there was no business so pleasing to God as exchanging bread for the Torah, and to judge from the number of loaves that the rabbi took, we should have become great scholars and even rabbis ourselves.

We often held little feasts in the cheder. There were about sixteen or twenty of us. Each of us gave what he could – a kreuzer or two. We bought white bread and herring and plum jam and honey and a little vodka for the rabbi, and we sat at the table with him and he treated us like grownups, like equals, and on one such evening we bought rather more vodka than usual, and he became talkative and explained to us *why he had never laid hands on a pupil as other teachers did.* He said that he always remembered *Joshua and Moses, the greatest teacher and the greatest pupil since the world began.* And, as he drank his third glass, his face looked cheerful and handsome and he began:

"The story is really about our Father in heaven and Moses and Joshua. One day the Lord called Moses up to Mount Nebo and said, with some embarrassment: 'Listen, my friend, you have had worry and trouble enough with the people by now, so I think the best thing would be for you to take a rest at last and come to me in heaven. What do you think, my son?' And Moses looked bewildered and surprised and said: 'No, thank you, no. First I must lead them into the promised land. After that, I'd be delighted. Excuse me, O Lord,' was all he said, 'I'm in a great hurry now.' And off he went.

"After a while the Lord sent for him again and said: 'You know, Moses, it is very dull here in heaven. My angels have been practicing on their wind instruments and their string instruments for a long time, and they want a celebration, and they keep asking me when they shall receive you. You know, my son, how much we all love you.' 'Yes, yes,' said Moses, 'I know, Father, I know, but tell me – what would You have said if somebody had interrupted You during the six days of creation? No one knows better than You that a work once taken in hand has to be finished. Forgive me, O Lord. I hope I shall not lose Your heaven and the angels, and besides, I will hurry as fast as I can, with Your help, of course, and then I shall be glad to accept Your invitation to eternity.' And he went away.

"And after a while Moses was called to the Lord again, and this time Moses began without waiting to be spoken to: 'Father, I know that the angels find things dull and want to celebrate and that there is a golden chair waiting for me – it isn't something else, is it? I am almost at end of my work, almost in Canaan. What is it this time? Please be frank and speak openly. I am in a great hurry now.' And the Lord in His eternal goodness and peace smiled and said: 'Moses, frankness deserves frankness. You know that I have always been with you and always will be, but even I have to follow certain rules. You want me to be quite frank, don't you? Well, you have a pupil, Joshua, who has been sitting on his stool for forty years, listening to you and following you around and doing everything for you. Now he has a long beard and gray hair himself, and waits and waits. *The time has come now when I have to make the pupil, Joshua, the teacher and the leader of the people.* Now you know, my son.' Moses only looked up at the Lord and said: 'Is that all? Why didn't You say so right away? Appoint him, then, to be the teacher and leader of the people, and let me sit on his stool and watch, only watch from far off what becomes of my undertaking, my work.' And the Lord said: 'Very well, Moses, my son, I cannot refuse you that. Go, and I will guard you and keep you.'

"When Moses came back, it was thundering, and lightning flashed, and his pupil, Joshua, got up from his stool and knew that the Lord was calling him, and he went to Mount Nebo, and the Lord spoke to him, and the people waited in awe; and then Joshua came and walked straight to the temple, and everyone saw the halo around his head, and everyone knew that the Lord had kissed him that day. And just outside the temple Moses took Joshua by the arm and said: 'Joshua! What did He say to you?' And Joshua shook his arm free and turned and went on and only answered over his shoulder: *'Did you ever tell me what he said to you?'* And left him standing there and went into the temple, and the people went with him.

"And no one noticed how Moses, bent and shamed, went hurrying by back paths up to Mount Nebo; and the Lord was there waiting for him, and Moses raised his eyes to the Lord and said, 'Father, take me up to You!'

"Now do you understand why I don't treat you like little children and pupils?" said our rabbi. "One can never know who is the pupil and who the teacher. One day one of you will be a great teacher and I his pupil. Now you sit and watch me and listen to me like real men, and I feel as if it were only yesterday that I first went to cheder. Then one day I went to bed a child and the next morning I got up with a beard, and now I have a roomful of children of my own. And now it is too late to learn a trade. Look at the carpenters, the cobblers, the tailors, the bakers. They don't have to hold out their hands" – he used actually to have to go begging every Thursday, and he suffered from it. "Learn a trade, quickly, for tomorrow or some other day you will get up and find hair on your faces and have children yourselves and troubles, like me and your fathers."

He sang beautiful melodies too, and was fond of telling gruesome stories about ghosts and devils and lost souls who are to be found at crossroads at night. Lost souls were his particular specialty. Often such a sinful soul could enter neither heaven nor hell. It would live in a dog that was beaten, or in a pig or a hen, and could be released only by the blessing of a really pious person who "recognized" the soul in the animal. He also liked to tell us about the different kinds of devils. One sort was really wicked, but little goblins only played practical jokes. When they came into your house at night, they turned everything upside down or scattered sneeze powder, nailed the doors shut, or sewed up your shirt sleeves; it was gruesome and funny at once.

And when we went home at night with our little lanterns, and came to the crossroads, I made everyone stop and cried: "Witches, ghosts, and devils, hear there, hear there!" And then: "Away, away, away!" Everyone trembled and ran home with his teeth chattering. I trembled doubly: for fear of the evil ones and in terror at having called them. But the feeling that the others thought I was not at all afraid gave me something that made me keep on doing it. Every night they bargained with me not to call the evil ones. I acquired old bones and bits of iron and buttons. The buttons they cut off their clothes and their brothers' and fathers' clothes; but every time that we came to the crossroads I could no longer contain myself, I forgot all the bargains and called the ghosts again, so that I could gloat over their terror. Yes, I was a sweet little innocent child!

Until one day, when my rabbi-teacher and I were alone, he said to me: "I know, I know – you are much braver and smarter than the others – and just for that reason, you should protect them and not frighten them. However, I don't intend to meddle in your business. I would rather leave it to your own judgment."

And I understood that he was right, and I never did it again; but really only to oblige my rabbi-teacher, Schimshale from Milnitz, for whom you would do absolutely anything.

13

Perhaps My First Part

We heard that a Jew, Herr Hirsch, was so rich that the Emperor had him come to Vienna and offered him great honors and title; and Herr Hirsch only said, "Thank you, great Emperor, but I cannot accept."

"Why?" asked the Emperor, astonished.

And Herr Hirsch had answered: "Great Emperor, God has made me rich, and you want to give me honors and titles; but in our country of Galicia there are so many little Yiddish children whose parents are so poor that they cannot feed or clothe or educate them. And since I have the good fortune to be in your presence, I should like to beg you to permit me to open schools there at my expense so that these children may learn something and when they grow up, they will make brave and intelligent soldiers for you."

Then the Emperor said: "Oh, I like that idea, I like it very much, my dear *Baron* Hirsch."

And so Herr Hirsch came home Baron Hirsch, and founded the Baron Hirsch schools in Galicia, and one of them was in Horodenka.

You could not compare the Baron Hirsch schools with the cheder. The cheder was dark and dirty, and Schimshale loved us and talked to us as "equals." The school was light and clean, and the teachers treated us like little animals and beat us.

But if you studied well, you were given a cap with a shiny visor, and if you studied more, you got a pair of breeches to go with it, and a really good student got a jacket too, and the best students were outfitted from head to foot, even down to shirts and handkerchiefs.

We were watched to see that we came to school washed and clean and even with our shoes polished; if not, we were sent home, which was a disgrace. The teachers dressed in European fashion, spoke Polish, and used to beat us. When we did our exercises badly or gave the wrong answer to a question, we had to hold out our hands, palms up, and the teacher hit them with a ruler.

Many of the teachers hit us mechanically, and it didn't hurt much, but one teacher, Herr Wieselberg, who taught us to read and write Yiddish, hit with the sharp side of the ruler. He was the first wicked man I encountered in my life. He had a golden blond Emperor Franz Josef beard, and on the slightest excuse he looked in a mirror and combed his beard, especially after a thrashing; on those occasions his face turned as red as an ape's bottom and he looked in his mirror and combed his hair and beard and made himself trim. On his desk lay his ruler, a very thin rattan stick for thrashing, and his comb and mirror. We were often laid across a bench and thrashed with the rattan stick. Boys who expected a thrashing used to stuff the backs of their breeches with small pillows or rags. When they were caught at it they had to take down their breeches, and the blows fell on their naked flesh. That hurt a great deal and was a disgrace besides. Herr Wieselberg was a master at these proceedings, and we hated him so much that we never spoke to his children, who went to the same school with us. He came to thrash, not to teach.

They all thrashed, even the woman teacher, whose name was Chameides. And that made us particularly angry. But we defended ourselves after our fashion. In winter we brought pieces of ice to class or little hard snowballs and we started small snowball fights in the classrooms. And in spring there were millions of cockchafers. We brought them to class by the hundreds and, at a given signal, let them loose, and they buzzed and hummed around and our Chameides became hysterical and screamed, and we looked innocent and rejoiced. Once during recess we stuffed her gloves with cockchafers, putting one in each finger, and when the class was over and she began to put her gloves on, she shrieked with terror and we with joy. She called the director, whose name was Berlass, a tall lean, dark-looking man, with a pale face and twisted mustaches, and he kept us in all day.

There was only one teacher who never laid hands on us; his name was Dreyfuss. When you took your exercise book to his house, he even gave you sweets. But he died suddenly, and someone wrote on his gravestone:

> *If only you'd left your beard grow,*
> *You'd be walking in heaven now!*

But the other teachers treated us like little criminals.

However, the fine clothes for holidays, and in winter the good thick bean soup, and the games outside the school helped us see it through. The good that Baron Hirsch did us, his teachers could not quite undo.

At home, life was more regular now, for everyone worked, and each had his particular duties. We younger children got up at four o'clock to help roll crescents and shape Vienna rolls. At about six o'clock we put the various sorts of bread and rolls into straw baskets and carried them to our customers and to the market stall. About eight o'clock we went to school. I always had bits of dough stuck under my fingernails, and I showed them to the other children proudly and boasted that 1 was already working at night like a real journeyman.

My brother Schabse, who was about a year older than I, was always tired and unhappy, and his eyes were red and bleary, as if he had not had enough sleep. In his spare time he studied his lessons and kept out of our street games, and when the teacher questioned, he stuttered unintelligible answers, nervous and frightened; but I knew what he meant. He had to sit down in shame and embarrassment, and when I was called on after him, I had only to repeat what he had just said; but I repeated it loudly and clearly; and so I was praised at his expense. My poor brother Schabse!

We sat on the third bench, and beside me sat two blond, spoiled boys with rosy faces, about my brother's age and mine. They had long blond curls down to their shoulders and wore light blue and pink sailor suits. They were the banker Jungermann's children.

Every day they brought some new kind of delicacy to school. Usually it was slices of white bread with chicken between them. Or rolls with butter and preserves, or honey, or sweet raisin buns. And fruit too: sweet or sour cherries, apples, pears, or peaches. Once during recess I was hungry, as usual, and I looked at their tidbits, my mouth watering, and asked young Jungermann to give me something. "No," he said, and looked at me coldly and went on eating. I felt the blood rushing to my face, and I was ashamed to have asked him, and ashamed because he had refused me, and I began to hate them both. I became very unfriendly, and every two or three days I thought up something unpleasant to do to them. I brought soot and scattered it on their side of the desk, and they got themselves and their books filthy. I put sharp stones on their seat, and they were both hurt and annoyed. One day I put a tack on my neighbor's seat, and he sat down on it and shrieked, and everyone laughed except me – I only looked innocent. And on another day I knew beforehand that the woman teacher was going to ask me something. So I took my inkwell out of its well, made sure it was full, and carefully set it in such a way that when I was called on and jumped up, the inkwell spilled over my little neighbor like a waterfall. His rosy face, his blond curls, his white sailor suit were covered with ink spots. The class roared with laughter. Little Jungermann cried, the teacher tried to calm us, I put on a serious, puzzled expression, but somewhere inside me there was something sweeter than his sweetest buttered raisin bun. And so it went on.

I would slip into our bench like a flash and hit our young banker in the ribs with my sharp elbow, or when we stood up, I would "accidentally" tread on his foot as hard as I could. I kept inventing new ways to plague him, and he watched me in terror, always expecting some fresh piece of malice.

But once during recess he came to me shyly and said, "Why haven't you ever asked me for anything again?"

I said, "And if I asked you, would you give me anything?"

The older brother spoke up and said, "You just ask."

And I said, "You just give!"

And I couldn't believe my eyes – they had a whole package of lunch for me, and a big pear too.

From then on I got something good to eat every day, and so I began to look forward to going to school. And the inkwell stayed properly in its hole, and there were no stones or nails on their seats, and I sat down carefully on our bench so that I wouldn't hit my neighbor's ribs with my sharp elbows, and there was no more treading on feet. And we became friends, and after school I took them both to the market to steal fruit.

We had long laths with nails at the end. When the market woman looked away, we brought the nail down on an apple or a pear, and they were ours and we vanished. We were a small, organized gang. And we rifled orchards, and when there was a fire we ran to "save things" and stole what we could like magpies. At the smith's, when no one was looking, we "found" bits of iron and horseshoes and nails and sold them all to Mord'chai, the old iron dealer, who pretended to be pious and who knew very well – we could tell from the prices he paid us – where we had gotten our wares. Mord'chai gave us a new and happy idea. There were five or six of us boys who were always together, so some of us offered him our booty and haggled with him, and meanwhile the others stole bits of iron from his own stand and then offered them to him, and he often bought the same horseshoe and the same nails two or three times over. He bought and paid for them every time, and that was wonderful fun. But in our overconfidence, we once stole an old samovar from his stand and offered to sell it back to him right away. He became suspicious, looked at us, looked at the place where the samovar had been, and began to take off his leather belt. We threw the samovar at his head and ran and never did business with him again.

Then one day the banker Jungermann sent his boys' private tutor to my father to complain that I not only was stealing, but was trying to make thieves of the Jungermann boys. Father said he was mistaken and threw the tutor out – his children were honest and upright. Let him bring proof and stop spreading such tales about our family. And when the tutor had gone, Father sent everyone else out of the room and said to me: "I believe every word the man said, but now I want to hear it from you. Say yes or no, because you are studying with a Godfearing man, Schimshale from Milnitz, and in the Torah it is written, 'Thou shalt not steal,' and until you are thirteen years old I and your rabbi must be punished for your sins. Say yes or no now, and tell me how many strokes I shall give you."

I said "Yes" and asked for twenty-five strokes on my rump, and Father said, "Good, my son, you are not a thief yet, because thieves are liars too; and promise me never to do it again, and I will let you off without the twenty-five strokes you asked for."

Then everyone came back, and Father only said, "Well, well, Jungermann is a thief himself. He steals from God and the world and his fellow men, so he is afraid that his children will take after him. We are honest, honorable people and do not have to be afraid of such things."

I did not understand him then, my wise, good father; but if there is such a place as heaven, he is sitting up there now and smiling and thinking: How *long* it takes for a child to understand such *simple* things!...

One Tuesday there was great excitement in the market place. A rope was stretched from the highest building, Herr Neumann's house, to the post office. A man, a woman, and a boy of about my size appeared, dressed in colored tights with spangles, the mother in green, the father in red, the boy in light blue. Father, mother, and boy climbed onto a high platform. The mother beat a drum, the boy blew three blasts on a trumpet, and the father made a speech. He explained that he spoke all languages but here he would speak Polish because the burgomaster spoke Polish too. Then he told us that they were great artists – witness the many medals he had received from all the crowned heads on earth – and that he had come to Horodenka to demonstrate his art just because we had such a fine burgomaster. He was almost weeping by now as he said that he staked the life of his only child on the chances of his art. His eight-year-old son, who was just my age, would walk through the air on the rope from one building to the other, and he asked for no money beforehand – and now there were sobs in his voice – because if anything were to happen to his child, he would have no use for the money; but if God helped his son to cross over to the other building on the rope, then he, his wife, and his son would permit themselves to pass the hat, and he did not believe that there were any people in Horodenka scoundrelly enough to simply walk off after the demonstration without contributing anything to the support of the artists who risked their lives and who had received medals from all the crowned heads on earth.

Thousands of people stood tense with expectation in the market place. The man tied two ropes around the boy's waist which hung down on either side, almost to the ground; the woman handed the boy a balancing pole; then they both climbed down, and each took the end of one of the ropes. Everyone stopped talking and stood looking up at the boy in silence. The father called something to him, the mother wiped away a tear, the boy crossed himself, and the father shouted in twenty languages, "Attention, attention, attention! Most honorable audience, the performance will commence!"

And, to the astonishment of thousands of spectators, the boy began to slide first one foot and then the other forward, and to try the rope, and to advance, balancing himself with the pole. He was walking, putting one foot before the other, and sliding them forward along the rope.

The crowd was electrified and stared tensely at the boy. The boy advanced, and came to the middle of the rope, moved his pole up and down, and cried in a heart-rending voice, "Father, the wind!" The spectators shuddered and crossed themselves. But behold, he went on. God be praised! Faster, faster, faster he stepped, balanced the pole, moved forward, faster, faster – then there were only five steps left – and at last he reached the roof of the post-office building.

The market place screamed and bellowed and jumped with relief. Father, mother, and son collected the money. No one went away, Everyone pressed around to give his mite.

I was close to the boy. I drank in the sight of him. A human being had risked his life, a boy like me. I marveled at him and envied him.

And Saturday afternoon I assembled my friends and the neighbors' children. There was a rope on the ground, and I took a bread shovel in my hands and tautened my muscles and shut my eyes and slid first one foot and then the other forward, feeling my way, and advancing, and I came to the midway point and swayed to both sides, and thought I was falling, and cried desperately, "Father, the wind! Father, Father, the wind!" And then I repeated the performance again, and again, and again.

The children were in raptures. My brother Leibzi stared at me with a faraway look, and the sweat ran down my forehead, and I did it over and over. By this time I went faster along the rope until I came to the middle, and again I cried, "Father, the wind! Father, the wind!" And once again I stepped along the rope, and once again I reached the middle and balanced the bread shovel to the left and right and thought I was going to fall from an incredible height and cried desperately, "Father, the wind! Father, the wind! Father, the wind!"

And the neighbors came and grownups, and the bakery was packed, and a deaf woman asked what was going on, and one of the neighbors shouted in her ear: "You see, it's terribly hot in the bakery, and he goes back and forth yelling, 'Father, the wind! Father, the wind!' He must have gone crazy, poor boy."

14

Moische, Does One Smash Windows?

There were several town idiots in Horodenka, but Moische, the water carrier, was a useful idiot. He was tall and broad-shouldered, always quiet and thoughtful, and he never talked to anyone. And when someone wanting to gloat over his helplessness asked him a question – which happened often enough – he would turn his head away and answer, and avoid meeting the questioner's eyes. His answers were short; he looked for words as if the words had just come into the world and there were always one or two among them that didn't fit the subject.

Once when we little street boys were passing the town bath, we heard him cursing and shouting. We thought that someone had attacked him and that he was defending himself and struggling with an adversary, who seemed to be about to choke him, so desperately and so close together were strange, newly coined words pouring out of him. We slowly opened a window from outside, and in the half-dark bathhouse we saw a strange scene: Moische was standing in the middle of the room, staring straight ahead and talking and gesturing to an invisible adversary. "A ladder grew up to heaven...and lightning bolts fell on mangy heads! And therefore does one smash windows? Whole wells spit into the face...and tree trunks shoved down the throat for dessert...And therefore does one smash windows? The Talmud shoveled with the thumb...and robbed heaven of its blue....And therefore does one smash windows, does one smash windows, does one smash windows?" he repeated softly over and over again.

We boys at first stood paralyzed with fear, but then we began to ape him: "Mangy heads shot up to heaven on ladders, does one smash windows, Moische, does one smash windows? Brooks and beams swallowed and spat out, Moische, does one smash windows? Talmud stolen in the...blue sky.... Moische, does one smash windows? Moische, does one smash windows?"

But he, seeing us, became quiet at once and lay down on the floor with his eyes shut, indifferent, apathetic, as if nothing had happened. And we soon ran off about some of our fifty other childish tricks. But from that day on we – and the whole town with us – called him, "Moische-does-one-smash-windows."

Moische-does-one-smash-windows was dressed in rags, yet his rags were different from the rags of the other town idiots. The rags on his body were not dirty, and around his legs they were carefully tied on with string. Summer and winter, he went barefoot. And he had handsome, even graceful feet. When he was hungry, he took two cans from the bathhouse and carried water. Water, for food. Usually he carried the water straight to the bakers and was given an old loaf of bread in exchange. You could not count on him as a water carrier, because he carried water only when he was hungry. As soon as his hunger was appeased he stopped carrying water and hid himself away in the town bath again or in a barn, on a pile of hay, where he would lie talking softly to himself, then holding his breath while he soundlessly answered his own arguments.

When we little street boys pestered him, he simply made no response. But when some grown-up loafer only came near him, he became dangerous and wild and his white teeth showed and his black eyes flashed in his dark hairy face. And the loafers kept out of the way of his strong hands, which otherwise hung idly beside his broad-shouldered frame.

Moische-does-one-smash-windows had his own manner of life, like a real personality. He was not from Horodenka; he came from somewhere or other, but no one talked about it. He had a great deal of dignity, and there was an atmosphere around him like a ring. One would think that there is no one poorer in the world than a town idiot. And yet everyone knew that Moische-does-one-smash-windows was a head above the average citizen of Horodenka, and compared with the other town idiots, he was an aristocrat....

Once, on a day in Passover week, someone gave him a clean shirt and a coat. He bathed and dressed, then he walked through the lower streets in the afternoon, looking strangely unfamiliar and handsome. People standing outside or sitting in their doorways or looking out the window stared at him as if they were seeing him for the first time. The women blushed, the men looked after him enviously. The simple workmen envied him his broad shoulders, and the learned his noble expression; and no one dared to mock at him that day.

And a whisper ran from house to house that Moische-does-one-smash-windows was not a mere "nobody," and certainly not an idiot. And when he was out of sight, little arguing groups began to form, and pious Channe Rachel, the prayer leader, swore that she had seen with her own eyes a shining halo over his head. And crooked Josie, the tailor, who was tubercular and always coughed, swore by what was left of his lungs and by his seven children that Moische-does-one-smash-windows was a Lamed Wownik, one of the "Thirty-six Just Men." And Chaim Zankie, the carter, maintained, in his own manner of speech, that, for such a one, heaven would one day open, and if Horodenka had behaved badly to him, he had only to crack the heavenly whip once and the whole of Horodenka would be wiped off the earth! Yes, said someone else, it was easy to see what great and dangerous power there was in him: a Lamed Wownik! After all, that means something – one thirty-sixth part of the whole world depends on him!...

But we know that he was no Lamed Wownik. He was a poor fellow from Brody, a small Galician town on the Russian border. There he was to be married to Channe Chifre, the maid of the rich shopkeeper, Mr. Horowitz. But an accident intervened. Madame Horowitz, who was sickly, lay down and died. And then the rich and portly Mr. Horowitz decided, to his own great delight and to the vexation of all Brody, to marry his full-bosomed and broad-bottomed maid himself.

And on the wedding night, when, according to the old custom, the newly married pair was being put to bed, Moische broke all the windows in their house and, covered with shame and disgrace, fled to Horodenka. It was in Horodenka that he went crazy, and began to carry water only when he was hungry, and to sleep in the town bath or on a heap of straw.

And that day in Passover week when someone gave him a clean shirt and a coat, people thought he was one of the Thirty-six Just Men. But we know that he was not. He was only a poor man, come of poor people, whom the children and the whole town used to call "Moische-does-one-smash-windows."

15

Our Family Grows Smaller, Our Poverty Greater

In all disorder there is order, a sort of disorderly order. Even in the muddled affairs of our family, there was a method. Thus, my elder brother used his dowry to help my father start a bakery, and now he was married and lived in the village, just as we used to live there. His wife bore him, just as my mother had borne my father, a child every year, and he came to have the same worried expression, the same furrowed brow, as Father.

And one day my funny brother Jankel packed his wooden box, made a new walking stick out of sweet-smelling sour-cherry wood, and Father came in and asked him what he had in mind. Jankel said that a very rich and childless man from Miskolcz in Hungary was lying on his deathbed and had sent for Jankel to make him his heir and hand him over his property. Father smiled and asked why the man had chosen Jankel, and Jankel said that someone had told the rich man how amusing he was and how many clever tricks he could do, and the rich man wanted to laugh once more before he died. And Jankel began to ventriloquize without moving his lips and to roll his eyes and bend his legs backward at the knee, and he barked like a dog and clawed at us and mooed like a cow and crowed like a rooster, and everyone laughed, and Father asked him when he would be back, and Jankel finished cutting the sweet-smelling cherry stick, and he would not look my father in the eye, and his voice became suddenly serious and sad and he said: "When?" – why, the old man had storerooms full of money, and after the man died and as soon as Jankel had finished counting it, he would return in a four-horse carriage with a wagonful of gold as a present for Father. And he took up his wooden box and said he would come back presently to say good-bye, and he went out.

And he never came back again, and when anyone asked after him, we used to say: "Oh, Jankel – he was very lucky, he became the heir of a millionaire away off in Hungary, and now he sits dressed in silk and satin counting the money in his storerooms, and when he has finished he is coming home to take us all away with him and share his good fortune with us." We waited all our lives for Jankel; he never wrote, and we never heard from him again....

Abraham, the second oldest, went to Lemberg with some carters one day and remained there. After a time he came home, dressed in city clothes and bringing us presents; he smiled happily and contentedly and asked Father to come with him, because he had found a bride in Lemberg and wanted to show her people that he hadn't been found on a doorstep, and Father must honor his wedding. Father was moved and proud, dressed himself in his Sunday clothes, and went with Abraham to attend the wedding. Then he came back and told us wonders about Abraham's beautiful bride, and how big Lemberg was, and that Abraham dealt in fruit and went about with prominent people, and no one in Lemberg called him by a nickname or laughed at him when he spoke, and the people in Lemberg lived on friendly terms with one another, and earned more, and had less time than in Horodenka to gossip and slander their neighbors. Yes, indeed, Lemberg was really a great city. Father's account made a tremendous impression, and each of us began to have an unexpressed longing to escape, to flee to some great city where everyone is busy and friendly and there is no time for gossip and jealousy.

Now the four eldest sons had all left. First Schmiel. Schachne Eber, the eldest, lived on in the village. Jankel went to count his millions, and Abraham married and settled in Lemberg.

When we opened the bakery, Sister Rachel had come home. She said she had been staying with Father's sister, Aunt Taube, in Wiznica, and had learned millinery and could make lovely hats out of wire and cloth and straw. No one mentioned her friend Ivan to her. Everyone was glad that she had come back and saved the family reputation. She looked more grown-up and prettier; every Saturday our house was full of her admirers, who found an excuse for visiting by pretending that they wanted to make friends with her brothers.

We suffered under it, for we ourselves spoke ill of other girls who went around with fellows. Partly as brothers, partly as youths reaching manhood, we were concerned for the honor of the family; partly, we were simply jealous. And she didn't care a straw what we thought. She only smiled and winked with her bright black eyes and showed her big snow-white teeth and her round face, which was always changing color, with its two deep dimples. She laughed and whinnied like a young foal at everything and at every word. We suffered under it and almost hated her, for we had heard the fellows making dirty remarks about other girls. And then one day we heard a fellow make just such a remark about our sister. We broke his skull for him with stones, came home full of rage, and grabbed our pretty sister by the hair and pulled it. Father came running and separated us; we wept, Rachel wept, and we explained that we didn't want a whore for a sister! Father punished us and said we mustn't even think such things, it was impossible in our family; and we never spoke of it again.

But Rachel seemed to become more careful – Father had taken her for a walk and had a long talk with her. She sat in our stall in the market place and sold the baked goods, which we children brought from the bakery in baskets. Then one day we found some handkerchiefs of Rachel's embroidered with mottoes and with her name and the name of the fellow with whom she wag secretly "playing at love." There was another explosion, and she finally ran away again to Aunt Taube's in Wiznica.

We had two helpers working for us. One was nicknamed "The Keg." He was fat and strong, and we paid him a gulden and a half per week, with board and lodging. The lodging was in the flour storeroom in summer and on the stove in winter. There we all slept together in a heap.

The Keg was an object of wonder to me because of his freedom and independence. He finished his work and went out for a walk and had money and could buy anything he wanted, while we of the family worked much harder and were given no money at all. I set myself to copy his businesslike way of going about his work, and after a time I became the fastest of all at rolling crescents and shaping Vienna rolls.

Leibzi was now the oldest brother left at home; he was sixteen, but looked older, for he was tall and broad-shouldered, but clumsy. He had not begun to walk or talk till he was five; he had been the fattest child in the family. He was light blond and cared nothing about clothes, but he loved to eat, and at night, before the others rose to work, he cooked himself various delicacies, which he shared with me, He was quiet, never quarreled, gave way to everyone; he was the best-natured of us all. People said of him that he had no gall, and ever since the time we both had typhus there had been a close friendship between him and myself. We complemented each other; I liked his thorough-going ways and he liked my quickness.

I was the only person who knew that after supper on Friday evenings he went to a brothel, always with a present, and he often sent me there on weekdays with silk stockings or a bright-colored kerchief or chocolates for the little whore Salka, whom he loved with a love that was fierce and silent. I usually brought him back a letter from her, which I would read aloud to him, for he could neither read nor write, and I used to write out answers for him from a "Polite Letter Writer." I knew three Polite Letter Writers by heart, and my brother was amazed at my mature wisdom. I also regularly kept back some of the money I received from customers and gave it to him: we shared a great secret. I admired his maturity, his manliness, and he my gift for quick repartee and the beautiful letters I wrote for him.

One day Salka fell ill, went to the hospital and from there to another town. My brother Leibzi became even more close-mouthed and began to grow thin.

One night we were both awake and he was broiling a piece of liver over the coals; he told me that he had a secret, and that this week I must steal at least two gulden. This I did, and Saturday after supper he whispered to me to slip out and meet him by the courthouse. I felt very important and mysterious and was there before he was.

From there we went to the outskirts of the town, and when we had the last house behind us we sat down by a ditch and he said that he could no longer stand it at home, that all grown boys left home, and he was going to leave, too. And then we cried a little, and he promised faithfully to let me come and join him later wherever he might be, and said that it was best for him, the elder of us, to go first and then he could take a look around for me too.

Then we kissed each other, and I stood there, as if I were paralyzed and could not believe my eyes. He walked on and turned around, then he waved his hat, then he grew smaller and smaller, and I looked after him until he was no bigger than the stub of a pencil and he disappeared.

And I walked home feeling utterly crushed, and as it was already night, I went into the bakery and did his work myself, mixed the leavening for the bread dough and the yeast for the rolls, and when Father came to work that night and saw that Leibzi was not there he only said, "My dear children are like birds – as soon as they grow feathers they fly away without saying a word to their father – well, perhaps that is how it has to be."

And I felt ashamed because of my secret, and I did Leibzi's work every day and silently wished that I were gone too. Six months later we had a post card from Leibzi. Father put on his glasses and read it aloud:

> *Dear Father,*
> *I have not written to you because you never taught me to read and write; now I have met a fine girl, and she writes for me. I am working in Stanislau at Seybold's bakery, and am – thank God – in good health. I hope to hear the same from you.*
> *Your faithful son,*
>   *Leibzi*

Father took off his glasses, put them in their case, and two big tears rolled down his beard. It was the first time I had seen him cry.

So the family became smaller and smaller, but our poverty grew greater. We had turned all Schachne Eber's dowry into bread, and we could no longer carry on the bakery. We were bankrupt. And we kept growing up, and soon I left school and went to work for another baker – our erstwhile rival – but I liked it better. I was independent; I was only ten years old, but I knew that I could support myself. And that was a consolation which has often helped me in my life....

16

My Brother Schmiel, with the Rich Imagination, Comes Home

Several years had passed after Schmiel's flight, and one evening, shortly before we left the village of Werbiwci, some peasants came in and said that they had seen Schmiel at the horse market. Then Uncle Leiser came to congratulate us – he had spoken to Schmiel at the market, he should soon be home. Then a few of his old comrades and friends came in – they had seen Schmiel at the market too and wanted to speak to him. Elikune from the village inn also came to congratulate us and to learn what had brought Schmiel home from the wide world – he too had seen Schmiel at the market.

The room was packed, everyone waited; we were all much excited and stayed up very late, but no Schmiel appeared.

But that very night Jus Fedorkiw's best horse – a three-year-old mare – disappeared from its stall. There was great excitement in the village, and next market day Jus recognized his horse among those displayed by the dealer Mendel Spierer. Spierer told him that he had bought the horse from a boy of a neighboring village, who was to bring him the papers that day. So Spierer had no proper title to the horse, and there was an explosion.

My eldest brother, Schachne Eber, who always looked out for the family's good name, went with the horse dealer and

Jus Fedorkiw to a tavern, where they sat down and drank several glasses of beer; they talked it all over in a friendly way and agreed to share the loss between them, and Fedorkiw got his mare back and the matter was forgotten.

That had all taken place several years ago; by now we were living in Horodenka. And the incident of the mare was still something of a puzzle. Now Schmiel came home. He was twenty-one and had to report for military service.

He was dressed with great elegance; he wore a handsome fur coat with an astrakhan collar, he had riding breeches and brown boots like a cavalry officer, and Saturdays he wore a black suit with patent-leather shoes and fine leather gloves, which he generally carried in his hand so that his many rings could be seen; and he always carried a heavy, flexible cane. His curly hair was parted, and he wore his green velvet hat at an angle so that the thick curls on the left side of his forehead were visible. And, to cap the climax, he insisted that he could no longer speak Yiddish, but only German.

He spoke German to everyone, even to little Mama, who begged him at least to speak Yiddish with her when no one else was present, so that she could feel that he was really her child. "No, Mudder," he said, in something that was meant to be German, "nix on Yiddish – me from Mislowitz" – Mislowitz is a little hole near Maehrisch-Ostrau, in old Austria – "where we speak Daitsch."

He had a thick wallet, too, stuffed with bank notes, which he proudly displayed whenever he had an opportunity; he would smile and say that he could even buy himself an estate now. On the next market day he bought himself a fine little horse and rode about the neighborhood all day, speaking "Daitsch."

One day he left his wallet lying around the house and Sister Rachel wanted to see how many millions our brother had brought home with him. She looked through it: there were sixty-five kroner in real money and a great many thousand-krone notes. The latter, however, were printed like thousand-krone notes on one side only; on the other you read, in large letters: "That's just what a glass of Pilsener is worth, and we sell one for just five kreuzer. – The Bell Inn, Mislowitz."

The secret spread through the lower streets that very day, and everyone was delighted that not even in Mislowitz did millions lie around for the taking; and our brother, who, until then, had been nicknamed "Horse" Schmiel, got a new nickname, "The Daitsch with the Millions." Father smiled and said it would last only a while, we should soon see that Schmiel would learn Yiddish again and get used to the fact that you could live well enough in Horodenka without having millions.

We had a distant relative in Horodenka, whom we called Aunt Henje. She dealt in geese and hens and had three grown children, two married sons – big, strapping men; one was a carter, the other a porter – and a big, rather stupid, cowlike unmarried daughter.

One Saturday afternoon Schmiel took the daughter for a walk outside the town; he got tired, and they both lay down to rest in a grain field. And late in the afternoon the girl was seen running through the streets, weeping and wailing.

Instantly a crowd gathered in front of Aunt Henje's house. The daughter could be heard crying, "Mama – Schmiel – in the field – he did something to me! Mama, he did something to me – help me, Mama! Help me! I'm so unhappy!" And she gnawed her handkerchief and sobbed and wept.

Aunt Henje sent for my father. The onlookers were asked to go home, and Aunt Henje and Father had a long, serious, worried, and amicable conversation. Father came home and said that Schmiel had learned bad behavior among the "Daitsch." We waited and waited, and at last Schmiel came home too.

It was already dark in the room, but we could not make a light because the stars had not come out yet: the Passing of the Sabbath. Father began: "Listen, my son, I said nothing when you spoke your silly 'Daitsch,' I said nothing when you played the millionaire with printing-press notes, I never asked you to tell me about the mare – but if you believe that your riding breeches and your fur coat and your patent-leather shoes give you the right to behave like a tramp, you are mistaken. Either I shall whip you with your own cane until you speak Yiddish and forget your swindling counterfeit money – or I shall send for Aunt Henje, and we shall celebrate your betrothal to her daughter tonight."

And suddenly Schmiel began to moan and gesticulate; he made unintelligible noises and tore at his tongue, and everyone was thunderstruck. Then he began to tear his hair and beat his breast. Someone lit the lamp; Father gave him pencil and paper, and he wrote with a shaking hand that he could not speak; he had been struck dumb and begged for help. A doctor must be sent for. Aunt Henje and her daughter and the grain field were instantly forgotten. Dr. Kanafass came, pounded him and examined him, fumbled in his mouth, massaged his temples.

The house was full of people. There was a crowd outside – everyone wanted to see our handsome curly-haired Schmiel, "The Daitsch with the Millions," whom God had so suddenly stricken dumb.

The doctor charged us two gulden and said that, as Schmiel was rich, there was nothing to worry about. For the present he would come every day, and meanwhile he would write to a great specialist in Vienna and ask his opinion; possibly, however, it was only a chill on the vocal chords. He would come again in the morning. He put Schmiel to bed and told him to take hot vodka and pepper, so that he would perspire and loosen up; then he sent everyone away and went himself.

Schmiel writhed in his bed, moaning, sobbing, and sweating, and fell asleep. The next morning he was as white as a sheet, and everyone looked at him pityingly. Father helped him to dress, and we all went to the wonder rabbi's house.

The house was packed. The rabbi made Father tell him the whole story, and all the while kept his eyes fixed on Schmiel's. Then he addressed Schmiel, who looked rather pale and frightened, as follows: "Schmiel, son of Aaron, in the presence of this congregation, of your father, and of the Father of us all, Who is always with us in our need, I exhort you now to pray with your whole heart and your whole soul."

And our brother's eyes were moist, and the rabbi said: "I see tears in your eyes; our words have found an echo in your heart, and I know that now you are pious and honorable. Let us begin." He turned to the congregation and added: "Help him to pray today so that the gates of heaven may open and our prayer may be heard."

And the prayer leader began and all joined in with fervor; the congregation sank into pious meditation, their faces turned to the "on high," their eyes closed; soon all were in ecstasy; and now, as the prayer leader cried out, "Hear Israel, O Lord our King, O Lord the One God," and as all chanted the holy appeal in pious rapture, we heard our brother's voice sounding above the rest.

And the rabbi cried: *"Mazltov, mazltov,"* congratulating him, and broke off the prayer. Schmiel, however, began to make signs that he was still dumb. Then the rabbi said: "I, and the whole congregation with me, just now heard you speak aloud; but if trying to make us believe that you are still dumb amuses you, do so, my son, do so. The important fact is that I and your parents and this congregation, who have all been helping you, now know that you can speak, thank God – and no one need worry any further about you."

In the meanwhile prayer shawls and *tfillim* were folded away, and everyone sat down at the great table, and vodka and honey cakes were served round. The rabbi had a glass poured for Schmiel and took a glass himself. They held their glasses in their left hands, and the rabbi gave Schmiel his right hand, and everyone watched and waited in suspense. The rabbi said, "May God help you, so that your tongue will obey you like every pious man's," and our brother said loudly and clearly, "Amen, Rabbi," and joy and rapture overflowed, and we sat together for a long time.

Years passed. I was living in Berlin, and Schmiel went to America by way of Hamburg and visited me on his way through. He could not speak a word of German. I asked him how that could be, when at home he had spoken German so fluently that he was nicknamed "Daitsch"; to which he answered that he spoke the "Mislowitz dialect."

Many years later I came to America, and my brother called himself Sam and was a rich man with grown children, all born in America, and free and bewitching as only American young people are. And he still told cock-and-bull stories just as he used to at home, and his American children believed him as little as we had. They loved and honored him just as we had done. He was never boring, he had the most highly colored imagination in the whole family, and he firmly believed in his tall tales. His children often talked to me about it. They said: "Father is always telling stories that we know are made up; but in the first place he is the best father in the world; in the second place we like him to have his fun; and thirdly we believe that most Europeans don't stick too much to the truth." I had just come from Europe myself, and I was somewhat embarrassed for my old continent.

17

Everyone Fights with the Weapons He Has

Father, my brother Schabse, and I were now working in Wolf's bakery. Father was paid the salary for all three of us, and we worked innumerable hours. We began Saturday evening and worked through, with intervals of a few hours for sleep, until Friday afternoon. Friday afternoon we went to the steam bath, slept at home Friday night, had Saturday free, and Saturday evening started in again, to work till the following Friday afternoon.

I knew the trade now like a real journeyman and began to think of making a getaway. The great holidays had arrived, the young men were coming home from the various towns where they worked and earned money. They came back well dressed and said that anywhere else in the world was better than Horodenka.

My school friend Rosenkranz's brother came back from Czernowitz, and he not only had a blue striped suit, but he wore a high stiff collar too, with a colored necktie, a light gray velvet hat, and kid shoes made of the finest leather, and their heels were fitted with two little disks of rubber, which caused a sensation in Horodenka. The rubber heels were good-looking and practical; when they were worn out, he told us, you could buy another pair for a few heller; your shoes were like new again, and you walked in them like a dancer, without making a sound.

They excited me so that I and my school friend kept following his rubber-heeled brother around, admiring and envying him.

It was not only the rubber heels. Everything about him – the way he walked, the way he winked at the girls, the glistening oiled curl on his forehead, the superior, self-satisfied "Czernowitz smile" that he had brought back with him, his gray gloves – these excited not only me, but the whole of Horodenka.

The holidays passed, and he went back to Czernowitz, but something of his rubber heels remained in the air. You could really see them and hear them; they kept whispering: "Break away – you can have us too – but not in Horodenka."

One Saturday afternoon we were all set: I and my school friend Rosenkranz, brother to the rubber heels, put on two shirts, one over the other, and both our weekday and Sabbath suits, and started off in the direction of Kolomea. Our hearts were pounding, and toward evening we reached my home village of Werbiwci and decided to spend the night at Aunt Feige's – not at my eldest brother's, because he would have sent us home.

The next morning we got up very early, stuffed our pockets full of green cucumbers from the garden, and were off again.

We had been walking along the highroad for half an hour when we heard someone calling us. It was Aunt Feige, at whose house we had spent the night – Aunt Feige, who never smiled, who was always warming over thin, tasteless soups. All her cooking was tasteless – she made soup of everything, even, I think, out of old wash water and rags, and there was always soup left over from yesterday and the day before; she warmed it up, she never started fresh. We asked ourselves when she could have first started cooking that soup she always had on hand to warm over! We called her our "warmed-over aunt," for she looked exactly like that: warmed over, thin and left over from day before yesterday!

So now Mrs. Warmed-Over caught up with us and went through our pockets and found the cucumbers; and Watery

Soup said that she thought we had stolen eggs, and she left us the cucumbers and went away. I felt so ashamed before my friend that I have never forgiven my watery aunt for it, not even yet!

After a half clay's walk we came to the little town of Gwozdiedz, which was even smaller than Horodenka. There we had our first experience of "hunger in a strange land"; without thinking it over, we sold our good clothes, bought fresh bread and cottage cheese and milk and butter, and ate and drank, and suddenly we felt cheerful and we had money, and we set out and walked again and by evening we had reached Kolomea.

In Kolomea I immediately went from one bakery to the other, and for the first time in my life spoke the bakers' password, *"Uschitz."* And the journeymen answered, *"Lemschitz."* I believe that these two words of comradeship are corruptions of *ohneschutz* ("without shelter") and *nimmschutz* ("take shelter"). Journeymen bakers frequently "traveled," particularly in summer. In winter they settled down somewhere and earned a small salary, but with the coming of spring you would meet hundreds of baker-birds on the roads, and you called out *"Uschitz"* and were answered with *"Lemschitz,"* and you felt a homey bakery warmth and solidarity on the road.

The journeymen bakers whom I now went to see talked to me as if I were a grownup, asked for news of so-and-so and so-and-so, and gave me bread and advice as to where to look for a job. They sent me straight to a master baker who had a small establishment and came from the little town of Jablonow, a wretched hole not far from Kolomea, and who was looking for a young helper like myself.

I found the man, who had once worked as a journeyman for us, and he hired me for twenty gulden a year with board and lodging. Sleep on the stove, two meals a day, and two kreuzer for breakfast, "to buy something to eat with your bread." I at once thought of the beautiful things I could buy myself for Easter, and particularly of rubber heels! My friend Rosenkranz found a job in Kolomea too, as clerk in a hardware shop; he earned much less, but clerking was more elegant.

Jablonow lies at the foot of the Carpathians. After working the first night, I was given my first two kreuzer to buy something to go with my bread for breakfast. I went to the market place and as I was bargaining with my *"huzul,"* a Carpathian peasant, for some nice fresh blueberries, I saw the back of a man who was getting out of a wagon and looking about, and I recognized that broad back; it was my beloved father!

I ran to him, and he took my trembling hand and said quietly and warmly, "Go and get dressed, my son – I will wait here."

Five minutes later I was back. We climbed into the wagon – it was Brother Schachne Eber's one-horse rig, which Father had borrowed – and we set off. He let me drive, because he knew how much I liked that. And all the way we talked about the Carpathian Mountains, about the good black earth, about what fine children my eldest brother had in the village, about prices in town, and about how he expected soon to go to see the wonder rabbi in Czortkow. My father talked to me about a thousand things that day, but he said not one word about my running away. Blessed be his memory!

When I got home I went to work for Jossie Bones. He had once worked for us, now he had married and set up for himself. He was a first-class workman and a fine goodhearted fellow, and he was especially fond of me. He paid me a gulden a week with board and lodging – and it goes without saying that I carried the money home.

I worked with a youngster from the small town of Obertyn; he was about my age, no one knew his name, and everyone called him "the mouse from Obertyn." We hated each other at first sight. He was rather taller than I, but thin, and he had a leathery, brownish-greenish skin, wrinkled like an old man's, a thin pointed snout like a mouse's, and he slobbered when he spoke and slobbered when he ate and was as clammy as a worm and as contrary as a sick rat. He found fault with everything, nothing in our town pleased him, he didn't like the houses, he didn't like the people. He never laughed, and was always finding fault with me. He told tales about me to the boss whenever he had a chance, and he tried in every way to become the "pet" of the boss's wife. He helped her in the kitchen, helped to clean the rooms, and even helped with the children, and she liked him and listened to his talebearing and relished the fact that I, the son of the man for whom her husband had worked, was now working for her.

One afternoon, when we had finished our work and had lain down to sleep on the floor between the oven and the wall, he began to pick on me and criticize me because I dressed nicely, and because I was conceited, and because I wanted to be grown-up, and because I already looked at girls, and because I was going to remain as small as a dwarf and wouldn't grow any more – in this vein he jeered at me.

I said to him, "Listen, you Obertyn mouse, if you don't leave me in peace, once and for all, you'll be sorry." He: "And what can an ignorant ruffian like you do to me?" I: "I can spoil your mousy face for you." He: "Your paws will grow lamed if you touch me." I: "Yes? But first I'll knock your filthy face off for you." He: "Oh, the devil take your bastard of a father!"

Then I gave him one in his loathsome face. He knew how I loved my father, he knew that I had once taken a hatchet to a man who had attacked him. He did not hit back, he only said it again, perfectly quietly, "The devil take your father!"

I let him have a second box on the ear. And again, with no change in his voice, he said, "The devil take your father!"

And I hit him in the face again, and now things went faster: he repeated the curse, and I struck him. It went on mechanically, like clockwork: curse and punch, punch and curse, curse and punch! Faster and faster – we no longer waited for each other, he cursed my father uninterruptedly and I hit him uninterruptedly. I began to feel tired, I looked at him and thought of other things, but the punches and the curses kept on. His eyes were wide open and expressionless, there was slobber around his mouth and nose, and he kept mechanically repeating the same curse – somewhat more softly – and I was hitting him more weakly and mechanically too, and I thought, "Is he going to let me hit him like this till morning? But," I thought, "he is defending himself, he is hitting back with his curses, that is his defense, that is his weapon." I felt a sudden weariness, a sudden nausea, as if I were pounding my fists into a manure pile, into a heap of clammy worms. My hand was wet with his slobber, and I was tired of repeating the same motion, and I went on hitting him, but with less force, and I wondered how I would feel if I were alone in a strange town and knew no one and someone were to hit me like that, and if I had a greenish-brown skin like his, and a pointed mouse face like his – and I stopped hitting him and shut my eyes, and then I was in a strange town just as he was, and I felt forlorn and dirty and covered with slobber and sick and helpless and unhappy and lonely, and I turned my face to the wall and my whole body shook, and shivers ran over me and I moaned and sobbed for a long time. Then I grew quiet and felt ashamed, and he was still lying there, motionless, with his eyes open and his face a blank, and I got up and went away, and I never returned to Jossie Bones's again.

And for many weeks I had a dull wooden sensation in my right hand; I had the feeling that it was still dirty from my blows and his slobber.

I kept thinking of a little homeless scabby six-year-old boy I had known who went begging and whom the other boys were always thrashing. When someone was about to hit him he used to say, "If you hit me, my dead mother will come tonight and throttle you with her long thin horrible fingers." That worked for a few days, but since his dead mother never came and strangled anyone, the boys began beating him up again, and he began to say, "If you hit me this time, my dead father will come– he was a butcher and had the longest knife in the world, and he'll butcher you." But that too only worked for a short time, and again he was beaten up. After that he used to say, "If you hit me, I'll stink," and that was a real threat. For he could do that, and he did, and the boys went away and left him in peace.

For that is how it is in this world: Everyone fights with the weapons he has.

18

People and the Awakening of Love in Horodenka

In Horodenka there lived also the Gloger family. People called them "the Yerischkes," after their eighty-year-old progenitor, Yerichem. This old man's face was always flushed and happy from the last vodka he had just tossed off. He had small, cunning, bright eyes which twinkled under his bushy eyebrows, and a thick yellowish-white beard that looked as if the wind had blown it to one side – in reality, it grew only on one side. And it looked as if it were made out of flax and wood shavings. He had eight sons, seven of whom were married; they were all glaziers and carpenters. They were simple, uneducated men, big and strong and daring.

Horodenka trembled before the Glogers, especially before the youngest, who was stocky and broad-shouldered and defiant. His name was Srul Kune. The Glogers had frequent violent quarrels among themselves, the wives in particular envied one another and were always wrangling, often one brother would not speak to another for years. But when one of them had a fight with an "outsider," they all rushed to help him.

And anyone who was in need and appealed to one of the Glogers would be warmly and generously helped. The youngest, Srul Kune, the most feared of them, was the readiest to help and the kindest. His circle of friends included the journeyman carpenters, the butchers, the horse dealers, and the porters, who followed him blindly. He often went with them to visit the poorest people to find out if they were going hungry. Then he went to the rich and used threats and blackmail to force them to help the starving poor. The rich hated him and wrote anonymous information and complaints against him and sent them to the county officials, but the poor and people of moderate means loved and revered the Glogers, particularly Srul Kune.

On Thursdays the poorest people always went from house to house begging, and Srul Kune and his friends found out from them who gave and who did not. Once on such a Thursday the rich and miserly Herr Offenberger was in a bad humor and threw the beggars out and said that he would give nothing and, furthermore, he was not going to let himself be blackmailed by that tramp Srul Kune and his gang any longer. Soon the town was talking of nothing else. And Friday night Herr Offenberger's house "accidentally" burned down.

Everyone knew that it was Srul Kune's work; everyone was pleased, but no one said a word about it.

Early on Saturday morning a crowd was standing by the burned ruins of Herr Offenberger's house, and Srul Kune and his friends passed and he said, "Good Lord, what a sin – to start a fire on the Sabbath! But certainly God Himself has done this, to punish Offenberger for his hardheartedness to the poor."

Offenberger was insured against fire, but in spite of that he suffered a large loss. He began to give alms again, indeed more generously than before; but he got the county officials to bring a new and harsh set of gendarmes to Horodenka. Among these new guardians of the law there was one sergeant who sported a twirled mustache with the turned-up points on a level with his eyes, so that his angry glances darted through the extreme ends of it and you had to avert your eyes when he looked at you. Anyone whom he did not like, he arrested on the least suspicion, and was always beating people up at the police station. He often visited Herr Offenberger, who treated him to a vodka, and he "bought" a great many things from him without paying for them; he would say, "Yes, Herr Offenberger, there will be order here now!" And Herr Offenberger always greeted him in friendly fashion with the words, "Greetings, Herr Order!" Soon the whole town was calling him "Herr Order."

Once, on a market day, Srul Kune got into a fight, and Herr Order came up and arrested him. His friends wanted to free him by force, but Srul Kune shouted to them, held out his hands for the handcuffs to be put on, and only said, "Yes, there must be order in Horodenka, and there shall be." So he was led away, and the town was in great excitement, and the next day he was let out, and he said not a word about it.

No more than two weeks had passed before Herr Order was waylaid one night, disarmed, and fearfully beaten, one of his two long-pointed mustaches was cut off and he himself was delivered at the hospital like a bundle of refuse. But his rifle, with bayonet attached, his saber and sword belt, his pouch with its chains and handcuffs and its gold sergeant's tassel, and his terrifying hard hat with its blue-black feathers were all delivered to the district police station with the following letter:

TO THE OFFICERS OF THE ROYAL AND IMPERIAL GOVERNMENT IN HORODENKA:

Tonight we found the sergeant of gendarmes completely drunk in a ditch, where he was soiling the Kaiser's uniform and the Kaiser's weapons; we carried the drunken sergeant to the hospital to sober up; we are herewith delivering his weapons, his uniform, and his helmet to the officers of the royal and imperial government. Long live the Kaiser!

SRUL KUNE GLOGER AND FRIENDS.

Froim Gloger, from whom we had rented the bakery, had a boy about my age, Moische Mendel. We went to school and to cheder and to steal fruit and to "find" horseshoes together, and shared a thousand secrets. We told each other everything we knew, everything we wanted to know, and everything we suspected. We were both beset with a great longing to develop our muscles and to satisfy our curiosity. When we devoured a fresh loaf of graham bread with butter in secret together, we immediately felt our muscles and were convinced that they had become harder. When we sucked a good marrow bone, we believed that it made our own bones stronger. When we ate heart, or kidneys, or lung, or liver, it was perfectly obvious to us that the corresponding parts of our bodies were thereby fortified. But we also believed that to be strong without being intelligent was not enough, so we began secretly buying boiled or fried brains in little restaurants in order to develop our minds.

About this time a park was opened in Horodenka, with plenty of gardenhouses and benches and trees and flowers and seesaws and swings and other amusements. It was called the "Promenade Garden."

Saturdays and Sundays and even weekday afternoons you could see hundreds of young men and girls gathered there. First there were groups of boys and groups of girls, then words and jokes would pass from group to group, then couples would begin to pair off, and soon people would be saying, "He and she are going together" or, "He and she are speaking together." And when he and she "went together" or "spoke together" for a long time, then people said, "He and she are playing at lovers" or "going as lovers."

Saturday was the day of real excitement. Early in the morning the young workingmen went to the synagogue, but more to meet one another than to pray. From there they would go to the shadier taverns, buy one another vodka or a bite to eat, begin to feel carefree, say a good word or a bad word for sundry hims and hers, and then they would walk to the Promenade Garden.

The girls would already be there – dressmakers, seamstresses, milliners, housemaids, and what not. Couples soon formed, and soon there were "romances" and "love affairs" and mocking songs and adventures and elopements and even small tragedies. Especially when some girl from the upper streets, from the "better circles," became infatuated with some bold handsome journeyman and "stooped" to love him. Then the parents on both sides rushed in and there would be a flight and a secret marriage and lawsuits and scandal and general excitement.

This was all quite new to Horodenka, for the older generation used to say, "We never dared to do such things!" Suddenly people dared. It was the first generation to manage without marriage brokers.

Every young fellow who thought anything of himself and wanted to be considered grown-up began to "go with" girls, or even to "play at lovers." The air in the Promenade Garden was heavy with rumors and gossip about love and lovers. You suffered the pangs of love, you sacrificed yourself to your feelings, you suffered in your soul, you pretended to be melancholy. You read novels that were so exciting that they made you dizzy.

One was the famous story of the suffering, despairing suitor who was locked in a tower by his rival and left to starve to death. Finally, utterly desperate, he jumped from the tower – and just as he jumped, his lady love drove up in a big hay wagon, and he landed in the hay and not a hair of his head was hurt! And lover and beloved fell into each other's arms and wept tears of joy, together with the reader.

Then there was the story of the young baron who, despite his wicked relatives, loved his own chambermaid. He was driven out and banished with her, and they wandered through the world, begging in rain and snow and frost, till at last they both collapsed and fell into a ditch and lay there together, and the instant before they breathed their last the postman roused them with a letter which said that the baron had at last inherited the estates of his dead grandfather, and he went happily home, and made his unfortunate beloved, the despised chambermaid, a real baroness....

Rich Herr Koffler had a little housemaid who was as pretty as a picture; her name was Riffkele and she came from the small town of Uscieczka. She was poor and simple, but she dressed neatly and prettily. Her clothes fitted tight to her slender fourteen-year-old body, so that you could see her firm, round curves. She had snow-white skin, silky brown hair, large dark burning eyes, two dimples in her firm little face in which the color was always coming and going, and two little rolls in her blouse. And when I would deliver Herr Koffler's bread in the early morning in my baker's uniform, my white baker's trousers, with an apron, and my shirt sleeves rolled up and a torn cap on my head to keep the flour out of my hair, Riffkele would call out in her laughing musical voice: "Oh, the torn cap has brought some really beautiful crescents this morning!" or, "Oh, the torn cap has brought rolls that aren't brown enough this morning!" or, "Oh, the torn cap has brought really crisp Vienna rolls this morning!" Every morning when I brought their bread, I got one of her "torn cap" sentences as a reward. "The torn cap" this, "the torn cap" that. The "torn cap" sentence would pierce my heart, and I was deathly unhappy when none was forthcoming. So I began to look after her, and even to follow her at a distance.

She had a friend, the other maid in Herr Koffler's house, and one time her friend gave me a wink which told me that they were aware that I was following them. Then I began standing as inconspicuously as possible in front of the house. And she began coming inconspicuously to a window with her friend, and they looked out in the opposite direction. This went on for weeks – not a word, nothing but pounding hearts.

One day I said loudly to my friend, who was with me, "You know, I'd like to go for a walk in the garden." And then she said to her friend, also rather louder than necessary, "I have nothing more to do except to tidy up. When I've finished, let's go for a walk, shall we?" Both girls vanished. We waited. Then they came out and went into the Promenade Garden.

In the garden we and they walked up and down the same walk, and we always met them just in the middle of it, coming the other way, and after a while my friend told me that I ought to speak to her, and I thought he was right, and we deliberated over the first sentence, and every time I met her I was so excited that I had neither the strength nor the courage to open my mouth, and the words stuck in my throat.

After several hours she said loudly to her friend that she was going home now, and we both followed them with our hearts pounding, and then we were standing in front of her house again. Then she came to the window with her friend, and all four of us talked, but not to one another. I would say something to my friend, and she would answer to her friend, and all the while we did not look at each other. On such an occasion one evening, the following conversation took place:

I to my friend: "When one follows a girl and doesn't speak to her directly, one knows just the same what it really means."

Then she to her friend: "If one knows what it means so well, why make such a secret of it?"

I to my friend: "It's no secret, anyone can see that I'm in love with someone."

She to her friend: "It's not enough that anyone can see it, Someone ought to say it to Someone right out."

I to my friend, with a melting block of ice in my heart: "Someone is going to hear me say it soon."

Then she, still speaking to her friend, ironically and provocatively: "Then Someone had better hurry, because Someone is going to Zaleszczyki next week, and then there'll be another Someone in another window." And both girls snickered.

All this time we had not looked at each other, and my throat was dry and I felt hot and my heart was pounding and I said to my friend: "If Someone goes to Zaleszczyki, I'll come to Zaleszczyki too. And then Someone will have to believe that this is serious."

She to her friend, laughing: "Good. I'm going Wednesday. And then we'll see how a man keeps his word."

So, feeling as if I had been hit on the head with a stone, I said, "Then I'll follow Saturday."

There was a solemn silence, and I thought of Wednesday and remembered that she had said "a man." And I raised my eyes and saw her beautiful long snow-white neck, her silky reddish-brown hair, and her two black bright eyes shining in the half-darkness. And we looked into each other's eyes seriously for the first time, and our eyes held each other, and I thought I saw tears in hers, and I felt all weepy myself without knowing why.

And then she said to her friend: "I still have a lot to do today," and, speaking directly to me for the first time, looking tender and fond, she said, "Good night, torn cap," and drew slowly back from the window. I stood without moving, as though paralyzed with emotion. Then she came back alone and opened the window slowly – she had on a sleeveless blouse now and an apron – and she said softly and playfully, "I hope I haven't hurt anyone's feelings with my 'torn cap.' It looks very well on him. Good night."

"Good night," I answered, already happy and grateful, "good night."

And she slowly shut the window, and I went home feeling happy and light, and my friend was in raptures over the way we had broken the ice, and everything in me felt glad and I went to sleep and had a long and detailed dream about how Riffkele and I went to walk in the park, and the garden was so big that it went to Zaleszczyki, and she was wearing her nightgown so I could touch her bare round arms, and it was cut low so that you could see the beginning of those two little gourds, and we played ball with the torn cap, and when we were hungry I baked some wonderful salt pretzels and caraway sticks, and they were crisp and hot and we were happy and laughed and laughed all the way.

On Wednesday Riffkele went to Zaleszczyki, on Friday my father sent me to buy five post cards. I thought of my flight and pocketed the money. Saturday afternoon after dinner I set off.

My friend went with me as far as the edge of the town. The sky was cloudy. We sat down by the ditch. I tied my shoes together by the laces and slung them over my shoulder. He gave me his best pencil to remember him by, we swore eternal friendship, and I set off.

After a good half-hour it suddenly began to rain, I felt frightened, and I hoped with all the strength of my piety that I would find a bit of iron as a protection against the rain spirits. I made a bet with myself: if I didn't find a bit of iron, that meant I must go back. Suddenly I saw half a horseshoe in the road, as if someone had put it there for me. I took it for a good omen and pressed on with renewed strength, and by evening I was in the village of Serafinez, which lies between Horodenka and Zaleszczyki.

I went to the village inn, which was full of Ukrainian peasants, who immediately plied me with a hundred questions: how old I was, how long I had been on the road, what the world political outlook was, why Turks wore red fezzes, if it was true of some people that the men wear braids, and whether there were men who had only one eye in the middle of their foreheads. I had an answer for everything.

The one who had asked the most questions invited me to come home with him to supper – which I, as a pious little Jew, politely refused. Then the peasant urged the Jewish innkeeper to invite me, which the latter declined, saying that he had his own children to feed. The Ukrainian philanthropist then presented me with four large rolls, a herring, and half a liter of beer, which at once gave me a headache, and I went to sleep in the barn.

I shivered all night, rose with the sun, and set off. I walked quickly and soon felt warm, and the birds sang their morning prayer to the Creator, and a twelve-year-old youngster was alone in a great wide world, and he was so small and so afraid to be walking alone in the huge world.

So I began thinking what they would be saying at home when they missed me, and that I really ought to have said good-by to Father. But how could I have explained to him about Riffkele? Ah, Riffkele! How she will stare when she sees me! The first words I will say will be: "A man does keep his word, and he doesn't go standing under other windows with other Someones as quick as all that!"

Suddenly I felt troubled. I had the sensation that there was someone behind me calling me in all this expanse. And so there was – I turned around and saw, far behind me, a big, tall fellow waving his stick and shouting and calling. Then I felt afraid and walked along faster, and I looked around and saw that the man behind me was walking faster too, and he was still shouting and calling! Run, Run! I thought – the wide world seemed so huge and the boy who was running away so small and the fellow who was chasing him so big! I ran with all my strength, but my pursuer was coming closer and closer. I ran, and my heart raced, and the horizon danced in front of my eyes, and sweat poured off my body. And I was already breathless, and I felt my pursuer nearer and nearer, and I shut my eyes and my heart jumped into my throat, and the fellow behind me was calling and shouting, and I thought: Where, in what spot, will he hurt you before he kills you? And my strength left me, and I fell, and saw a thousand twinkling stars dancing in my head, and I lay where I had fallen, knowing nothing.

I lay there for quite a time. I thought it was an eternity; then I opened my eyes in terror, and there was a young peasant bending over me, and I saw his sweaty, kindly face. He shook me and said, "You little devil, you can run like the wind."

And he smiled and wiped the sweat off his forehead with his linen shirt and took his bundle, which was tied to his stick, and opened it, and I watched him, frightened and suspicious. And he brought out a chunk of good black country bread with goat cheese, and he broke it in two and handed me the bigger half and invited me to eat with him. And I ate, half because I was afraid and half because I was hungry, and he said jokingly that he was sorry there was no inn here, otherwise he would buy me a vodka too. And we ate without speaking.

Then he said, "Tell me why you ran away so fast?"

And I said, "Why did you run after me?"

And he, "I ran after you because you ran away from me."

And I said, "I ran away from you because you ran after me."

"I see. And aren't you going to Zaleszczyki?" said he.

"Of course I'm going to Zaleszczyki."

Then he said, "That's what I heard last night at the inn. And I'm going there because today is market day. So I thought we should go together and keep each other company."

We had finished breakfast, and we set off together and talked as though we had known each other for years, and we told each other funny stories and laughed a great deal. And about noon we reached a suburb of Zaleszczyki, and there we took leave of each other like old friends.

I liked the clean pretty town, around which the Dniester flowed in a curve; and the people looked and talked like the people at home. I looked at the baker's displays, and was standing in front of one which I thought particularly fine, and there was a short fat man with a blond beard and a kind smiling face standing beside it, and he kept watching me, and suddenly he said: "Say, you're not from these parts. This is the first time I've seen you here."

And I said that I had just come from Horodenka and that I was a journeyman baker and was looking for work. But he smiled and said, "You mean you're half a journeyman; you can't be a whole one yet, you look like a fifty-percenter," and he gave me his hand, and he left his wife to take care of the stall and said, "Come along with me."

And he took me to a taproom and bought me a vodka and pretzels, and I would much rather have had milk, but I was afraid to ask for it because I wanted to pass as a grownup. And he asked how long I had been a baker and what I could do. And I said he had better try me out for one night and see for himself. And he swallowed his vodka and looked at me and laughed and said, "Well, at least you don't brag about yourself," and he took me to his bakery.

There were four journeymen there: an old man of seventy named Antosj, and Raffael, who had a long, well-kept beard and a wife and children, and two others who were unfriendly; and I made the fifth; and the boss himself worked with us at night, and he watched me and made me do various things, such as kneading dough for white rolls, mixing leaven for bread, shaping loaves, and when I came to shaping Vienna rolls and rolling crescents, I saw him smile with satisfaction, for at home I was already the best hand at those particular things.

And, early in the morning after we had finished, as I was carrying the wares to the stall, he suddenly came and walked beside me and said, "Come and have a drink with me, we must talk business."

And then he said, "I know well enough that I can hire you dirt cheap until Passover, and don't tell me how much you want; I'll pay you exactly what I pay Raffael, the one with the long beard and three children. You'll get a gulden and a half a week and board and lodging, and you'll stay with me till Passover. Is it a bargain?"

"It's a bargain," I said happily, and we shook hands. And I saw myself getting home for Passover in a blue suit with stripes, and new shoes with rubber heels, and with presents for Mother and my little brothers and sisters, because now I myself was a big brother to them, and I was grown up and alone in a strange town, where I had followed my "love."

And Menasche Strum suddenly said, "Well, Fifty-percenter, what are you thinking about now?"

And I answered, a little embarrassed, "Home."

And he said, "Well, go and get some sleep, and you'll feel at home here too." And I did.

And how my new home received me, and how I found her for whose sake I had come there, I shall tell later.

19

Away from Home It Is Cold – but Instructive

Now I was on my own; I did not have to obey Father or Mother or my older brothers and sisters, there was no one to make demands, I was responsible to no one; but by the same token I had no one to protect me.

Menasche Strum's wife had borne him six children, and six times he had wanted a boy, and six times it had been a girl. He was a good father to them, but he was unhappy because he had no sons, and he conceived a liking for me at once and took me everywhere with him, even to the synagogue. However, in the first place it bored me to go with him, in the second place the other journeymen kept taunting me, saying that I was trying to become the boss's "pet," and in the third place the boss's scrawny, sickly wife was jealous of me; she thought that her husband was fonder of me than of his own children just because the poor things were girls.

She was mean and miserly, and he was lavish and a spender. He went to various small taphouses to drink, and invited anyone who happened to be next to him to join him because, much as he liked to drink, he could not swallow a drop without company. When he wanted a vodka, he first had to find someone to drink with him, and what he liked to do best was to invite all bystanders. Many a sly fellow was well aware of this and followed him when he went into a bar and stood near him; and when the same face reappeared at his elbow five or six times during the same day he would usually say, "Oh, do come and drink a vodka with me, I haven't seen you for years."

Menasche Strum liked very poor people, particularly beggars. Every Friday night and every Saturday he had a dozen or more beggars at his table, and they were served in style and the food was excellent. Among them were men who had traveled all over the world and could tell fine stories. They felt perfectly at home in his house; they did not behave as if they were guests, as if they were receiving a favor – they believed that by accepting his hospitality they were giving their host an opportunity to do a good deed, for which his sins would be forgiven him and whereby he could assure himself of a good place in Paradise.

For there were whispers about some great sin that Menasche Strum was supposed to have committed. The story went that a girl, who was a poor relative of his and who had worked in his house, had a child only four months after she was married and that he had bought tickets for father, mother, and child and shipped them off to America. People would say, "Well, well, Menasche Strum is a good, generous man, he gives his relatives children four months after they marry, and he feeds poor beggars."

I began to look for Riffkele. Because, after all, she had been the main reason why I had run away from home, and she was the main reason why I was here. Many weeks passed before I became used to my new surroundings and began to find my way about. And there was no one I could ask about her.

Finally, I heard that young men and girls met one another at the house of a journeyman baker, who worked in another bakery, and that his wife, Channe Kozak, with her fresh young laughing eyes and her faded face, and her blond three-story hairdo, ran the place. She sold beer and vodka and served various delicacies there.

I became acquainted with her husband, and he invited me to the house. So I went, and I found a boisterous gathering – fellows of twenty or younger and girls; and Channe Kozak, the baker's wife, was the center of everything and a storehouse of gossip, and she helped bring people together and separate them, and everyone told her everything, and she had a finger in every pie. She had already heard of me and reproached me for not having come sooner and gave me to understand that she was always glad to do a service for a friend, but first she must have proof of my friendship.

I began going there every week and spent part of my salary there and saved and bought her material for a dress, and then she made an appointment with me for a weekday and I had a long talk with her about Riffkele.

She said that I was still so young and Riffkele was older, and the girl had not known that I really meant it so seriously when I said I would come after her and so, since such a long time had passed, Riffkele was now going with Max the coachman, who was known as "the Curl."

Max had a rubber-tired carriage, and he took officers out driving, or drove them to see their girls, or drove people to the newly opened railway station. He was nineteen years old, stocky and broad-shouldered, had a cold, impudent face, wore loud clothes, with his cap on the back of his head and a bunch of thick black curls hung over his right eye, from which he got his nickname, "the Curl."

"Yes," Channe Kozak said, "Max the Curl is really serious about Riffkele, and it will be very hard to get her away from him, if it's possible at all." She did not give me a chance to answer, but went on and unfolded a plan so that I might see she was truly my friend. We must first try to make friends with the Curl, and then talk things over with him, because the Curl was a "good guy" and would do anything for a friend. She advised me to buy him a present at once, to soften him up, and then to invite him to her house for vodka and a breakfast early Saturday morning – that way we could come to know each other and he would be well disposed toward me. My objection that I wanted to speak to Riffkele herself, she simply waved aside, because that would prejudice the terrible Curl against me beforehand, and all would be lost....

"All would be lost," I repeated to myself, and I thought of that conversation under the window in Horodenka, of my running away, of home, of Father, to whom I had not said good-by, and I felt completely miserable and I choked back my tears, and Channe Kozak asked me how old I was, and I added three years to my age and asked for a vodka and drank it down like a man, and I went back to the bakery and couldn't say a word to anyone, and I had the "far from home" feeling in my stomach and I couldn't eat, so I lay down on the stove and fell asleep and dreamt of devils and evil spirits. I saw Raffael, the journeyman, in the shape of Beezlebub, and after him came the baker's wife and Channe Kozak and the baker's six daughters, and they all yelled and danced and acted like witches, and the whole of Zaleszczyki looked like a witches' sabbath, and even Menasche Strum plunged his head into a gigantic cask of vodka, and besides his blond beard he had horns now and he laughed at me and said, "Hi, you Fifty-percenter, everyone here is a devil in disguise, we enticed you here from Horodenka, just for fun." And then the Curl appeared, likewise in the shape of a devil; he was riding a horse with a wild mane and a long tail, and I was tied to the long tail, and he galloped up and down the market place, dragging me along, and the whole town laughed and yelled, and Riffkele was the wildest of all, and she pointed at me and screamed, "He is so little, just twelve years old, and already he wants to play at love!" And then I tumbled off the stove and bumped my head and the other journeymen woke and asked me if I was crazy, screaming like that in my sleep, and someone pressed a knife against the bump on my forehead, and then I went to work and worked all night without speaking a word.

Many weeks passed, and Channe Kozak, the bawd, met me in the street and told me that the Curl was coming that Saturday morning, and everything was so pleasant at her house these days, and why had I stayed away? And I had saved money again, and I bought Channe Kozak a Turkish shawl for four and a half gulden, which was exactly three weeks' pay. And Saturday morning I went to her house again.

The room was packed. I ate and drank, though I had no appetite, and the Curl arrived, and my heart pounded, and I wanted to go away, and suddenly the Curl spoke to me, "Hi, you from Horodenka, I hear you're a 'regular guy.' Come and drink a vodka with me."

And he ordered two vodkas and I ordered two vodkas, and everything in my head began to whirl, and I did not know what to say to the Curl, and suddenly Riffkele came in, and she gave me one look and blushed, and my heart raced, and the Curl looked at his watch and said insolently, "Hey, you, I don't like people to be late," and he shook hands with me and walked out, and Riffkele walked behind him, and she gave me another look and blushed again.

After a while I walked to the Dniester and felt sick and vomited and went back to the bakery and lay on the stove all day, and loneliness and the "far from home" feeling crept through me like icicles, and I shivered on the hot stove.

The following week Channe Kozak told me not to lose heart and advised me to buy the Curl a present. And she went to the shop with me and helped me to choose a beautiful long whip with an ivory handle, which cost me four weeks' pay, six gulden. We went together to his station, where several wagons and carriages stood, and he was tremendously pleased with my present and boasted to other coachmen what a fine friend he had in me and winked at them, and Akim with the crooked mouth said, "Hey, you, for a whip like that I can get you ten women."

And the Curl said roughly and angrily, "You keep your crooked mouth shut."

And Akim said, "Can't a man make a joke if he feels like it?"

And the Curl winked at him again and said, "Yes, but not about a friend of mine."

And he took me aside, put his arm around me, and said he wanted to take me somewhere with him Friday evening and do me a favor in return. Then two young officers came along and got into his carriage and named two girls. Then everyone laughed, and the Curl cracked my whip and drove off, calling back to me, "Friday evening, at Channe Kozak's!"

And Friday I was waiting at Channe Kozak's, and she said slyly and equivocally, "See what I've done for you! Tonight you'll get what you want."

And I was ashamed to ask her what, for fear that would not be like a man, and the Curl came in and we ate and sat around, and he asked me if I could lend him three gulden, and I could. And he gave Channe Kozak a gulden and a half for two glasses of beer, and it was midnight, and we walked across the market place to the apothecary Kalmus's house, and he took me in by the back door and we sat down in the kitchen and waited. I heard two people in the next room laughing and talking and joking and playing – a man and a woman. And then the door opened and out came Riffkele in a sleeveless nightgown, and her face was red and her silky red-brown hair was all disordered, and the Curl said roughly, "Go and get ready!"

And she suddenly saw me, crouching in a corner, and she blushed to the roots of her hair and cried, "No! No! No! No! Not with him! Not with him!" and burst out crying, and the Curl said, "You'll do what I tell you, you dishrag – get dressed!"

And Riffkele ran back into the other room, and I was bursting with rage and shame and despair, and I jumped up and spat in the Curl's face and trembled and could only cry, "Swine! Swine! You vile swine!" and I rushed at him. Then I felt a blow on my temple from an iron knuckle-duster and I fell, and another blow, and then all I felt was a warm pleasant moisture running over my head and face, and I saw a thousand little sparks dancing before my eyes, and I fainted and knew nothing...and when I came to, Kalmus the apothecary was washing the wounds on my head and face with cotton and alcohol, and he bandaged me up and begged me not to tell anyone that it had happened in his house, and he said I could come every other day and he would treat me for nothing. And I promised and went home through the darkness and felt many years older, and my heart was divided – half of it pitied me and half of it comforted me – and my teeth chattered with a cold, strange loneliness.

The next day I did not go out, and I told them in the bakery that some drunken soldiers had attacked me, and everyone said I could consider myself lucky, because people had often been killed in such fights.

I did not go to Channe Kozak's again or look for Riffkele any more.

One day Menasche Strum brought home a young man who had a bundle of books under his arm, and he said that the young man was going to teach his daughters. He was a Russian student by the name of Czerniakoff, who had left Russia to study here.

Czerniakoff took a great interest in me. He went out walking with me, asked me numberless questions, and encouraged me to question him too. And he gave me little thin books to read, which I did not understand, and told me things which I thought unbelievable but which were very amusing to listen to. The most amusing was what he tried to tell me about the heavens: that every star was as big as our world, and that the stars were there by day too but we could not see them because of the sun, and that we turned round and round like a merry-go-round without ever getting dizzy, and that it had taken millions of years to create the world, not six days. And many other things, which I simply did not believe; for, though he was very intelligent and kind, he was certainly not more intelligent than my father and Schimshale from Milnitz.

In any case he had a warm voice and kind eyes and wore a beautiful wide drooping necktie, and it was much pleasanter to talk to him and listen to him than to go to Channe Kozak's and drink vodka, which gave you a headache and made you vomit and parted you from your hard-earned money.

I began to save, and winter came, and one day my father appeared. Suddenly he was standing in front of me in the bakery, and I put out my hand with the traditional greeting, "Peace be with you," and Father took my hand and looked straight into my eyes with great seriousness and answered, "With you be peace." Then, still holding my hand in his, he said, "I hear that you have agreed to work here until Passover."

I: "Yes, Father."

He: "And are you going to stay till Passover?"

I: "Yes, Father."

Father, still holding my hand in his, said: "My son, I know that when you are my age you will be far more clever than I am. But at the present time I understand more about life than you. Will you promise me that, when, the next time you want to leave home, you will talk it over with me first?"

I: "I promise, Father."

He: "And I promise I will not keep you from going."

Then we went for a walk, and Father told me how things were at home, and about our neighbors, and what other boys had left Horodenka. Then he said that my boss had invited him to dinner, but he could not accept the invitation because I worked there. And that, just as I had talked it over with my friend, Moische Mendel, before I ran away, I could have talked it over with him too. Of course, he would rather have me go on studying, but since he was so poor and I, though still a child, had to go and work for strangers, he wanted me to feel that he was not only my father but my real friend too.

Then we went into a restaurant, and I ordered vodka and beer and a good meal. And people came up and greeted my father and praised me to him. And a beggar woman came in, whom I had seen at the bakery, and asked if that was my father. And then I paid the bill, and we went out.

Then Father said to me: "Well, my son, that was the first meal you have given your father, and you are not thirteen yet, and now I shall leave with a good feeling: you can support yourself, thank God, you're already smarter than others of your age, and when you come home at Easter I want to take you to see the wonder rabbi from Czortkow, who will be visiting in Horodenka then, and ask him to bless you."

Then I walked with Father to the sleigh in which he had come, and the other passengers were already waiting for him, because they wanted to be home before nightfall. But we walked as far as the bridge, and I bought a thick warm shawl and a beautiful silk kerchief for Mother and promised to be home for Passover. Father also told me that my elder brother, Leibzi, who was now serving in the artillery in Stanislau, would be coming home on furlough too, and we took leave of each other at the bridge like two men of the same age, like two good friends, and my heart was filled with pride and joy and with delight over my poor dear good father's visit.

The following Saturday afternoon I was sitting in front of the bakery, when suddenly the beggar woman, with her husband and a boy of about my age, appeared; and the beggar woman asked me if my father had gone yet and began to chatter and gossip, while her beggar husband smiled approvingly at her. She let herself go on the subject of my father and scolded and criticized him for allowing me to work so hard away from home. She and her husband were only beggars, but their little boy of my age still went to school and had round rosy cheeks and soft hands and looked well taken care of, but I ought to look at myself in the mirror, with my baker's pallor and my huge baker's feet and my big baker's hands, and she showed me what delicate hands her son had, compared with mine. And the beggar man smiled, and I felt myself dirtied, and I got up and went away and thought: "Why didn't you answer them that you would work day and night a hundred times harder, rather than let your parents go begging for you, and that you would rather have feet and hands ten times as big than such a half-idiotic face as their weakling of a son?..." But the right answers never came to me until too late, and that annoyed me, and then I felt even more annoyed at being annoyed by it. But my hands, my big hands – I have often looked at them. Yes, those big hands – they stayed with me for years and years....

Weeks later Channe Kozak came to see me and told me radiantly that the Curl and Riffkele had broken up, and now Riffkele was going somewhere in Czernowitz, into some sort of a "house." Then she said that the Curl was very sorry for the way he had behaved and had said that I was a "regular guy" and hadn't tried to sue him, and to prove it he was going to give a big breakfast at her house on Saturday and pay for it himself, and he wanted to become reconciled with me before our mutual friends and apologize to me.

My fellow workers at the bakery advised me to accept, for by then everyone knew more or less what had taken place.

On Saturday the other bakers and the Curl's friends took me to Channe Kozak's, and we sat at a properly laid table and ate and drank, and the Curl sat beside me, and after a few vodkas I suddenly felt that I had turned pale, and I trembled and thought of my experience in the kitchen and of Riffkele and of the humiliation and the shame he had caused me, and without saying a word I picked up my heavy beer glass and hit the Curl in the face with it as hard as I could, and I felt better, and I said, "That makes us square. Now you can hit me back," and he threw himself at me, and the others separated us, and blood was running down the Curl's face and out of his mouth, and there was a general free-for-all, and most of them were on my side, and Channe Kozak, the bawd, howled and the other women screamed. And the Curl was washed and bandaged, just as the apothecary had washed and bandaged me the time before. Then peace returned, and we were reconciled, the others urged us to shake hands, and after a while I went home.

From that day on I avoided Channe Kozak and the Curl and their whole circle. I spent more time with the Russian student Czerniakoff, who was like an older brother to me, and

I told him everything, and he always listened to me sympathetically, and then one day he said to me: "Look, maybe your father can't send you to school, but if you think over everything that has happened to you here, you will learn more than any Ph.D. Because life is hard and merciless, it teaches and forms and kneads, just as you knead your dough. You have learned more in this year away from home than many students do in ten years at school. Riffkele and the Curl and the beggar woman – all of them have hit you, but today you are more than all three of them put together. And someday you will discover much more important things in life, and you will stop thinking about these experiences."

Then came the day before Passover, and I bought myself a new suit and a shirt and collar and a wide red Windsor tie with black dots like Czerniakoff's, and kid shoes with rubber heels, and traveled home with my heart pounding and wondered whether many people would envy me my red tie and my rubber heels as I had envied Rosenkranz his rubber heels a year before....Funny, now that I had that which I used to envy someone else for having, I longed to have someone envy me too. A curious emotion: you not only want to get what you desire, you want to be envied for having it, besides!

20

Curiosity

The Russian student Czerniakoff, who in the course of time had become my friend and teacher, came to me one day shortly before Passover and said that he was leaving for a large town where a number of his friends from home were studying. But he could not tell me where that was. Then, having made me promise to say nothing about it, he explained to me that he belonged to a society, a group of friends, who had made it their task to educate the people of Russia and lessen their sufferings. To this organization belonged not only poor, simple people – such as workers from the towns and peasants – but also great scholars and writers and students and professors as well; and many of them were languishing in prisons or had been exiled to Siberia. Some had escaped and now lived abroad and continued their work from there. They printed books and pamphlets and newspapers, which told the truth about the czarist tyranny and taught men how to fight it; and they found means to smuggle these into Russia.

He told me that there were such people all over the world, and they met in different places and discussed various plans for improving the condition of the workers in Russia and in other countries. It was all a secret, and he had known me all this time and had not told me a word about it until he had felt sure that he could trust me completely. And someday, he thought, when I got to the larger cities, I would learn much more about these matters from other workers.

Then one day he disappeared, without saying a word to anyone else or even saying good-by. And I kept his secret to myself and held long imaginary conversations with him. And Zaleszczyki was suddenly empty and boring without him.

I began getting ready to go home and bought presents to take with me: a Bible in Yiddish for Mother, a walking stick and a package of the best Turkish tobacco for Father, bright dresses and beads for my two little sisters, Matele and Lubitschka, a little pair of top boots for red-haired eight-year-old Senderl. I had a blue striped suit made for myself, and bought a blue hat to match and a flowing red Windsor tie with black dots à la Czerniakoff, and kid shoes with rubber heels. I packed everything carefully into a new wooden chest, painted with green and red flowers.

Then came the day of my departure. I hired a seat in a conveyance which took passengers to Horodenka, and Menasche Strum, who was very busy all those days, found time to invite me to drink a vodka with him and said many nice things to me – among others, that I could come back at any time, he would always hire me again, and even pay me a higher salary.

And now we were driving back over the same road that I had walked ten months earlier, and we came to the place where the good-natured Ukrainian peasant had run after me, and I had been frightened to death, and he had given me bread and cheese. Then I thought of Riffkele again, for whose sake I had come to Zaleszczyki, and of the Curl, and Channe Kozak, the bawd, and good, serious Czerniakoff, and I said good-by to them all there in my mind.

Then I thought of the faces that I should find at home; how they would receive me...

And suddenly I was in Horodenka and I saw the town and the market place and the church with its onion-shaped dome in which the two bricks were still missing, and I saw familiar faces. And everyone we passed gave me a friendly greeting, and my heart pounded, and suddenly I was standing in our room, and I held back my tears, because I was thirteen now and a grown man. And the neighbors came in, and my little brothers and sisters showed them my beautiful new chest, and I was their big brother now. And I unpacked my presents, and I had nice things for each of my five little brothers and sisters. My two little sisters, Matele and Lubitschka, were particularly demonstrative and hugged me and were delighted with their dresses and beads and admired everything about me and everything I had brought. And there stood my elder brother, Leibzi, in his brown artilleryman's uniform with shiny brass buttons. He was taller and broader than Father now. And the two of us, who were not only brothers but real friends, were especially happy, and he told me that he had already found a job for me at a bakery in Stanislau, and when his furlough was over, I could go right back with him. And Father interrupted and said that I must first begin to put on *tfillim*, and he wanted to take me to the wonder rabbi from Czortkow, who would be in Horodenka for the second half of Passover. And I could go to Stanislau afterward by myself.

Meanwhile I handed out my presents. Mother wept for joy over her Bible and said that I must read aloud to her out of it. Father immediately rolled and smoked a cigarette of the yellow Turkish tobacco I had brought him, and said that it tasted so good that he understood now how pleasant it must be to be rich. "Or," said a neighbor, "to have children like yours!"

But when I unpacked the elegant little top boots for my eight-year-old brother, Senderl, faces were suddenly turned away. And Mama sobbed aloud, and I looked around and saw no Senderl. And Father quieted little Mama and said, "Children, please, let us not desecrate the holidays!"

Then he turned to me. "My son," he said, "it has pleased God to take your brother Senderl to heaven, only a few days before I went to visit you in Zaleszczyki. But I did not want to make your heart heavy with the news while you were far from home." Later I was told the whole story.

In our district there lived an old man named Lazar Kukuck. A remarkable, jolly old fellow. No one ever knew from where he appeared or whither he vanished. He was respected, almost feared. He talked to everyone with great familiarity and went around in the district searching for poor old spinsters who had been left on the shelf, in order to make marriages for them.

He lived on soup and milk and grits, was always cheerful, smiling with his birdlike face and toothless mouth, and always carried a knotted sack on his back, which he never opened. He used to say playfully that he had become a child again, because his hundredth year was already far behind him, and every day he continued to live was a gift from God Himself. For the Lord allowed him to stay on earth only in order to straighten things out a bit, as it was not right that poor old maids should not find men. He was always smiling happily and contentedly, and you could hardly see any of his toothless, birdlike face – his thin tobacco-yellow beard began right under his eyes, and his bushy eyebrows hung down to his beard, and between them his cheerful little mouse eyes shone through.

When he discovered a poor old spinster he would first talk to her as if he were her father and find out whether she wanted to marry and what kind of husband she would like him to find for her. Then he went from town to town in the vicinity, collecting money from the rich and prosperous. He did not beg. He demanded specific amounts, he laid assessments. To some big grain dealer he would say, "Listen, you, didn't you just ship five hundred sacks of wheat to Vienna?" If the answer was "yes," he demanded a hundred kronen. If the man said "no," Lazar Kukuck would say, "Well, you'll soon be selling a shipment that size," and insisted on his hundred kronen. People liked him and bargained with him. He usually received half or a third of the sum he demanded, and in this way scraped together a few hundred kronen. Then he looked around for an old bachelor, or a divorced man, or a widower with children, and thus found a husband for a poor old spinster.

One day he came to us and said to Father, "Aaron, I have married off my last spinster and I should like to die in your house." He sent for the head of the congregation, the gravedigger, the joiner, the stone mason, paid for a plot in the cemetery, ordered a coffin made to fit him, arranged for four pallbearers, which duty the head of the congregation, my father, and two other pious men took upon themselves, and at last opened the sack which he always carried, and there were his grave clothes with a prayer shawl and even a bag of earth from Palestine. He arranged everything seriously and cheerfully and took leave of everyone as if he were going on a long journey. And he got into bed, and three days later he was dead.

At the funeral the bag of earth from Palestine was missing. Someone ran home to bring it and, to his great horror, found little Senderl playing with it. Now there was a superstition that anyone who played with any of the things that belonged to a corpse would very soon have to follow the dead person into the Beyond. Even in the cemetery people began whispering that little Senderl had played with the bag of earth. And the rumor spread through the whole town. Neighbors came in to sympathize with poor, frightened, superstitious Mama, who watched her little boy nervously, full of forebodings. The other children suddenly became distant and frightened and stopped playing with him and told him why. Everyone regarded him as the next victim, who would soon have to follow Lazar Kukuck into the Beyond.

The boy became melancholy, and wept and cried in his sleep, and sat in a corner all day without speaking, and refused to eat and began to grow thin. After a few weeks he sickened, developed a high fever, and died.

So my homecoming was completely ruined. No one noticed my blue striped suit, my red Windsor tie with black dots. Even the rubber heels on my kid shoes made no impression, for rubber heels were now for sale in Horodenka too, and most people wore them.

Among the many soldiers who had come home on furlough was Srul Kune Gloger. He was serving in the Kaiserjaeger and wore a tight-fitting dark uniform with green facings and a stiff hat with blue-black feathers like a gendarme. There were about twenty soldiers home on furlough, and they created a sensation, because they all looked wonderful and they served in different regiments and were always meeting and telling one another funny soldiers' tales, and they bought wine and barrels of beer together and drank each day in a different house.

Then suddenly one day we heard that the wonder rabbi from Czortkow was coming. There were two big synagogues named for him in Horodenka, and his followers, young and old, put on bright soldiers' uniforms and hired horses and carts, and everything was gaily decorated – even the horses had red and green and yellow and white wool braided into their manes and tails, and bells were hung round their necks and on the shafts, and the children had rattles and trumpets and whips, and the colorful, noisy masquerade set out to meet the rabbi. Funniest of all were the old men with their long white beards and their bright hussars' uniforms. The workaday world was forgotten, all were in pious ecstasy, their cares banished. The rabbi was met and conducted into town amid dancing and singing. He took lodgings at the largest inn, Herr Kugelmass's, and from then on the place was packed within and besieged without, day and night.

Finally, one day Father and I were received together. I was already in the room, where the delicate, pale rabbi with his sparse, silky, blond beard was sitting. I can still see his small, long thin hands resting on the table. And before him stood the rich wood dealer, Srul Dicker, after whom it was to be our turn.

And Herr Dicker said: "Rabbi, a week ago I was the rich Srul Dicker, with the biggest lumberyard in the district, and then there was a fire that burned everything, and it all went up in smoke. Now I have nothing left but the shirt on my back." And tears came into the eyes of the big man with the thick red beard, and he said, "Rabbi, I could not bring you even a small gift today, I am poorer than anyone!"

And the rabbi smiled and said softly: "Listen, Srul Ben Hersch, fire comes from God, and water comes from God, and His ways are hidden, and we must take everything as it comes. But where there was once a spring, it always returns." And he put his small white hand into a silver bowl which stood before him, full of coins and bank notes that the previous visitors had brought. He took as many of the bank notes as he could hold, without counting them, and said, "Take it, Srul Ben Hersch, take it, it is blessed, and it will re-establish you."

Herr Dicker took the money, and he had hardly left the table before Jungermann the banker and the other rich merchants rushed at him, and each one asked him for a single bank note from his blessed money as a first payment on the big credits they were going to grant him for large deals in the future…and in a very short time Herr Dicker was even richer than before.

Then Father and I were received. Father laid on the table a note which explained the reasons for his visit. The rabbi read it slowly and from time to time looked at me searchingly and somewhat worriedly; then he said, "So, Isaiah Ben Aaron, you were named after that friendly man, Shaiko Wisdom?"

"Yes," said Father, "hasn't he his eyes, Rabbi?"

"Yes, he has just his expression," said the rabbi, and stared at me rather skeptically, but with a little more inquisitiveness. "You are just thirteen, my son, and you have already spent a year away from home, and you are going to another town again," he said, glancing at the note that Father had laid before him. "Isaiah Ben Aaron," he sighed, rather solemnly, "may the Lord bless you and guard you from curiosity. You see, my child," said he, "the Creator of the world keeps every secret locked in His eternity, and men can come to know and understand only what pleases Him. And He does not like it when men are too curious. It happened even to Moses that, when he was to choose between fire and gold and inquisitively reached out for the gold, an angel pushed him into the fire and he burned his tongue, and he lisped all his life. Let it be a lesson to you, my son, that even great men burn their tongues when they are too curious, and may the Creator guard you from it and bless you, so that your father may have great joy in you!" And he touched my head with his cool, delicate hand, murmured a blessing and said, "Amen," and Father and I repeated, "Amen," and were dismissed.

But the rabbi's blessing was never fulfilled. My chief characteristic was and remained curiosity. Curiosity in every direction. It was curiosity that made me frighten the children at the crossroads when we came home from the cheder at night. It was curiosity that made me fasten my rabbi Schimshale's beard to the table with wax. It was curiosity that made me stand under Riffkele's window and follow her to Zaleszczyki. It was curiosity that made me hide in the bushes by the river to watch girls bathing. It was curiosity that made me listen to the Russian student Czerniakoff when he talked about stars and worlds. It was curiosity that now made me want to go to Stanislau! And lo, he, the rabbi, knew what was going on inside me and warned me not to be curious and blessed me against it! And it turned everything inside me upside down, and I secretly vowed to repress my curiosity.

But this curiosity of mine never left me. I could think of nothing else, and however much I hoped and prayed that the rabbi's blessing would be fulfilled, yet, while I hoped and prayed, it remained deep in my heart, it nestled snugly in my mind, stood before my eyes, whispered into my ear, and grew with me year by year, just as my longings grew deeper and greater and my body grew stouter and stronger. Until I finally gave up and stopped wishing it would go away. And then it stayed with me and beside me, without leaving me for an instant, until at last I told myself that not all wishes and blessings can be fulfilled. And I became accustomed to my curiosity, I even became friendly with it, and I have kept it to this day, and now I would not be without it for as much as my life is worth.

A few days later I left Horodenka with a light heart. The whole family and our neighbors and friends conducted me to the newly opened railway station. And when the train started, I saw Father's brown eyes fill with tears, and two big drops rolled down his face into his beard. That was the second time I had seen Father cry, and the last time that I saw him in my life.

Nor was the rabbi's wish that Father might have great joy in me fulfilled, for he died a few years later and I never saw him again. May the earth lie lightly on him, for this life brought him burdens enough!

21

It Is Good to Have a Big Brother When You Are Far from Home

My experience in Zaleszczyki, my last visit to Horodenka, my little brother Senderl following Lazar Kukuck into the Beyond, the Rabbi of Czortkow's blessing against curiosity, my father's last look of farewell with the two tears rolling silently into his beard, the journey to Stanislau, all this weighed on my heart like an invisible sack of stones. My only comfort was my brother Leibzi, who was serving in the artillery in Stanislau and had left me the address of the baker Pietrogradski in Zosina Wolja Alley, where I was already expected.

Stanislau was the next largest city after Lemberg. Stanislau had an electric street railway that ran out to the suburbs. It was the garrison town of the Fifty-eighth Infantry Regiment; there were uhlans and dragoons stationed there as well as the artillery regiment in which my brother was serving. It looked like a toy town. There were beautiful white houses several stories high with ornamental grounds and gardens and flowers and avenues of trees; there was a big clean market place with rich displays of all sorts of wares; and at night the electric lights burned, and it was as bright as day but much gayer.

One side of the principal street, the Promenade, was popularly known as "Line A," the other as "Line B." There the young people met. Pretty, well-dressed girls walked up and down, chattering and laughing with students and smart-looking officers. There were coffeehouses where you could listen to music, an arcade where one had rendezvous, and restaurants. Plenty and delight and a gay enthusiasm were everywhere. There were dance halls and amusement palaces, there were a hundred times as many people as in Horodenka's Promenade Garden, only here everything was more daring, freer, more light-hearted; it was contagious, everyone laughed and joked and had rendezvous and trysts. You heard Polish and German and Ukrainian and Yiddish, and the people you saw looked so important and were all so busy and so excited.

And about ten o'clock the street lamps suddenly went out, and the hubbub ended, and Line A and Line B were empty. Everyone left the streets. Here and there you would see a belated couple or a solitary carriage. And at many a door stood a soldier with a servant girl, and they looked around to see if they were watched, and when no one was looking they embraced and kissed, and if someone came by they stood there like thieves caught in the act, embarrassed and silent.

I asked several people where Zosina Wolja Alley was, and they looked me over suspiciously and cheekily. I learned later that, besides containing the artillery barracks and Pietrogradski's bakery, the greater part of it was full of whores and whorehouses, and to ask how to get there was not the proper thing to do. Until finally a half-drunken soldier took me in charge and said, "Come with me. Who knows, maybe we'll become brothers-in-law tonight!" On the way I was several times spoken to by strange girls; I knew what they meant, thought of Riffkele and my sister, and felt ashamed for them.

Now I could see the big steam bakery from afar. I entered it and asked a good-looking gray-haired man with a short pointed beard where I could find Herr Pietrogradski, and he answered proudly, "I am he."

I said that I was the journeyman whom the artillery soldier had sent. He looked me over from head to foot, called his wife, who limped a little but was very pretty, and then two journeymen came in, but I could see that they were his sons. Then a fat schoolboy appeared who was about my age, for he had three silver stripes on his uniform, and a girl of perhaps ten. They stared with suspicion, hard enough to photograph me, and whispered and laughed and nodded at my little wooden chest with the green and red flowers. I felt riddled by their scorn.

Suddenly Herr Pietrogradski said, "Are you hungry?"

"Yes," I said.

Whereupon he remarked loudly, "I can well believe it; anyone could tell that by looking at you," and everyone laughed at his joke. Then, turning to the others, he said, "The only question is, can you do any work?"

His wife said reproachfully, as if I had been lying to her all my life, "Huh, how can such a big strapping soldier have such a weak little brother?"

I blushed and felt embarrassed and ashamed because I was so small, but I felt glad that even they had been impressed by my big strong brother.

Then the baker said, "All right, you will work here for a week on trial, then we'll see." He turned to the fat schoolboy: "Hi, Professor, show him his boudoir so he can store his elegant flowered chest."

Fatty answered simply: "No, I won't. Someone else will have to."

The father began to unfasten his belt and growled, "I'll teach you to say 'I won't,' you fat jellyfish," and his lame wife interrupted, scolding him in Polish so that I should not understand, "Don't you understand, you ignoramus, that he can't do that? He is a student, and it's not proper that he should."

The elder of the other two sons put one hand on his hip like a girl and held the other spread out daintily near his cheek and said in a high falsetto, "Oh no! 'Students sniff roses and shit in their trousers!'"

I had to laugh, it was all so new to me, and so funny. But the fat dumpling of a schoolboy hissed at me. His mother put her arm around him and caressed his fat, shapeless face as if he were a baby, calmed him down, and threw me a look full of hate.

The elder brother said, "Come with me, kid, I'll show you your palace."

He led me out through the back door, then across the court to a room which was used for storing flour, and said: "They're all crazy – the best thing to do is to pay no attention to them. I'm their own son, and even I can't stand them. I've already spent a year in Lemberg, and I am going away again. The Old Man is from Russia and acts like Nicholas himself; *she* wants at least one professor in the family, so that she can have something to boast about. So now the booby is going to school. She coddles him and spoils him until one of these days the fat balloon is going to burst. Come along back with me, there's smoked brisket today, and the old miser keeps it locked up in his strongbox. Afterward you'll have to bring in wood to heat the oven. I'll show you where everything is."

We went back to the shop. The father was already cutting slices from a smoked brisket. You could take as much bread as you wanted. I took the portion he handed me, went back to my corner in the flour room, sat down on half a sack of flour, and devoured my supper alone like a strange little puppy. The chest they had laughed at watched me, and I felt sorry for the poor beflowered little thing from Zaleszczyki, which my two little sisters, Matele and Lubitschka had stroked so tenderly and so lovingly. And the little chest smiled at me with its red and green flowers, as if it wanted to remind me of the wise Ukrainian proverb, "Every dog is a king in his own yard."

Then I was called to work. The sleepy, yawning journeymen, who had just been wakened, were in a bad humor; they had not had their fill of sleep, and they looked me over ironically. Especially one – his name was Joine Burlak, and he was four or five years older than I, a rough and uncouth fellow. He leered at me and asked me where I came from. When I said Horodenka, he grinned and said that was the hole where the goats grazed on the roofs. And the others, tired as they were, grinned their applause.

The work of the bakery was divided between the helper, who looked after the oven, the "white mixer," whose duty it was to prepare the dough for rolls, and the "black mixer," who was responsible for the leavening and the rye dough. Then there were those who formed loaves, rolled rolls, twisted crescents, shaped Vienna rolls, and braided twist rolls. Finally there was the *jidl*. My job there was to be the jidl.

The jidl is the handy man. Why the Austrian bakers called the handy man, who had to do the dirtiest and the hardest work, the "jidl" is a secret we may leave to them. The jidl had to serve everyone. His was the heaviest work: fetching wood, splitting it, firing the oven, heating water, moving flour sacks, sifting flour, carrying the trays of uncooked loaves out where it was cool so that they would not rise too much, bringing them back to the oven, carrying away the finished product. And all quickly and smartly. When, after a night's work, everything was finished and everyone could go and rest, the jidl had to scrape out the troughs, clean the scales, clean and oil the dough cutter, sweep the bakery, put everything in perfect order, and then fetch wood again, put on water....When the others worked fourteen hours he worked sixteen; when the others worked sixteen hours, as they did at Pietrogradski's, the poor jidl had to work at least eighteen. And, as there were errands to run besides, I worked from eighteen to twenty hours a day, and collapsed on the stone floor of the bakery exhausted, like a dead man, and it was hard to shake my young bones out of their deep sleep.

At first, when they wakened me, I was roughly seized and pushed and shaken. This was always done by my fellow journeymen, who had to get up to prepare their leaven. Next they tried shoving and slapping. Joine Burlak thought it was the best fun to tickle the inside of my nose with a feather or simply to poke me with a piece of wood. But I was half dead, and my body became accustomed to being punished, and I slept on. Then Joine had another funny idea: to pour cold water over me. And that worked. I always jumped up then, in a fright, felt unhappy and sleepy, and longed for Friday and Saturday, when I could sleep twenty hours at a stretch.

After a week I was taken on permanently as the jidl, and from then on after that I met my brother outside the bakery or in his barracks, and to avoid the awkwardness of handing him money I always slipped my salary into his pocket. Because, first, I did not need it, and, second, I was very glad to help him. We were friends, and not merely brothers.

Among the journeymen, it was this Joine Burlak who persecuted and tormented me from the first minute on. He was even more angry now because I received the same salary as he; and although I was smaller and younger, I was a better and faster worker. The other journeymen and Pietrogradski's two sons, who were paid just like the rest of the workmen, were always teasing Joine about it. And he hated me and hit me when he could and called me the "small-town pig"; for he came from the "big town" of Kolomea, and I only from Horodenka. The others laughed at him too, because I could read and write and he was illiterate.

His greatest amusement was to "wake" me. He used to get up earlier than he would otherwise have done, to indulge in this enjoyment. He was always thinking up something new; he rubbed my face with handfuls of soot; he held my mouth and nose shut so that I could not breathe. After a while I simply turned over on my stomach. Then he tickled me behind the ear with a straw. But what he liked best was to pour a pail of water over me. By now I had become accustomed to only four or five hours' sleep, and I did my work quickly and smartly, and everyone was satisfied with me.

Then something very important happened: a baker's union was organized in Stanislau for the first time. And because, ever since my days at the Baron Hirsch school, I had been able to read and write Yiddish, Ukrainian, Polish and even a little German – an unusual accomplishment for a baker in those days – I was elected secretary of the union. Our first oven worker, bright little Shimele Ruskin, had nominated me himself.

Shimele was about forty years old, clean-shaven, could neither read nor write himself, but had a very wide-awake and clever head. He despised Joine Burlak and always took my side; not that it helped matters much.

A baker's working night is long, and many things are discussed while the bread and crescents and Vienna rolls are being made. From then on, the others teased Joine even more – he had come from the big town of Kolomea and had been in Stanislau a long time, and the little jidl from a small town was the one on whom the honors had fallen, who had been elected secretary of the organization! So Joine Burlak made life harder and harder for me. I accepted everything without a word or a protest, I felt ashamed to complain to my brother, whom I wanted to impress with my independence and manliness. I thought to myself: someday he will grow tired of tormenting me and leave me in peace.

Besides, I was extremely pious. When I had finished work, I put on my *tfillim* with their phylacteries, went into my corner to pray, and sank into meditation and told my Creator everything that I hid from my brother. I wept silently and opened my heart to Him. And it became easier for me to bear it all. None of the other journeymen prayed, nor did Pietrogradski's sons. They joked about me and my "fanaticism." In that, however, I was invulnerable. There, no one could touch me – on the contrary, I even felt a little sorry for them all. I had only to think of my father, or of Schimshale, or of the wonder rabbi from Czortkow, and all their scorn and arrogance vanished like a soap bubble.

Little Shimele Ruskin was on my side too. He said that he was against letting any rabbi tell him when to fast or when to pray. He simply did not do it. But if a man was sincerely pious, no one had any right to interfere with him in the exercise of his piety. But Joine Burlak, the tough guy, was of a different opinion. One day when I was thus lost in meditation, opening my heart to the Lord, I suddenly had a *matschke* thrown in my face. A *matschke*, in bakers' language, is an empty flour sack dipped in water and then in soot. It not only hurts, it covers your face with flour and soot and water and glues your eyes shut, and it is a humiliation besides – with the dirt, you swallow shame and disgrace and insult, too. Everyone laughed – except Shimele Ruskin, who was disgusted.

I said nothing and went on praying and asked God in my thoughts whether it was agreeable to Him that Joine should do this to me just when I was praising Him. And I felt that He answered me and said that it was only another trial, because those whom He loved He tried ceaselessly. So I became more and more pious, and meditated more and more, and sought and found comfort in prayer. Shimele Ruskin became more and more distant with the ignoramus Joine, and influenced the other journeymen until they began to take him to task for picking on someone weaker than himself. But he, instead of stopping, became more and more bold and mean....

One Saturday I was walking along Line A with my big brother, when we met Shimele Ruskin. We stopped and spoke to him. And he was amazed to learn that I had a big, strong soldier for a brother. He took my brother aside and talked to him alone. I saw my brother turn white as a sheet after they had talked a short time; then he gave Shimele his hand and I heard him say, "Thank you, thank you for everything."

Then my brother and I walked away together; first he spoke about other things, and then suddenly asked me if it was true that Joine Burlak was in the habit of hitting me. I felt ashamed and tried to lie. Then he said: "Would you lie to our father too? I am your elder brother, and here, away from home, I stand in our father's place. Has Joine hit you, or has Shimele Ruskin been telling me lies?" Then I told him the whole truth.

That same night, about three o'clock, when we were all at the trough table rolling crescents, my brother suddenly appeared and said with great friendliness, "Good evening, bakers!" Everyone answered him. Then he said, "Which of you is Joine?"

And Joine called out loudly and gaily, "I am, soldier, what do you want?"

And my brother said, "I want to tell you, you swine, in plain soldier's language, that the kid here you're always beating up is my brother."

And he let him have a right and a left, and another left and another right, and another and another! And Joine covered his face with his hands, and after one more punch in the head he reeled back against the wall and said nothing.

The journeymen all grinned at one another, and Shimele Ruskin said, "We always warned you, Joine."

Then my brother said, "Now I'm going, you shit-arse, and I warn you that if you touch him again I'll send you to Kolomea in a coffin as a present to your whore of a mother!" And he went out.

There was a tense silence. I was the most excited of all. Because, much as it had done my heart good, and proud and grateful as I was that I had such a brother, still I shook at the thought of what would happen next.

Everyone continued to work, and no one spoke. Joine and I too. Suddenly he shouted wildly at me, "Hey, you, what do you mean by not telling me you had a brother in the artillery here?" The artillery barracks were near the bakery, and the others burst out laughing.

And Shimele Ruskin roared and cackled with delight and said, "Oh, Joine, you're not only a louse, you're a fool! Why should he have told you, when his brother could come and do it so clearly himself in that soldier's language of his?"

"The lily-livered swine!" said the baker's eldest son. "He didn't even try to defend himself! But hit a little helpless kid – he could do that all right!"

Then there was silence, and work went on as though nothing had happened.

My tormentor Joine never touched me again after that night. Not even in fun.

And so I learned how good it is to have a big brother to protect you when you are far from home.

22

Malka

Joine Burlak left the bakery, and I was given his job, which was much easier, and another *jidl* was hired and toiled in my stead.

Working conditions became more and more unbearable, and Shimele Ruskin, the chairman of our local, said that we belonged to the big organization and we must report to them about it. He dictated long letters to me addressed to the Vienna Trade Union Center about our conditions, and one day a union official came out from Vienna. The official, who had been a journeyman baker himself, explained that there was only one thing to do: we must present our demands collectively, negotiate, and see what would come of it; and if the other side showed no signs of meeting us halfway, then was the time to use the workman's strongest weapon – a strike. All this was something entirely new to us. Then he told us about the workers' fight in the big cities of Europe and explained that a strike was our last and most sacred weapon. For the strike was the weapon of the workers' solidarity and friendship and comradeship and pride and consciousness of themselves; for though workmen are poor, they have a morale that is worth more than the others' wealth. We lads were simply full of enthusiasm about it.

Then the various demands were discussed, such as better pay, shorter working hours, more hygienic conditions, and the abolishment of corporal punishment for the child workers. It was all written down, a strike committee was elected, the demands were presented to the master bakers, and we were to receive an answer in three days.

The first night after our demands had been presented, Pietrogradski, our boss, came into the bakery and made fun of our union and our demands, teased the workmen, and joked about the whole affair.

The master bakers refused our demands as a whole, without even entering into negotiations. And suddenly we were all out on strike!

We met every day. And one week followed another. The bakeries kept going; the work was done by the master bakers, their wives and children, people picked up in the streets, and a few strikebreakers – of whom Joine Burlak was one. The older workers soon lost courage and were afraid of losing their jobs. Wives came to our meeting place, raging and inflamed by provocateurs, called their small strike benefits "beggary," cursed the strike leaders, dragged their husbands home and made it hot for them. After five or six weeks a few gave in to the pressure of their wives and went back to work one by one. Our morale suffered. The man from Vienna made reassuring speeches, which had no effect, talked of compromises and adjustments. But the master bakers laughed at the strike. Gradually more and more men went back to work, under the same bad conditions. The union leader returned to Vienna, and all the strike leaders and everyone who had spoken at our meetings, and all who were suspected of being for the strike were punished: locked out and not rehired.

It was a great, grim defeat. Shimele Ruskin was the only one who did not lose his head. He held that even a lost strike could be made to have a value for the workers. If you learned from your mistakes, you would win the next strike, or the one after that, because the workers had to win the last strike – that was a law. I did not entirely understand him, but it was good to listen to him and believe what he said. After a time he left too and went to Lemberg.

I was now locked out and without a job – for the first time in my life. I went to the railway station, helped passengers carry their baggage, was chased away by the professional porters, slept in the waiting room, was pounced on by the guardians of the law, arrested, let go again, hunted, driven. And it was winter. The icy cold penetrated my thin clothes, the snow crunched under my feet. To a locked-out youth the nights are endlessly long, when cold and hunger and loneliness and curiosity and sexual awakening are all mixed up in him. He trudges from place to place, confused, uncertain, unable to think anything through, his heart as heavy as lead. Such nights are torturing eternities.

On my wanderings I encountered a variety of outcasts. They told me that you didn't have to worry about a place to sleep in Stanislau. You had only to go to a brothel, sit down in a corner of the waiting room, and so pass the night sleeping in a warm place.

One night, with my heart pounding, I went to Zosina Wolja Alley. There was one house after another. There was noise, confusion – a market of living flesh. Old men, high-school boys, soldiers, alone or in groups, went in and out. Furtively, like thieves: they walked unconcernedly along at first, then suddenly they made a rush and dove into one of the houses....

Worn out by my wanderings, by the daily chase, and unhappy, I hung around outside a house. And suddenly along came a group of men, and I stepped in among them and slipped in with them – and there I was, inside Herr Bretzele's brothel.

Bretzele was only somewhat bigger than a dwarf but had unusually broad shoulders; he looked like a huge cube, with his thick turned-up mustache and his heavy bull neck; when someone tried to get tough, he called out in his oily voice: "People behave themselves in this place – it's take your girl, and pay, and leave. And anyone who gets fresh is likely to find a knife between his ribs." So everyone became quiet, and

Bretzele retired to the rear of the establishment with a square bottle of vodka and resumed his post at the foot of the stairway which led to the second floor.

Eight or ten girls sat there, some of them quite young, looking tired and embarrassed. Some were older, with painted bright red cheeks, and all wore very short skirts, and you could see their thighs above the tops of their stockings, and sometimes even higher. I sat down in a corner and saw one of the guests rise and point to a girl. She stood up, and a full-bosomed wide-hipped woman with a three-story red hair-do and a bunch of keys handed her a key and a towel. The guest gave the woman some money and followed the girl. Another man did likewise, then a third and a fourth. Then the first girl came back and lit a cigarette. Some of the guests left, others came in. And the same process was repeated. And just as I had trembled with cold outside, so I trembled with a strange, oppressive excitement here. However, I made myself inconspicuous in my corner and fell asleep.

Toward morning I was wakened by the red-haired lady with the three-story hair-do. The house was closing. And I went out into the cold, cutting winter air, shivered and clenched my teeth and succumbed to cold and hunger and loneliness. I was locked out of the whole world. No bakery, no work, no brother, no Shimele Ruskin. Nothing but shame and strangeness and despair. In this condition I could neither return home nor go to Lemberg, where two of my brothers were.

So one day slipped by after another. I wandered about like a homeless dog. And at night I hung around the brothel again, and when a party came to Herr Bretzele's house, I mixed among them and crept into my corner and went to sleep. And thus many days and nights passed.

After such a night as I have described I was waked toward morning by the red-three-story hair-do. But tenderly this time, as a mother wakes her child. I was startled, and she stroked my forehead and said, "Boy, what makes you come here to sleep so often?"

"I have no job and no home and nowhere else to sleep."

She looked into my eyes softly, and took pity on me, and made me tell her how it had all happened and where I came from. And tears came into her big, kind, cowlike eyes, and she took two keys from her bunch and said one of them was to the outside door of Number 26 Zosina Wolja Alley, on the same street, and the other one was to the door inside that you saw right opposite you when you had opened the house door. That was her room. I was to go there and lie down and sleep. I accepted her offer thankfully, found the house a few blocks farther on, and unlocked the door of the room, in which there was a bed, a clothes chest, a little table with a kerosene lamp on it, and a chair. The room was so small and cramped that these few pieces of furniture filled it so that you hardly had room to turn around. I lay down on the clothes chest and went to sleep.

Later, my benefactress came in – her name was Malka – bringing some fresh rolls, and I got up and split some kindling. In the wall of the house by the entrance there was a little cooking place. I made coffee, set the table, served breakfast, and afterward shined her shoes and my own.

That very first morning she told me that she came from Jassy in Rumania, where she had had an unhappy love affair with one of "the Twelve." "The Twelve" were the terrible twelve brothers, great fighters, before whom Jassy trembled as the people of Horodenka trembled before the Glogers. But the Twelve were Christians, and she was Jewish. So her family had repudiated her because she went with a goy, and his brothers had waylaid her lover and beaten him because he was carrying on with a Jewess. They had lived together on the edge of the town and had already had a little daughter. One night he came home drunk and beaten up. He threatened and cursed her and said, "See here, you Jewish whore! It's on your account that my brothers have given me this lesson." She answered: "And all for nothing. There'd be some sense in it – if you loved me!" At that he went wild in his drunkenness, took the big chopping knife and bellowed and called her every filthy name, laid his thumb on the table and cursed and yelled, "Say that again, say that again, you worn-out whore, say

I don't love you!" And in her despair she cried: "No! No! No! You don't love me! You don't love me!" And he brought the chopping knife down with all his strength and cut off his thumb and ran out of the house bleeding. She wrapped the severed thumb in cotton, bought a jar of alcohol and put the thumb in it; then she left her child to board with some poor people and went to Czernowitz and into a whorehouse. She kept the jar with the thumb in it under her pillow and showed it to me.

Now she ran Herr Bretzele's house for him – she was "madam" and manager. She earned enough to support her little daughter Sonjutschka, who was ten years old and went to school and must not know that her mother lived in such a house.

She wept bitterly as she told me her story. I felt embarrassed and comforted her with the cheap stories of which I had a plentiful stock from reading trashy novels. She was impressed by my being able to read and write, and she immediately asked me to write a letter to her ten-year-old Sonjutschka. I composed a heart-rending, high-flown letter, compounded from several "Polite Letter Writers" which I knew by heart and a trashy novel about an unfortunate princess who suffered the tortures of the damned as a stablemaid until at last one day a real prince recognized her and delivered her.

Malka was in ecstasies over it and asked me to go to the brothel with her early that evening so that I could read my letter aloud to the other girls. I did so, and most of the little whores wept with emotion.

From then on I read cheap novels aloud to the girls every evening. And later when the guests began to arrive I went home and went to sleep on the clothes chest, and by the time Malka came home I had had my fill of sleep – I got up, split wood, made breakfast and served it, shined our shoes, and we chatted, or I read to her until she fell asleep.

During the day I wandered around; at nightfall I went back to the brothel. One day she said that I mustn't sleep all night on the hard clothes chest – I could lie in her bed until she came in, and then sleep on the chest. And so several weeks passed.

One Sunday night I stayed up very late with her and the girls, and toward morning, just as they were going to close the house, a drunken dragoon appeared who blustered and cursed, smashed things with his saber, grabbed one of the girls by the hair, and when Malka tried to rescue her, he attacked *her*. All the girls screamed and ran into corners.

In a flash I was up on a table behind him. Boiling with rage, I sprang at him, pulled him to the floor, punched him again and again, grabbed his saber, which he had been brandishing, and broke it over my knee. He lay there, vanquished, like a heap of offal. I dragged him out by the legs and across to the gutter. The house door was locked.

The whole affair had not taken three minutes. The owner of the house, Herr Bretzele, came down from the second floor, where he lived; he had a bottle of vodka in his hand, and he said, "I've heard all about it already. Here, have a drink with me!" And he filled two tea glasses with vodka and offered me one.

I took the glass and said, *"Prosit*, Herr Bretzele!"

But he said, "If you call me 'Herr' again, I'll break the bottle over your head, you son of a bitch. We are friends."

And we both swallowed our drinks in one gulp. Then he poured out two more, and gave Malka and the girls each a drink too. Malka brought in a bite to eat, and Bretzele said, "Let me tell you, you son of a whore, I like kids with courage like you." He reached into his pocket and threw me a gulden, saying, "Here, buy yourself some smokes."

And Malka said proudly, "Or a new book – he can read and write, and he always reads aloud to us when there are no guests around."

"Here's another gulden," he said, "and be here every evening. You won't lose anything by it!"

The next day about noon, when the girls in the alley went to visit one another, the story was that I had beaten up several soldiers single-handed. By two o'clock it was twenty soldiers; at five it was a gang of forty or fifty ruffians, whom I had knocked down and thrown out one after another with exquisite and masterly science. Toward evening girls and pimps from the other houses came to see the "marvel," the fellow who had vanquished a whole squadron of dragoons single-handed. And thus I became a famous hero overnight.

Malka took my two gulden, added something to it, and bought me a coat and a cap. She combed my hair in a smart curl on the right side of my forehead and made it stick with plum juice, put my cap on the back of my head so that the beautiful curl was well exposed to view, and only regretted that I hadn't a sign of a mustache. But, she said, if I would begin to shave, the mustache would follow. When I looked at myself in the mirror, I felt daring and strong. Bretzele gave me a steel knuckle-duster like the one the Curl had hit me with, back in Zaleszczyki. I began to swing my shoulders when I walked, the way Bretzele did. I flexed my muscles and looked the guests over distrustfully, like a watchdog, ready at any minute to jump at one of them and try out my knuckle-duster and my strength.

I always ate supper with Malka and the girls and became a sort of deputy lord and master of the house. I continued to read aloud, and wrote letters not only for Malka but also for the other girls, for which I was sometimes paid, sometimes given a little present.

Now I knew everyone's secrets, and I felt tremendously superior and strong and dangerous and daring, and I waited anxiously for the next fight.

One morning Malka came home; when, as usual, I started to get out of her bed to take my old place on the clothes chest, she simply said, "Oh, stay where you are," and she undressed and lay down beside me.

And when it was time for breakfast, she would not let me get up, she crawled out of bed herself, covered me up again, and tucked me in tenderly and carefully.

She split wood and she lighted the fire –
She set the table and she made breakfast –
She shined the shoes and she waited on me –
Because now I was a man – her man!
And she was my first wife....

23

The Theater

I lived with Malka, sat in the brothel at night, read to the little whores and wrote letters for them.

One of the younger girls was a little thing named Sosja – she came from Zaleszczyki and I knew her father. She was sixteen, but looked younger. Her hair was ash blond, she had a small, slim body like a boy's and big blue-green, melancholy eyes. She had run away when her father brought home a wicked stepmother who hit her and pulled her hair. Sosja claimed more of my time than the other girls. She opened her heart to me. She was very unhappy in the brothel and confided to me that she was going to run away to Lemberg someday and become "respectable" again and get a job as a servant girl. She asked me to teach her to read and write and paid me five kreuzer an hour for lessons and gave me little presents. One day she surprised me with a half dozen handkerchiefs, which she had embroidered with my initials in red silk. Another time it was a flowered tie.

When Malka became aware of this relationship, she stopped speaking to me. I became silent too. She left her job at Bretzele's, and every afternoon about four o'clock she put on a loud costume with a much shorter skirt than she had worn before, painted her cheeks red, took a big key, and went out into the street. At night, somewhere around ten o'clock, she would come home, and she always had money.

One day she asked me to go out with her. She took me to a shop, bought me a new suit, two shirts, and a loud tie. When we got home I asked her what all this meant. It was the first time we had spoken in weeks. She exploded like a volcano and screamed, "Do you think I haven't seen how that syphilitic whore, that Sosja, that stinking rag, is trying to get you away from me?" And she grabbed a pair of scissors and cut Sosja's handkerchiefs and tie to bits. "I can buy you things myself! I can earn more with my behind in an hour than she can in a month! I helped you when you had nowhere to sleep! I am your woman, and I know what you need!" She fell on my neck, kissed me again and again, and wept and moaned. Then her misery got the better of her. "I have no one else in the world," she howled; she would do everything for me, if only I would not leave her!

I didn't like this at all. I suddenly felt uncomfortable, tied, responsible. I scolded her and told her just what I thought. Then she began to laugh and cry at once, and screamed, "Yes, yes, yes! That's right! Abuse me! Strike me! I know you're strong. Show me that you're a man! My man! My sweetheart! Make me afraid of you, let me feel you! But if I ever hear of you going with that cheap whore again, I'll scratch her eyes out, I'll pour boiling oil over her, and then jump in the river myself!"

That made me perfectly miserable, and I lay down on the bed, without attempting to answer, and tried to sleep. She became calm then, begged me to forgive her outburst, put on her short skirt, painted her cheeks, gave me a caress, covered me up carefully, kissed me, begged me to go to sleep and forget everything that had passed, took her big key and went out into the street as she did every day at that hour.

I lay there feeling oppressed. It all ran through my head: Malka's outburst. Then I thought of Sosja too, the innocent little whore, who suddenly reminded me of Riffkele, and I had a horrible feeling; but at the same time I felt flattered too. So, I thought, little Sosja loves you too! You are a man.

Two women are already fighting over you, you're not so helpless, as you were at Channe Kozak's in Zaleszczyki. I turned the pages of my new "Polite Letter Writer." I was overcome with weariness. I tried to compare my situation of a year ago with the changes that had taken place since, and I fell into a light sleep.

I saw myself promenading down Line A and Line B in my new suit – but it was the Promenade Garden in Horodenka too – and it was all in Zaleszczyki, the girls from Horodenka and from Zosina Wolja Alley, from Herr Bretzele's house, and Sosja and Malka, with her high three-story hair-do and the bunch of keys at her side, were coming toward me smiling – and Channe Kozak came running up and told me that Riffkele cried for me now day and night and was sorry for everything and was so unhappy – I ran to Riffkele, took her in my arms, and forgave her and said, "Men *are* faithful!" And she laughed her clear, ringing laugh through her tears and called me "Torn Cap" again – and my brother Leibzi was there too – and we bought three gigantic tickets and sailed to America – and I baked pretzels and crisp caraway sticks again – and Riffkele kept feeling my muscles and made my brother look and see how strong and mature I had become – and she told him about the horde of soldiers I had defeated, and how I had even beaten up the Curl and Joine Burlak. I awoke when Malka came home.

From that day on I had a feeling of estrangement from Malka. We lived without quarreling, slept in the same bed, were friendly to each other, but it was more like living side by side than living together....

So several weeks passed, until one night someone knocked on the window and gave a short cough. It was my brother Leibzi. I knew him even before he called out my name. I answered, wildly excited, jumped out of bed – Malka was frightened. I explained that it was my elder brother, slipped quickly into my old clothes. Malka stared at me all the while with wide-open eyes.

I ran out without saying good-by and suddenly found myself standing in the dark beside my big brother. He was dressed like a gentleman, in a dark suit and a short topcoat, he wore a derby hat and carried a cane, and we walked to the station together without a word. He took only a sidelong look at me once or twice and then asked me jokingly why I swung my hips so much. I felt embarrassed, thought of the way Bretzele walked, and resumed my normal gait.

When we arrived at the station he bought two tickets to Lemberg, without consulting me, and was told that the next train left in half an hour. We sat down in the waiting room, where, two months before, I had tried to snatch an hour's sleep and had been arrested for it. He bought some salami and pretzels and beer and told me that he had married Sheindele, who was the youngest daughter of Shaiko Wisdom, the man for whom I was named. So now I was not only his brother, but his father-in-law. And we both laughed and boarded the train for Lemberg.

Then he began to tell me about my other brother, who had a sweet wife too, and big handsome children who all spoke Polish and went to school, and that he and our elder brother dealt in fruit, and things were going very well for them. Then he told me that he had run into Shimele Ruskin in Lemberg, who had told him about the lost strike, and that Shimele was working for Tabaczynski in the newly opened electric bakery, and that there was a job for me there too.

I suddenly began to think of all that had happened since the lost strike, how I had wandered around at night, and how I first slipped into the brothel, and how Malka had helped me, how she had offered me her little room, how she had stared at me that day with her great sorrowful eyes, and how I had not even said good-by to her. I ought not to have run off like that, I thought. She deserved better than that from me.

Suddenly it was no longer trees and telephone poles that were rushing past the window. It was houses. And my brother put on his derby and his topcoat and said, "We're almost there." And we drew into the great railway station. We were in Lemberg, Lwow, the capital of Galicia.

The noise and confusion were immense. Hundreds of people were getting on and off trains, pushing, calling to porters with trucks and luggage, engines breathed, puffed, blew, squealed, whistled, screamed. People rushed busily in all directions – and, lo, out of all the confusion a group approached, laughing and waving, and came to greet us! It was my elder brother Abraham, elegantly dressed, with his wife and his grown children. Leibzi's ash-blond Sheindele was there too.

Everyone fell on me, hugged me. Abraham's children called me "Uncle." Sheindele called me *"Tatku,"* which means "Little Father." There was a battle between the sisters-in-law – both wanted me to come to live with them. Through their talk I heard Abraham remark to Leibzi that I looked like a lean herring and ask whether he had found me lying in a barrel!

Leibzi grinned and said, "No, he's been lying next to a barrel." Then it was decided that I should spend alternate months with each of my brothers, and the first month I was to go to Leibzi's, because he had no children.

From the station we all went to a good restaurant, and my eldest brother ordered a wonderful meal: gefullte fish and roast goose. We ate and drank as only the richest people in Horodenka did on high holidays.

The next morning Shimele Ruskin came and took me to Tabaczynski at the electric bakery. I was hired for two and a half gulden a week, with a loaf of bread and twelve rolls each day besides.

The same day Leibzi went with me to a shop. We bought material for a suit and an overcoat, which he arranged to pay for in installments. Within a week I was dressed as I had never been in my life before! I got a new haircut. The curl on my forehead, which Malka was always sticking down with plum juice, was cut off, and I abandoned the swinging gait that I had imitated from Bretzele. A new man in a new town, in new surroundings, began a new life.

In the meanwhile I was shown Lemberg, with its beautiful clean broad principal street, the "Kazimierzowska," and the big shops with their show windows, the long Bahnstrasse, where little cars drawn by horses ran on rails, and the electric railways in the other streets. Jews with long beards and high silk hats stood on the corner by the Exchange and talked about big deals. Along the sidewalks and at the corners stood fruit dealers. At one such corner my brothers had a fruit stand of their own.

There were placards advertising various soaps, Kathreiner's malt coffee, restaurants, and a circus with dancing horses, a Polish opera, Ukrainian plays, Yiddish singers. And all the market places! Particularly the one in front of the synagogue, where, amid tremendous confusion, everything was bought and sold; books and fish and shoelaces and *pirogen*, meat raw and cooked, butter, cheeses, iron, mirrors, bread, dresses, kvass, suits, soup, puppies, cats, children's toys – all together. Every day there was the same tumult, and the more I was impressed by it all, the more I was reminded of Horodenka. It was bigger – ten times – a hundred times – but I found nothing that surprised me, nothing to make me wonder. The difference between the village of Werbiwci and the little town of Horodenka was much greater than the difference between Horodenka and the capital city of Lemberg.

But one evening we went to the theater. And there I found something different – vastly different from anything that I had yet seen or heard or experienced! For there I found another world, an unknown, a new world!

Even the preparations! "Going" to the theater! How they all talked about Gimpel, the director. How we turned into Jagiellonna Street, came to the small court, the crowd of radiant faces – everyone looked in such a holiday mood. My brothers bought tickets at a little window, spoke to friends and acquaintances. Simple people like themselves. I felt that I knew them at once. And everyone talked about the actors, about their latest doings. How Schilling had looked when Guttman said such and such to him – how old deaf Rosenberg read the words on the others' lips, about Kalisch's Ben Ador and Zuckermann's Bar Kochba – how Frau Fischler drank the poison as Chasja, the orphan – how Frau Rosenberg ties her fast by her pigtails and beats her – how Palepade laughed – and how Frau Karlick danced – and how Mellitzer, acting in *The Wild Man*, had really gone mad and had to be sent to an asylum. And that Frau Fischler was really married to a rich doctor, but when she played Chasja, the orphan, she forgot she was rich and wept bitter, real tears. Everyone had something to tell. Everyone was in raptures with what he had seen and heard.

Of all this I understood not a word. I knew only one thing: it was in just this fashion that the pious Chassidim in Horodenka talked about holy wonder rabbis. No one said a word about work or business or weekdays, or even about his own family. I envied them their familiarity, their air of being on the inside, and my curiosity began to itch somewhere in the region of my heart.

Then a bell rang, a long warning summons, and everyone obediently began to enter the theater. There were men at the door to whom you had to show your tickets, others directed people to their seats, which were numbered. The house was brightly lighted. We sat in the thirteenth row. Behind us, people – in front of us, people. The house was already crowded, and more people were coming in, laughing, bowing, waving. The bell rang again. The noise in the house grew even louder, the doors were closed. Many still stood talking to their neighbors. Then the bell rang for the third time. It became quieter.

Down in front, beyond the first seats, there was a cloth wall, with a picture painted on it: a man dressed in nothing but a pelt was playing on a shepherd's pipe; an almost naked woman, whose breasts were only half hidden by her hair, listened to his playing. Suddenly a gong sounded, the lights went out – the house was dark. Other lights suddenly came on at the foot of the cloth wall. Another stroke on the gong – music playing somewhere – now the house is perfectly still – a third stroke on the gong – my heart nearly bursts with expectation.

And now the cloth wall rises. Two long flights of stairs against a background of painted clouds, girls sitting on the stairs in long blue nightgowns, with big wings hanging from their shoulders, costumed as angels. A little too large for angels, perhaps, but I'm already convinced that they really are angels. They sing that they counsel men only to good, and now the devil appears in person! Dressed in the reddest of reds – and he limps – he has real devil's horns on his head, and he explains gaily and impudently how boring it is on earth, he says nasty but clever things. Then we hear God's voice, praising a pious Torah writer, Herrschale Dobrowner. And the devil incarnate laughs his grating laugh in God's face and makes a bet with Him that he can tempt the pious Torah writer to destruction with money and wealth. And then the cloth wall goes down.

What a world! What splendor! It is a hundred times more exciting than the most exciting dream! The sweat runs down my face! What will happen next? My brother Leibzi looks at me, smiling and curious. I cannot speak a word. There, now! The gong sounds! Darkness again! The cloth wall goes up. It is a poor, plain, ordinary room, such as I have seen hundreds of times, such as I know from my own home in the lower streets. It is winter – one of the windows is stuffed with rags, the other with an old pillow. You can actually hear the wind whistling outside. On the table lies a rolled-up Torah scroll, wrapped in a covering. An old grandfather is saying funny things, playing with one of his grandchildren, who is already a big girl; and a woman is sitting peeling potatoes – she has a toothache and cannot laugh at the old man's jokes. Neighbors come in – there is talk about Herrschale Dobrowner, the Torah writer, about whom we just had seen the devil make a bet with God in heaven. But the people up there do not know what we know. They say that Herrschale has gone to take a bath before he writes the word *"Adonai"* and the last sentence of the Torah. And now he comes in himself: a poor but delicate man, as beautiful as a picture, with a pale, noble face – he looks like the wonder rabbi from Czortkow. Now he washes his small, beautiful hands, sits down without saying a word – everyone waits tensely. He writes the last sentence, pronounces a blessing, everyone congratulates him. There is general gaiety – he is urged to play something on his violin. There is such peace in this poverty – all the people are so friendly and kind to one another! Suddenly a knock at the door. The door opens, a rush of wind – and in walks the devil himself, the one we saw before in heaven but dressed like a man now – like a traveling salesman – and he says his name is Mazik. But I recognize him at once by his impudent laugh and his cutting voice. He says that he sells lottery tickets. Obviously only an excuse! Herrschale Dobrowner smiles – he won't buy any. I should say not! Besides, he hasn't a penny. But Mazik with his devilish tongue talks him into taking one of his tickets, presses it upon him – for nothing! And all the time he is making very daring but very clever remarks. And when the tension is at its height, he gives a loud, grating laugh, and down comes the cloth wall again! The other world is shut behind it once more.

Around me there is a babel of voices. Everyone is talking at once, as professionally as if they were all a part of it. I go over the happenings and the speeches in my mind. Again the gong sounds, again it is dark, again the cloth wall rises. Now the room is bright and richly furnished. So the poor Torah writer won the lottery! He wears fine clothes – but the devil is beside him and whispers vile, false advice into his ear. The noble Torah writer succumbs to his influence. They decide to open a prayer-shawl factory. The man who was so poor and so noble before is rich now and treats his wife and his friends and his father badly, as the rich people in Horodenka treated theirs. For shame! Now he even decides to get divorced from his wife. The devil talks him into marrying his niece. The old grandfather and the others, who were happy and gay in the beginning, now sit sad and mournful in the richly furnished room. Then the curtain again.

Now he makes one mistake after another, one stupid error after another. I want to call out to him not to heed the devil's advice! He is really an intelligent man! Good God, how is it possible? How can such a clever man be such a fool? Then another intermission. We go out into the air for a while. I am feverishly excited and furious with that impudent Mazik. The villain! I'd like to give him one in the face with my knuckle-duster!

Then the bell sounds its summons. We go in, and the play continues. And now something really terrible takes place: in the factory that he and the devil manage together, a wheel has torn off one of the workmen's arms, and the workman is the son of his best friend, Chazkel Drachme, and he is lying there dying! But now his friend speaks out and gives Herrschale Dobrowner a piece of his mind! What a good man he used to be, and what he has become! How he had treated his father and his friends before, and how he treats them now! How, when he was poor, he had lived in peace with his wife, and now that he is rich he has simply thrown her out! How his wealth has demoralized him, and could he answer for so many evil deeds? "Yes," Herrschale replies, but already somewhat taken aback. "Every man must answer for his deeds, and nothing will be left out of the reckoning!" But then his old friend cries in a heart-rending voice, pointing to a bloodstained prayer shawl: "Your reckoning is false! No man can pay for so many evil deeds! Think of the wife you have cast out! Your father! Your friends! And here is a prayer shawl from your factory! A product of your false riches and your false friends! That prayer shawl is soaked in my son's blood and my son's tears! Here! Add that to your reckoning!" and he throws the prayer shawl in his face and leaves him. The whole house shouts like a storm! Raves! Claps its hands! Stamps its feet! "Bravo, Drachme! Bravo, Rosenberg! Well done! He's right! God bless him for it!"

And I shout too, and rejoice with the rest, and feel a wonderful relief.

The enthusiasm and the noise in honor of the departed friend last a long time, and now the rich man sits there, bent and silent. His young wife enters – she has gone mad, probably from a bad conscience and boredom – babbles unintelligible words, something about his violin, which had grown silent, and goes off. Everything is topsy-turvy! Now he takes his violin, which he has not touched since he became rich, begins to play it very sadly and to accuse himself the while he plays. He acknowledges all his faults and is deeply repentant, picks up the bloodstained prayer shawl that his friend had thrown in his face, sobs and weeps bitterly. "The reckoning is too high," he admits, then makes a noose and hangs himself from his safe. The devil appears, in a fury at losing his bet – and it is all over!...

What a world! In three short hours! A whole life! Many lives! What utter, what more than real, reality!

We poor wretches live and die, and so it goes from generation to generation. The poor remain poor, the rich remain rich, the bad bad, and the good good! But here before your eyes, in three short hours, men and worlds and the whole of life change! What a magical miracle! I cannot grasp it all yet. But how unimportant everything I have experienced suddenly appears! It has gone on for so many years, and I am not even at the beginning. Everything moved so slowly and so torturingly. But here, in three hours by the clock, good men become bad, poor men rich, young men old, the evil are punished, the good rewarded. This justice! This settling of accounts! Those wise speeches! This marvelous life! Yes, here even death is something beautiful!

This is the world where I belong! Here is where I want to live. Here I will speak out, cry out, act out, explain my curiosity and my dreams! And my longings! Within me there was now a silent, iron resolve to walk that road! To force my way into that world! I did not know how I should manage to enter it, but one thing was absolutely clear to me: no power on earth could keep me back or block the road into that world for me!

There my father must talk about God with Jus Fedorkiw, and "Little Pity" and "Thank God" must appear. "Little Pity" falling into the well, and "Thank God" covering "Little Pity's" grave and freezing there. Schimshale from Milnitz, the wise teacher who went begging – he too must be shown there; and Menasche Strum, the good-natured drunkard. And Riffkele – how we stood under the window, how I ran after her, and how she was led astray by the Curl, and perhaps even how I was to find her again! There too could be shown how Joine Burlak tormented me and how my brother beat him up. But in that scene, I wanted to be, not "I," but my brother! There everything – yes, *everything* – could be told and shown and felt, and others could *feel with it all* and take part in it all. *And in that world no one is alone!* And everything goes on before your eyes and is over in an evening, in three hours! A whole life! And the next day, yet another life, other people!

On our way home and the following days I went over all that I had seen and heard. I repeated Herrschale Dobrowner's speeches, Chazkel Drachme's great tirade with the blood-stained prayer shawl. I was particularly good at the devil's impudent laugh. My brother Leibzi was surprised by my memory. He told my other brother that he had already seen the same play several times and had not remembered a word of it. The next day I went to Gimpel's theater again, saw another play, and it was just as exciting.

Then I began to go there alone and in secret every free evening and in the afternoons as well. When I worked during the day, I went at night; when I worked at night, I went in the afternoon. I always went to the gallery, the cheapest seats, and that was the best place to be, too, There I met young fellows of my own age who had the same thoughts and longings as myself. We had long conversations, and I made friends with some of them. Among them were a tall fellow named Wolf,

Iziu Wandel, and Schluesselberg. We told one another our secrets, we all wanted to follow the same road. Some of them even knew this or that actor personally. Only Schluesselberg did not want to become an actor. But he said that no one was better qualified to become one than I, after I had once bellowed out Drachme's tirade and laughed the devil's laugh for him.

Between Schluesselberg and myself a great friendship developed. He completely understood my resolve to force my way into that world, and he confirmed me in my intention and strengthened it by his deep conviction that I belonged there. We always went to the theater together, and spent all our free hours together too. His father was the owner of a large bakery, and Schluesselberg, in order that we might see each other oftener, got me a job there.

One evening in the theater something very exciting happened: The play to be performed was *Chasja, the Orphan*. Chasja comes from a Ukrainian village, is young, healthy, and very pretty, and she tells people exactly what she thinks. Her poor village father brings her to her rich relatives in the city, where she works hard as a maid and waits on everyone. She falls in love with the son of the house, a good-for-nothing. Now they are all dressed up and in great excitement. They, on the stage, are going to the theater! Then Chasja sees the son of the house, with whom she is in love, steal a gold brooch and hide it. The aunt wants to wear the brooch, and everyone looks for it. There is great confusion. Suspicion falls on Chasja. Now the wicked aunt asks Chasja if she knows where the brooch is. She says, "No!" "Swear by your dead mother that you do not know where it is!" But Chasja will not swear by her dead mother. The aunt is now convinced that Chasja is the thief, seizes her by her two long blond braids, ties her to the bed with them, and screams, "Where is the brooch?" And Chasja says, "I don't know!" And now the aunt gives her a left and a right and repeats the same question and gets the same answer and goes on hitting the poor orphan again and again. Chasja kneels there, tied by her braids, taking the blows and looking proud. The house is in tremendous excitement. We all hate the aunt and sympathize with Chasja. Now the aunt bellows even louder: "Where is the brooch? Where is the brooch?" and boxes the poor orphan's ears without ever stopping. And suddenly a man who is standing near me in the gallery pulls a revolver out of his pocket and shouts out louder even than the people on the stage: "Beast! Untie her this minute or I'll shoot you down like a dog!"

The blows on the stage cease. The house is in tumult. Everyone turns and looks at my neighbor, a devil-may-care youth of about twenty, who, now was white as a sheet, has pocketed his revolver and is trembling with excitement....

The cloth wall has already been lowered. The lights are turned on in the house now. Groups are quarreling, arguing, all at once – the young man has disappeared! Chasja's poor father – Motje Schtrachl, otherwise Jidl Guttman – is standing before the curtain; he raises his hand. Little by little the people quiet down, and he begins to speak very softly: "My dear listeners, may I say something?" Some clap, others call: "Speak up, Guttman, speak up, Motje! Quiet! Quiet!" Gradually there is silence. And he begins again: "My dear friends, it is a hard thing for me to step out of my character, but I must say a few words in explanation." And he begins, gently and quietly, like a father explaining something to his children: "You know that Madame Fischler is married to the famous Dr. Fischler and has a father and mother – God be thanked, and may they live to be a hundred and twenty! But art demands that, for this evening, she is an orphan. You know too that Madame Rosenberg has six children and is the best mother in the world and has a heart of gold – but art demands that tonight she is the wicked aunt and hits Madame Fischler. I myself am the president of the Bnai Jakob Synagogue – but art demands that this evening I am Motje Schtrachl, Chasja's poor father. And so I could go on and tell you who all of us are in real life, and who we are obliged to be for art's sake.

Every afternoon around five o'clock you can see us all sitting in the Café Abazia, and we are the best of friends. Even our children are friends. And Madame Rosenberg and Madame Fischler are particularly intimate friends. Now here's a young man – I'm sure he has a good heart, but he doesn't know all these things I have been telling you – he gets excited and threatens to shoot his revolver. I ask you: Is that right?" "No!" shouts the house. "Throw him out! Bravo, Guttman! Bravo, Fischler! Bravo, Rosenberg!" Again and again there are shouts and thunderous clapping. The poor old father, the actor and president of a synagogue, Jidl Guttman, raises his hand, and there is quiet again: "Well," he says, "shall we go on?" And again there is a thunder of applause and agreement and cheers! And the house is darkened, and the play begins again where it had stopped. Chasja's wicked aunt, Madame Rosenberg, who is a mother herself and has a heart of gold, again asks Chasja, the orphan, who is really the wife of Dr. Fischler and – thank God – still has her parents: "Where is the brooch?" And she answers more loudly and strongly than before, "I don't know!" "What, you don't know?" says the wicked aunt and the good mother, Madame Rosenberg, and grabs Chasja the orphan, Dr. Fischler's wife, by her braids, ties her to the bed again, just as before, and shouts threateningly, "Where is the brooch?" And Madame Chasja, the orphan, cries, "I don't know," and Aunt Rosenberg gives her a left and a right again! And again Chasja cries loudly and with pride, "I don't know! I don't know!" and lefts and rights land on her ears again and again and again!

So, that evening, because of an excitable young man, who surely had a good heart, the delicate, beautiful Madame Fischler was beaten twice over! Poor Madame Fischler.

But thought I, for art's sake, it is worth it to be beaten twenty times over. And it was a marvelous evening!...

24

A Dog, a Cart, and a Woman

Of the acquaintances I made in the gallery, Schluesselberg became my friend. Already as a child friendship had been something sacred to me. Father often talked to us on the subject. He taught us that to have a friend or to be a friend was a wonderful piece of good fortune. Friendship is a sacred thing, and has its own laws, and reaches further than kinship and family, he used to say. Because you are born into a family, but friendship is something that you find. The family is like the earth: you live upon it and it nourishes you; but friendships are like precious stones and veins of gold and other treasures: hidden deep in the earth and rare; and only very fortunate people find such a vein of gold – a friendship. And it makes you happier to give friendship than to receive it, but the finest thing is when the friendship is equal on both sides. Father considered Jus Fedorkiw, who was a Christian, his friend, and nearer to him than all his coreligionists who prayed to the same God and spoke the same language and had the same traditions and customs. He used to point to the relations between us, his children, as an example. We respected our older brothers and sisters and obeyed them, but, in general, we were merely "brothers and sisters." But between some of us there were real friendships, as between Schachne Eber, the eldest, and funny Jankel, or between Leibzi and me.

I had always been on terms of friendship with someone. First it was Leibzi, then Czerniakoff in Zaleszczyki, then Shimele Ruskin in Stanislau. But to them I had always looked up, because they were older than I. Now for the first time I had a friend who was my own age, who was my equal. And in spite of the fact that I came from a small town and Schluesselberg had been brought up in a large one, I was the leader and the giver. For he was lonely and unhappy and sometimes melancholy, and I became for him what Czerniakoff had been for me. His situation was a sad one. He had lost his mother very early. And his father, a prosperous and energetic man between fifty and sixty, had brought home a second wife who was only half his age and could have been his daughter.

Herr Schluesselberg, who was hard and harsh with his workmen and employees, whom he was forever berating and cursing, was quite a different person at home: silent, mild, and timid. He smoked cigars like a small furnace. When he scolded, his cigar danced in his mouth. He never called his men by their names. When he waked a helper to heat the oven, he usually bellowed: "Hey, you bastard, are you deaf? Can't you hear, you son of a whore? It's six o'clock already. Time to heat the oven, you damned dog! What are you waiting for, you mangy cripple?"

Or when he wanted the coachman to harness up, you would hear him yelling across the court: "Hey, you crooked dog, you scum! Are you going to harness up or not? Look at the way he shakes his lame bones! Deliver the bread to the restaurants and the station, you mangy animal! And I hope they bring you back a corpse, you blind beast!"

One-eyed Piotr smiled at all this, and Schmiel told me that the old man had been working for them for eight years and was used to Schluesselberg's curses.

The bakery, which was on the ground floor, opened onto the big courtyard; and across from it, one flight up, were the family's living quarters, with a balcony from which Herr Schluesselberg, standing with a cigar in his face, would bellow his orders down to the courtyard, like a captain on a sinking ship in a stormy sea. But as soon as his frowzy young wife appeared, he stopped. Because in the house it was *she* who did the bellowing.

She was rather pretty, but she was never properly dressed. She slopped around in her fur slippers, and her clothes hung loosely on her wide-hipped and full-breasted body, and there was always a button off somewhere, and you caught glimpses of her flesh shining through rents and rips in the most unlikely places. She was bone-lazy, was always chewing on something from morning till night, but she managed to make it appear that she was continually busy. She never stopped chewing except to scold. Simply because she could not do both at once. He, however, could scold and smoke at the same time, whereby his cigar had learned to dance. She often sat on the stairs to the balcony, with her legs apart, chewing. The workmen said she never wore drawers, like other women. Sundays and holidays she sat on the stairs too, dressed in silk and jewels, gazed into space, and chewed. The workmen said that she did not dare to go into the street in her finery for fear her jewels would be taken. But even when she had on silk and jewels, she wore her old fur slippers and she chewed. She chewed like a ruminant, like a real cow.

There was another member of the household too – a little girl of six or seven – Frau Schluesselberg's gift to a husband twice her own age. The child was as pretty as a picture and had a childish eccentricity, the little darling – to wit: she did exactly the opposite of what anyone told her to do. If you said, "Run into the street and play with the other children," she crawled into bed. When she was asked to stay at home, she ran away. If she was forbidden to strike matches, she did nothing but burn matches the whole day. When she had a glass and you asked her to be careful of it, the glass crashed to the floor in a thousand fragments. When you gave her something to eat, she spit it out. When she was forbidden to touch hot bread, she stood in front of the oven and ate hot rolls until she got a stomach ache. Lately she had not only found a pair of scissors, she had tried them out. Towels, tablecloths, dresses, suits, curtains, all bore mute witness. Her mother often beat the little creature, who never cried. As for her father, she pinched his legs and spat in his soup, the sweet darling, and when the family was sitting at dinner and nothing else occurred to her, she was quite capable of suddenly getting up and simply making pee-pee in the middle of the room! Her father, however, did not dare to touch her – usually he jumped up, ran down to the court, bellowed senselessly at his employees, and made his cigar dance in his mouth. Meanwhile his wife bellowed in the house, let fly at her stepson, and scolded and cursed until the neighbors came and passers-by stopped in the streets to listen.

In such a confusion, in such a hell, lived my friend Schmiel. In our free time we went to the theater together, preferably to mournful plays teeming with lonely orphans and wicked stepmothers. And we wept and sobbed with the suffering creatures and hated the wicked stepmothers and the weak-willed fathers who delivered their poor children into the hands of strange, wicked women. But up there in the higher world, up on the stage, there was more mercy and more justice. There something good, something beautiful, always came to the suffering and innocent. Even when everything was going wrong there were wonderful, uplifting moments for the "good" and punishments for the "wicked."

One day, looking out of the bakery, I saw little Rickele – the untamable child – standing in the court looking questioningly at me with her great black eyes. So I said to her, "Rickele, you aren't allowed to come into the bakery!" And she ran in and stood looking at me defiantly and provocatively. "There are hot rolls over there," I said. "Eat some." She looked at me wrathfully, puckered up her mouth and said, "No!" Then I handed her a glass and said kindly, "Here, Rickele, break it! Go ahead and break it!" She took the glass and set it carefully down, and there we stood, grinning at each other like two old horse thieves. "All right," I said, "now you'll have to stay here in the bakery with me," whereupon she was off like the wind. I told my friend about it, and he tried the same thing with his wild little sister, and from then on he could make the child do anything he liked. He had only to demand the opposite. She understood what was going on and took great pleasure in the topsy-turvy game.

But finding a game that would work with his stepmother was a different matter. Usually it worked in the following manner: When his father was on good terms with the frowzy lady, my friend was scolded and tormented and thrashed. But when some little incident shattered the peace between the spouses and set his father and his stepmother to quarreling, my friend was forgotten. So the thing to do was to think up some way of disturbing their peace.

"We must drop a fly in their ointment, a hair in their soup," I said to my friend one day.

"Yes, *soup*," said my friend, laughing. "Father is so fond of soup," he added thoughtfully.

And the next day, Friday, the famous Heymann from America was to act *The Wild Man*, and, as we could not go unless his beloved parents were quarreling, what was simpler than to throw a handful of salt into the soup early that morning when his stepmother shuffled out of the kitchen? We should soon see what would come off!

The next morning my friend only whispered, "It's done!" Noon came, and I stood at the bakery window, as fascinated as if I were at the theater. But this time Herr Schluesselberg was the villain! How will he play his part? I wondered. And then it began: Herr Schluesselberg tasted the first spoonful and made a face. He could not bring himself to believe that there could be so much salt in a soup. My friend had been lavish. At the second spoonful Herr Schluesselberg jumped to his feet, coughed, took his plate of soup and flung it into the court! And then the familiar concert began! My friend was forgotten, and in the evening we went to see *The Wild Man*, a sad play, and we thought of the soup and laughed in the wrong places until the others in the balcony were ready to murder us, and we left the theater without learning whether the guest star, Heymann, was really a great actor or only a bluff.

We used the salt trick several times more, until the stepmother beat little Rickele so unmercifully that we felt sorry for the child, who was as innocent as only a child can be. And we abandoned that trick. But after that there were a number of quarrels about "wholly unsalted food." Then peace returned to the house, and my friend found it as much of a curse as before. Trouble descended on him again, and this time he was persecuted and thrashed, on my account too, for "going around" with a mere salaried employee of his rich father's.

From that time on, we met only outside the precincts of the bakery, and our friendship became more and more intimate. One day "Frowzy" came into the bakery and ordered me to go out and do some shopping for her, which I refused point-blank because it was not a part of my job. She began to scold and swear: "I'll teach you not to obey a lady, you tramp!"

I answered her right back, what I said being a mixture of what I thought of her and what I had heard people say under similar circumstances on the stage. It was a long canting monologue, which ended with, "And a lady is just what you are not – you don't even wear underdrawers, you draggle-tail!"

Whereupon in her fury she lifted her skirts and showed me that she *did* wear underdrawers. All the eight journeymen began to laugh at her, and she ran scolding and howling into the courtyard. There she bumped into my friend, who could not contain his laughter either. She pulled off one of her fur slippers and belabored him fearfully. At that moment his father came home; she made a scene, whereupon the old man gave me a week's notice. I held a consultation with my friend, and we planned revenge.

The next day the draggle-tail was sitting on the balcony steps sewing her fur slipper, which she had ripped to pieces over my friend's head the day before. She used a curved packing needle. That wonderful packing needle was to be our fate.

I made my friend steal the needle, together with the slipper from under her bed. And at night, when everyone was asleep, I helped him to work the needle into the sole of the very same slipper with which she had thrashed him. We did it very carefully, so that more than half the needle – which stuck out at a slant – awaited her warm foot as the hook awaits its victim in a mousetrap.

That night neither of us slept. And early in the morning everything really went off according to plan. Our draggle-tail woke, grumbling and scolding as usual, and, still half asleep, slid her warm feet into her soft fur slippers. And there! The cleverly arranged needle slid into her warm flesh like butter, until it was stopped by a bone. A long shrill scream roused the house and the neighborhood. The scream was almost as good as the one that Frau Fischler gave in a play where she suddenly came upon her dead child. The plan had worked! A doctor was sent for; the dear needle, which had such a cozy berth in her flesh, had to come out, but it had done harm enough: the lady was confined to her bed for quite a long time. I never saw her again. Because now my friend and I had decided to run away.

Herr Schluesselberg always kept his cash in his pocketbook through the week, and Friday afternoons he would send my friend to the bank with the money, and my friend would bring back the receipt. It was almost a tradition. And we decided to break the tradition for once and run away with the money. But the amounts were too large – somewhere between four and six thousand kronen. And we knew that his miserly father would do anything to catch us for the sake of such a large sum. But a week came in which there were two holidays, and the total that Friday was 830 kronen. This was what we had been waiting for for weeks.

Every Friday we put on three shirts and two suits, one over the other. We wanted always to be ready when the chance came, and we didn't want to take a trunk or a bundle or a package with us. I knew that, in a flight such as we were planning, a package or a bundle is not only a burden, it is actually a traitor and a spy. A package or bundle beside you or in your hand is forever leering at people and whispering: "Look, look! I belong to someone who is on his travels, someone who wants a change, someone who has got out of the rut. Someone who is changing his domicile, running away! Just take a good look at my owner! How pale he is, how nervous, how suspicious! Just ask him where he is going, and why!" You can't make a bundle like that hold its tongue, so there is only one way left: simply don't take it along! No burden, no spy, no traitor.

And now we were standing in a dark doorway; my hands shook; I was counting money that was not mine and that I was about to appropriate. How clammy and disgusting such money feels! Well, thank God, I was not really "stealing" it. My friend "took" from his own father what in any case he would have inherited later – he was only inheriting it a little sooner. No, no, no, I went on talking myself and my friend into it – we are not thieves! So let's put our hands in our pockets, look indifferent – and off to the railway station!

Two tickets to Cracow – I bought them smiling and unconcerned, never even looked at the man, as if it were something I did every day of my life. But the train had not arrived yet. We had almost an hour to wait. So we waited. A loathsome, horrible wait! But we betrayed nothing – we made our way unobtrusively through the station.

The great waiting room in the front of the station was being repaired – there was not a soul in it. So we slipped in. Look! Outside the window – that was Herr Schluesselberg coming, with his cigar dancing in his mouth. He looked furious and was cursing to himself. I saw two tall ladders near the entrance. "Quick! Up that ladder!" I hissed to my friend. And I rushed up one of them, and after a few minutes I half opened my eyes and, from my dizzy height, saw the old man glance around the empty, disorderly room and vanish. A few minutes later I saw him through the window again – he got into a carriage and drove away.

We streaked down our ladders, almost bursting with excitement, passed the ticket taker, reached the track. The train pulled in. My friend's face was a greenish yellow, he was trembling; I whispered to him, "Smile, man, smile, look happy – think of the comedian Schilling in all his roles!" A few more minutes and we were both on the train to Cracow, locked in a toilet.

We heard our names called on the platform several times. It gave us a start each time. But I said, "Schilling!" and I saw my friend's sallow, sweaty face break into a faint smile. I grinned at his expression, though I was at least as frightened as he was. But, I immediately thought, he thinks that I am not afraid at all. And that gave me a certain superiority and the strength to hold on to myself.

When the train pulled out we went into separate compartments so that we should not be seen together. At Przemysl our names were called again, but mechanically and indifferently. Then came Okocim, later Tarnow. Our names were not called.

Just before we reached Cracow I went to his compartment and slipped him a note, in which I told him to keep me in sight and we would stop and wait for each other when we got outside the station. So he waited for me in the street, and we fell into each other's arms as if we had not seen each other for years.

Then we strolled through Cracow's old, narrow streets until we found a small inn, where we ordered hot tea and something to eat and spent the night. The next morning we thought we were in Lemberg, only in some other street – the people and the bustle looked so familiar. We picked up an acquaintance with the houseman at our "hotel," a chap of my own age and a great talker. He took us for Russian refugees, because it was after 1905 and an endless stream of Russian emigrants, students, and intellectuals flowed over the border into Austrian Galicia, and from there on to Vienna, Berlin,

Paris, or London. He boasted that he had a trick of his own for smuggling people over the German border, but his price was a hundred kronen a head.

We pretended to be quite uninterested, invited him to drink a glass of beer, and told him that, as Austrians, we did not intend to go to Germany, but to Vienna. Then he proudly told us his trick. Having first collected his fee for smuggling them, he took his clients to Oderberg, where there was a little wooden bridge which led to the German border town of Annaberg. There, passing yourself off as someone who worked in Oderberg, you paid three kreuzer to cross the bridge in order to go and drink some good German beer in Annaberg. It all looked as plain as a pikestaff.

And the next morning we were in Oderberg; in the afternoon we saw some workmen taking the road to the little wooden bridge. We mingled with them, paid our three kreuzer to the civilian border officer – and there we were in Annaberg, in Germany!

We changed our Austrian money into German marks. We bought two tickets to Berlin – bought a needle and thread too, and while we waited in a field for the train, I sewed the money into my breast pocket, leaving out only a small sum for our traveling expenses.

That night, in Breslau, a station policeman took us out of the carriage and, because we had no papers, was going to arrest us. Whereupon we both began to weep bitterly. It was not only because we were afraid of the fierce policeman. We suddenly felt so wretched in this foreign darkness, and were homesick, and simply wept in a sort of despair. A few people gathered around us and were obviously touched; a gruff conductor with a kindly gray mustache joined them. The engine whistled – he shouted: "All aboard, all aboard! The train is leaving!" Then, turning to the policeman, he said, "Man, didn't you ever run away when you were a boy? Or do you think they've murdered somebody? My own boy ran away a few weeks ago too!"

The policeman turned around, and the conductor growled at us, "Get in, you boobs!" The train was already moving – we tumbled aboard.

And about midnight we pulled into the Schlesische Bahnhof, in Berlin.

The gray mustache appeared once before we got out and recommended a flophouse near the station where we could spend the night. We found the place; there was a large dark room where more than a hundred "guests" like ourselves, of various ages, were lying on cots set close together, performing an evening concert of snores. We decided that one of us should sleep and the other stay awake, to guard the treasure sewed into my breast pocket. My friend fell asleep instantly, and about five o'clock our fellow guests began to get up. My friend and I were the first to leave, and there we stood shivering and freezing on the Schlesischestrasse, Berlin East. It was foggy and half dark. Lights were turned on and off in high, unfriendly, black houses. The giant, Berlin, was beginning to rub his eyes and get up.

The first thing we saw in the empty street was a two-wheeled cart, loaded high with cabbages. There was a big dog harnessed to it – his tongue was hanging out of his mouth – and beside the dog there was a woman, also in harness, tugging at the shaft.

A cart, a dog, and a woman.

That fixed itself in my mind as a symbol of the drudging German people!

A cart, a dog, and a woman.

Alexander Granach and wife Martha Guttmann, Graz 1914

Granach with his mother, Galicia 1915

With son Gerhard (Gad), Berlin 1919 and 1925

As Shylock in *The Merchant of Venice*,
Schauspielhaus, Munich 1920

As Judas Ischariot in the film *I.N.R.I.*,
directed by Robert Wiene, 1923

Granach (middle) in *Pankraz Awakens*
by Carl Zuckmayer, Deutsches Theater, Berlin 1925

Giving a telephone interview,
Westerland-Sylt 1926

Ticket sales for a performance with Alexander Granach,
Poland 1934

Tilla Durieux with Granach in *Hunting with the Hounds* by B. Blume, Berlin 1928

Granach (right) with fellow stage actors, Sylt 1928

25

First Steps in Berlin

So with my friend Schluesselberg I arrived in Berlin; we were both sixteen. In Horodenka, in Zaleszczyki, in Stanislau, in Lemberg, I had been able to look about me, to observe, discover, register impressions, make comparisons. But here I had not come to a city; here a city came over me. Here I felt myself pounced on, attacked, pulled in all directions by a new rhythm, new people, a new language, new manners and customs. I had to hold on to myself, keep my eyes wide open, my muscles tense, to prevent myself from being run down and broken and crushed to bits.

My longing for the theater, with all my plans for getting into it, vanished into the background. Each day brought its own demands: work, food, lodgings, rent. I had no proper papers – nothing but a little book, an identification card: I was a member of the Austrian Bakers' Union.

So my first visit, several days later, was to the Trades Unions Building, 12 Engelufer, to the bakers' employment office. And there – why, it was "colleague" and "comrade," everyone was most friendly, and no one seemed surprised that two traveling Austrian journeymen had packed up and made their way to Berlin. I was given information, a call number from the employment office, financial assistance, and advice about places to sleep and eat. When we left the Trades Unions Building my friend envied me for being a workman, for having a trade which gave me a prospect of finding work and independence in this strange world, in this terrifying city. It was a wonderful thing for me too. Berlin! It was as if a giant had given me a friendly smile. Yes, I had been afraid. The giant had inspired me with awe – but 12 Engelufer was friendly, called me "colleague" and "comrade" and gave me its hand. My heart warmed with self-confidence, and that day I fell in love with Berlin.

We boarded a streetcar and rode for two hours through an ocean of houses to the end of the line and back and acquired a vague impression of something enormous and terrifying that still seemed to receive one kindly.

When we got back we found a cheap tavern with a window displaying slices of bread spread with tongue sausage, with boiled beef and pieces of aspic, with Swiss cheese. Ten pfennigs apiece. We went in and ordered one each, and a fat bartender with a round bald head and long mustaches sized us up and said, "Sandwiches?" And I said "Yes."

My friend looked at me doubtfully. "What's that?"

Meanwhile the bartender had covered another piece of bread with dripping and laid it on the spread slice and cut the whole through in the middle and handed it to us. And I said, "There you are – sandwiches!"

And we ate "sandwiches" for the first time in our lives and washed them down with beer. Boy, was that marvelous! A "sandwich!" A "sandwich" with tongue sausage, and another with boiled beef, and another with cheese! Travel, good food, bread and butter, meat and cheese, beer, the prospect of work. Yes, I'd like to see the one who wouldn't shout for joy at all that! Then I saw him, he was sitting opposite me: my friend, who suddenly felt homesick and was crying.

When we reached Berlin, he had written home. I had not, for I didn't want to write until things were going well with me. And that morning he had received his first letter from his father, who begged him to come home – all would be forgiven, he would even get money for his journey back. His father, who had never liked me, enclosed a polite letter for me too. He wrote to me as to a grown man – I must send him back his son. I felt flattered and responsible.

Weeks went by. Our money was almost gone. Late every afternoon I went to 12 Engelufer. There the unemployed were called by number for steady or temporary jobs. One day the man in the employment office called numbers for a job as helper in a Jewish bakery – they had to have a man who could make braided bread. He called many numbers, but none of them knew the art. Then he called my number, and I took the job. I was told how to get to the Scheunen quarter, and when I got off at Lothringerstrasse, Schoenhauser Tor, suddenly in the middle of Berlin I found myself, in a district that looked like Lemberg.

Grenadier, Dragoner, Muladkstrasse, Ritterstrasse, Schendelgasse...

Short, narrow, dark alleys with fruit and vegetable stands at the corners. Women with painted faces and big keys in their hands strolled by as they do in the narrow alleys of Stanislau and Lemberg. Dozens of shops, restaurants, egg, butter, and milk stores, bakeries, with signs reading "Kosher." Jews walked about dressed as in Galicia, Rumania, and Russia. Those who did not keep shops dealt in pictures and furniture on credit. Some peddled tablecloths, handkerchiefs, suspenders, shoelaces, collar buttons, stockings, and ladies' underwear. Others went from house to house buying old clothes which they sold to wholesalers who, in turn, sent them to their old homeland. Most of the people in the neighborhood, however, were workers, who had jobs in Manoli, Carbati or Muratti cigarette factories. There was a brisk community life too. For the pious there were numerous houses of prayer, named after their sects or their rabbis. There were Zionists of all shades. There were Social Revolutionists, Socialists, and Anarchists. There were theaters and cabarets. The comedian

Kanapoff appeared in the Koenigs Café. The Loewenthal Restaurant had a small stage where plays were given. Minor actors or supernumeraries from the good theaters in Russia, Rumania, and Galicia played there and boasted in huge letters and pictures on billboards that they were famous international stars.

My friend and I rented a room in the Lothringerstrasse which we shared with six other boys. I went to work in the bakery to which I had been sent, and soon felt at home in this Berlin. My friend also found a job with an old-clothes dealer who had a shop in a cellar; everything he bought or sold, my friend had to write down. He was an elderly man who dressed in European style and lived with his daughter and son-in-law and grandson.

One day my friend came to me, white as a sheet and much upset, and told me that the old man kept locking the cellar when they were down there alone and would kiss and caress him and wanted to be embraced in return. It had already happened several times. At first my friend had thought that it was some sort of city joke – but the old man had become more and more insistent. My friend was crying and said that he was really afraid of the old man and that the whole thing made him feel sick.

That very day he had received another letter from his father, who again implored him to come home. His flight and the money he had taken had been long forgotten. And to prove it, his father had sent him money for the journey. My friend wanted to go home too – Berlin was so horrible. Fat old men trying to make you do such dirty things – it was sickening! His father again enclosed a letter to me, in which he begged me, as I honored my own father, to send him back his poor helpless son. My friend left it all to me, and I suddenly felt grown-up and superior and sent the unhappy father his prodigal son, to whom Berlin was personified by an old man who kissed him as if he were a girl. "No," he said, "no one can live in such a city!" So he went home. And since Berlin did not bother me with such things, I remained there gladly.

I was alone now, and I began to make acquaintances. I often went to Herr Loewenthal's theater, where a Herr Bleich and his wife and daughters and sons-in-law gave well-meant but bad performances – regular barnstormers. There was a new play every two or three days, but if you watched closely you saw that the play was always the same. It was always called "A Drama with Singing and Dancing." I often went there, saw some of the same plays that I had seen in Lemberg, made comparisons, criticized; naturally I found the gallery full of young people, as in every theater, and we joked mercilessly about the bad plays and the bad actors – and kept going back. Often, too, stars came from abroad: wonderful wild actors, the Guttentags from Rumania, the Schitjicks from Poland, and guest stars from America. They would assemble their own companies and perform in little halls in the suburbs. I never missed a performance.

One day I ran into a small, pale man with long hair and a Windsor tie who, like myself, was complaining of the bad acting and the cheap, trashy plays, and we got to know each other. His name was Schidlower. We became friends and were often together. He was the first actor I met who had a sense of social and cultural responsibility. He saw the theater not only as a place of amusement, where people laughed at cheap jokes – he believed that the theater should be the successor of synagogues and churches. The stage is higher than the pit in order that it may lift men out of everyday living; it raises their spirits, it creates a festive mood. So he refused to act in these trashy plays of the professional theaters – he would rather put on "better" plays with young people and simple workers who had the same beliefs as he.

We often met, and he introduced me into a circle composed of Russian cigarette makers, who worked in the Manoli and Carbati and Muratti factories. The circle was made up partly of married, partly of unmarried men and women – all much older than I. Most of them had fled from Russia in 1905; I was given books and pamphlets to read about what had happened there. In the evenings or on Sundays they read and discussed together. There I heard words and ideas that were entirely new to me.

I had been brought up piously and in great awe of God's world. The rich, who had gained possession of this world, we pitied or despised, we did not hate them. But these people thought very differently. They held that the "order" of the world was "all out of order" and that there was a great deal to be changed. They differed only about the "how." The thing to do was to study, get an education, read different books on these subjects, and discuss. I was not able to join the discussions. I only listened and asked questions. We would eat together at the lodgings of one or another of the comrades; everyone contributed something and helped to cook, wash up, and serve. It was very homelike and gay. Some of them were without jobs at times, but all kept house together. There was a general opinion that you must not let yourself be too much exploited by those who had work to give – better go without Sunday clothes than work all week. Because – so they thought – for every mark you earned, the boss made twenty-five. So if you made two marks less a week, the factory owner was poorer by fifty. And that satisfaction made up for the lack of Sunday clothes.

When I had arrived in Berlin I had decided not to write home until I should be sure that I was on the right road. One day when I thought I was sure of it, I sat down and wrote my father a letter. I said that I had sinned against him by not having written to him, and that I wanted him to know that I had resolved to follow a desire I had not been able to put into words before but which, now that I knew I was on the way to my goal, I wanted to tell him about: I intended to become an actor. In answer, I received the following letter from my father:

My Son:

You write me that you feel you have sinned against me — yes, my son, you are right, but I pray and fast for you every Monday and Thursday and I am sure that the Lord will not count this sin against you, for you have not hurt me intentionally but because, as you write to me, my dear son, you are choosing a new calling, going a new way. I do not know your new calling, and no one among your friends and relatives has had such a calling. But for that reason I understand that it is a new way. And because I know that new ways are hard traveling, I wish you strength and courage to follow it. I am ill and would much like to see you. If that is not granted me, know that my hopes and wishes are always with you, in this world or the next. May my blessings warm your heart through all eternity.

Your Father

Some time later I received word from my eldest brother that our beloved father had died. It was a great shock. I went to the synagogue to say the prayer for the dead. My new friends sympathized with me, but one of them made an impious remark which hurt me deeply. I asked them to leave God out of the matter; this gave rise to long and serious discussions, and we decided to go to the Free Religious Congregation every Sunday.

There we heard lectures on "Man in Nature" and "God in Man." For me it was new and exciting, and it nourished my thirsty soul. Evenings we went to the Free High School, where there were good lecture courses on world literature, the drama, the theater, and art. In addition there were occasional orientation lectures on culture and politics given by Russian intellectuals who lived in Berlin or were passing through.

Before I knew it I was a member of an anarchist group. It was called *The Workers' Friend*, after a newspaper of the same name which was then coming out in London, published in Yiddish by the non-Jewish Rhinelander, Rudolph Rocker. Through my association with this group I began to read Kropotkin and Bakunin, John Most and Nietzsche. Later, even Max Stirner's *The Ego and His Own*. There were some fourteen or sixteen of us, and our teacher and leader was named Moritz Riebler. He could answer the most difficult questions, guided our discussions, explained and analyzed the most complex problems. When a complicated argument threatened to lose its way, he would smile, take the argument by the hand, like a big brother with a little sister, and lead it back to the right path which he had marked out for it. Yet he was a simple cigarette maker. I honored him and loved him, for I learned a great deal from him. Many years later this international anarchist discovered his national heart, and became a Zionist.

All the members of the group were foreigners, and hence were not permitted to belong to any sort of political organization in the Berlin of that time. In order to reach a wider circle, to give these "world-shaking" ideas a broader base, we decided to found a "harmless" theatrical society, and thus to bring the non-Jewish Rudolph Rocker's ideas to the Jews. The professional actor Schidlower was made director, and we launched the Jacob Gordin Theatrical Society. At that time Jacob Gordin was living in New York, where he produced plays with great actors such as Jacob Adler, David Kessler, and Madame Lipzin, and was already the author of seventy plays and very "revolutionary." He was for the poor and against the rich. For whores and against fine ladies. For orphans and bastards and against the legitimate and the secure. He was for me too, and I learned his heroes' parts by heart in a frenzy of enthusiasm.

Our theatrical society grew, acquired more and more members. We organized lectures and evenings of conversation, pleasant gatherings over coffee and cakes with dancing and recitations. Little Schidlower conducted these evenings. I learned poems by Rosenfeld, Edelstadt, Bowshower, Gustav Herwey, and others. They were all complaints against the rich and the high-placed and hymns in honor of the poor and oppressed. On our cake-and-coffee evenings, when people would be chatting pleasantly and dancing, I would break in with one of these wild melodramatic poems. I bellowed them out with such vehemence that people put their fingers in their ears. I took it very seriously, and at certain moments in my performance I threw myself on the floor and writhed and shed tears and sobbed so desperately and so realistically that my audience felt with me and people said that I was an "artist." Which I was more than willing to believe; yet I kept my unshaken desire to become an actor a secret. I liked it even better when one of the older married women – for I had no contacts with girls of my own age – told me that I ought to try to get on the stage. I listened gladly and thankfully, and from my gratitude sprang friendship and love.

In the meanwhile Schidlower was rehearsing the first act of a play by David Pinsky, *The Zwie Family*. It is a portrait of a Jewish family in old Russia during a pogrom. Every shade of opinion, every reaction of the people, is represented: The old grandfather, a preacher, lashes out at his people and warns them to hold to their old beliefs, because all things go as the Lord appoints. The father, a shopkeeper, is interested in nothing but his business. One son is a Zionist and urges a return to the Promised Land, another son is an Assimilationist and preaches amalgamation and final loss of identity in other peoples. One is a socialist and believes that only his ideals can free the poor and the oppressed. His name is Rubin, and I played him.

It was my first part. Suddenly everything around me became unimportant. Day and night, in the bakery, at work, in the streets, I thought of Rubin and of nothing else. No, not *of* Rubin, but *as* Rubin. I ate as Rubin, I slept as Rubin, I waked as Rubin, I walked as Rubin, I argued as Rubin. Anyone I could catch underwent a Rubin lecture, a Rubin cataract. The rehearsals were exciting, electrifying. Every sentence was shouted and whispered, laughed through and wept through, a hundred times. Yet Rubin was not a particularly big or particularly important part – but for me it was the biggest and the most important thing in the world. Why, the world itself was unimportant, was nothing but an excuse for Rubin, a stage prop for Rubin, had only to revolve around Rubin.

It was not all plain sailing. Although we were simple workers and amateurs, the atmosphere of a real theater was not long in establishing itself: jealousy, grudges, gossip, intrigues. I suddenly found myself with friends and enemies. The friends were encouraging, but the enemies criticized, put their hands over their ears when I bellowed. There were explosions, reconciliations, even fights. It was now known that I wanted to become an actor, and one of the company, a Herr Urich, who peddled pictures, a smooth young man with cheap imitation rings and a mouthful of shining gold teeth, explained that you had to be born an artist, or, for that matter, anything else. Kings, musicians, poets, and actors – they were all born to be what they were. All this he expounded at great length during one of our rehearsals; some agreed with him and eyed me ironically. I was hard hit. My Rubin was hurt. We were both wounded. But there was a quiet older man in the company. His name was Herschel Simmenhaus, and he had told me that if I found myself in difficulties I must come to him. So I went to my friend and opened my heart to him. He smiled kindly, gave me *Twenty-six Men and a Girl* to read, and said: "The man who wrote that was once a baker, and he calls himself Maxim Gorki! Gorki means 'bitter.' You can imagine what he had to go through in order to become a writer."

I devoured the story, in which a real bakery is accurately and vividly described, and that story healed my wounded heart like balm. I drew the obvious conclusion for my own case: "If a baker can become a writer, why can't another baker become an actor?" So Gorki, the "bitter," filled me with a sweet strength that put all the critics and the head-shakers out of my mind. I let my hair grow long and bought a cape and a broad-brimmed black hat like Gorki's. I laid his name away in my heart as something holy, and I have carried it there all my life, as I carry Schimshale from Milnitz, as I carry my father.

Then suddenly one evening I was on the stage – an experience that I have never forgotten. I had never before been so conscious of my body. I could feel my fingertips and my scalp, my toes and my heart, but especially my stomach. The other members of the cast were no longer my personal friends or my enemies, but real relatives, my family: grandfather, father, mother, brothers. Then from the packed ranks of the spectators there came a something that is hard to describe. It was as if, from their eyes and their ears, from their breathing and their attention, there came an invisible force that penetrated me, that strengthened me, that poured into me, that I sent forth again intensified. The spell that I had felt the first time I went to the theater came over me now from a far different source, hypnotized me and bound me. At last! I tasted it, I relished it and now came the great hunger, the great thirst: theater! theater! theater!

The anarchist group that had thought to disguise itself as a group of actors became to me simply a disguise which gave me an opportunity to act. Our director began to put on entire plays. Most of them were by Gordin. One time I played a rough-hewn locksmith, another time a gentleman. Now a young man, now an old one. Good and bad, sane and mad, priests and pimps, saints and criminals. And I was just eighteen years old.

One night we were giving *God, Man, and the Devil.* I played the Devil. In a fiery-red costume with horns, with my face made up white, and deep furrows on my forehead and at the corners of my nose and mouth, with the hair at my temples made up gray, and a pitch-black pointed beard, with rolling eyes, a grating laugh, and cloven hoofs! It was really something wonderful! I swam in the joy of acting and in sweat. After the performance I was as exhausted as a sow that has dropped a litter of fourteen piglets.

I had taken off my make-up, the beard was gone and the furrows, when a tall, elegant gentleman in a frock coat came backstage to congratulate the performers. He asked for the actor who had played the Devil. When we were introduced, he thought the others were playing a joke on him; he was even more enthusiastic when he learned my age; and asked me to come to see him the next day.

There I had my first sight of a studio, with paintings and engravings. He introduced me to his pupil and assistant, Joseph Budtko, who, like myself, spoke in homely Yiddish. The gentleman said: "Budtko is a painter, and painting speaks all languages. But for you as an actor, Yiddish is too limited. You must learn German and become a German actor!"

He had put into words what had long been my secret desire. He gave me a letter of introduction to Professor Emil Milan. Emil Milan, the greatest speech teacher of his time, took me as a free pupil and began to teach me to act in German.

But the man who made possible this most important connection of my life was the etcher Hermann Struck. Hermann Struck was the first to give a helping hand to a baker's boy from a foreign country, and so opened the door for me to a new, wonderful world, which for us "poor people" was bolted and barred. When I tried to thank him, he smiled and said, "Well, when you are a famous actor, you can thank me in your memoirs."

Which I here reverently do. Today my gratitude and love flow from a full heart to Hermann Struck.

26

The Word

When I went to Emil Milan with Struck's letter of recommendation, he was most friendly, but he was in the midst of packing. He told me that he was about to go on tour, then he would take a vacation. Now it was May, he would be back in August; he took my address, promised to write to me on his return, and dismissed me. That was a hard blow. My hopes, which were already sky-high, had to creep back into the darkest corner of my heart. It was not the first time I had knocked at a door, seen it open, only to have it slam in my face. A humiliated, homeless puppy, I slunk away, convinced that I had only encountered another of the polite ways to get rid of people.

But my resolve to become a German actor was not abandoned, and I began to reorganize my life so that I should be ready. First I must change my job. In the evenings, when everyone went to the theater or to lectures, I had to go to the bakery. I hated the bakery for another reason too. I still remembered the beggar woman in Zaleszczyki, who, years before, had said something about my "big" hands, and "big" feet – it still stuck in my mind and tormented me. In the course of time I had acquired another of the marks of a baker, baker's legs, knock-knees – and no matter how sure I was that I had the stuff in me to be an actor, still I feared that these marks of my trade would interfere with my career. Didn't most actors have small, delicate hands and feet? I often thought that perhaps people would not notice mine, or – who knows? – perhaps there were roles which called for big hands and feet – as for my knock-knees, I had long since planned to get them straightened. In any case I must stop working as a baker.

It is easier to lose a job than to find one. After a long time I got work in a gramophone-horn factory. They made tin gramophone horns and sprayed them with fresh colors. And they also washed off old horns and repainted them. It was in this paint-removing section that I worked.

The horns were left in vats of lye overnight and washed off the next day. You wore rubber gloves at work. When one of your gloves became even slightly torn, you burned your hands. After a few weeks I had burned my hands so often that I saw a new danger in this for the career I had undertaken. So I gave up that job too. The struggle for existence in a "new homeland" is hard enough. But when it is coupled with a new plan, a new longing, it is even harder.

After a while I found work again, this time in a coffin factory. There my job was staining and polishing coffins with a brown stain and varnish, and soon my hands were a dark yellow-brown, almost black on the palms, and no soap would take off the stain. I suffered under that too, but I had my evenings free, I was able to study German, attend various courses at the Free High School, go to the theater, and frequent theatrical societies, where I could let out what I learned by heart – that is, declaim to the members over coffee and cake. I already knew Bern's *Declamations* by heart backward and forward.

In those days life for me was like a river: I was hustled and carried along, tossed hither and yon, went aground on some bank, where I stuck fast, became apathetic, hopeless. Until another current came along, lifted me off, and carried me farther.

Then one day Karl Emil Franzus's novel, *Pojatz*, fell into my hands. Pojatz intoxicated and enthralled me. Already Maxim Gorki's example had strengthened me, and now here came Pojatz. He was from my neighborhood too. I suddenly saw towns and villages, people from my home. This boy in the book wanted to be an actor too. He had just the same troubles, the same plans, the same longings, the same difficulties. He too saw a play that excited and transported him, and compared the characters in it, with their outlandish names, to people from his village, his home. I must get that play! I flung myself on it, read it, devoured it – no, it flung itself on me and devoured me. It was *The Merchant of Venice*. It was Shylock:

"Hath not a Jew eyes? hath not a Jew hands, organs, dimensions, senses, affections, passions? fed with the same food, hurt with the same weapons, subject to the same diseases, healed by the same means, warmed and cooled by the same winter and summer, as a Christian is? If you prick us, do we not bleed? if you tickle us, do we not laugh? if you poison us, do we not die? and if you wrong us, shall we not revenge?"

I burst into tears, mourned over Shylock, and tasted his deepest despair. "S-h-y-l-o-c-k," the book said, was the same as "S-h-a-y-e, Isaiah," my own name; the man was close to me, an intimate. Shylock and Pojatz and I were all one. No, were all I. Because I lived not only my experiences; whatever I read I took as a personal experience, as something I personally had lived. The only thing that I did not like was Shylock's going so out of his head over his ducats. I imagined what my father would do if my sister had done to him what Jessica did to Shylock – certainly he would never have made such an outcry over his money, and certainly it would never have occurred to him to want to cut off a pound of Antonio's flesh, even if Antonio was his enemy. So I ignored Shylock's meanness and concentrated on his sorrows and pains. I immediately learned his great accusatory speech and tried it out at several theatrical societies. It was well received, and my friends, male and female, discussed it at great length with me and encouraged me.

I went on polishing my coffins and felt that I was getting nowhere. I became more melancholy and more desperate, suffered attacks of world weariness, and thought that no one was as lonely and as unhappy as I. On the other hand I began to believe that I was something extraordinary, and became conceited and suffered from delusions of grandeur. I had, at one and the same time, delusions of grandeur and delusions of littleness. Added to all this were troubles with girls and friendships with married women. I suffered and I caused suffering, suffered again because I had caused others to suffer, felt noble and enjoyed my sufferings. Everything was confused in me – like a paprika goulash cooked up with plum jam. I was very low.

One day I saw a big placard, which announced: "An Evening of Recitation by Emil Milan. Program, 'Signalman Thiel,' by Gerhard Hauptmann." So, I thought, of course – it is already late in August – he has been back for a long time. But he has other things to do than to remember me, the knock-kneed baker, the cleaner of gramophone horns, the coffin polisher with the stained hands. However, I will buy a ticket and hear him.

The evening was still six days off. At the corner where I lived there was an advertising pillar, and another opposite the coffin factory. Every morning the two placards laughed and sneered at me: "You idiot, you dung heap with delusions of grandeur! Did you imagine that you'd caught your bird with that letter of introduction, your rag of paper? You have the 'bird,' my boy!" I knew that much Berlinese already. "Bird" meant "crazy." If only that day were past and the placard pasted over with another, so that I could forget it! I had already got the whole business off my mind when those damned placards were put up.

The day of the evening came – I said nothing about it to anyone. I wanted to go alone and swallow my shame and my defeat by myself. It was Saturday. I came home at noon and washed. Suddenly the bell rang – a pneumatic-tube letter! A fine, small, strong handwriting, like copperplate; sender (printed on the handsome blue envelope): Professor

Emil Milan, Sybelstrasse 12, Charlottenburg. It contained a few lines:

> *My dear Herr Granach:*
>
> *Please excuse me for not having written to you sooner. Here are two tickets for this evening. Come and see me in my dressing room afterwards, so that we can set a time to begin work.*
>
> *With cordial greetings,*
> *Emil Milan*

I read the note through several times, holding it in trembling fingers; finally I simply lay down on my bed and wept with joy. Then I went to a motherly friend, opened my heart to her, and that evening we went to the recitation at the Bechstein Saal.

There was a distinguished audience: preachers, actors, lawyers, directors – most of them Milan's pupils and admirers. He came out in evening dress and received a stormy greeting. His face was tanned and radiant, his blonde hair and beard were beginning to turn gray. There was nothing on the platform but a comfortable chair. He sat down slowly and quietly, leaned forward a little, put the tips of his fingers together – the hall became quiet, but he waited, and when it was so still that you could hear your own breathing, he began to tell the story of Signalman Thiel. Not a trace of declamation, of the theater: it simply flowed on; he recited the story from beginning to end from memory. Just as Jus Fedorkiw would tell my father a story. He spoke to his audience as simply as Schimshale from Milnitz used to speak to us when we were children. When it was over, the audience cheered him. He returned to the stage again and again. Then everyone stood up and clapped him a "good night."

Afterward, with my heart pounding, I went to his dressing room. I found a priest there and a number of ladies and gentlemen. He introduced me to them as his pupil. They were all drinking champagne. I had a glass too – the first in my life. One of the ladies was named Johanna Burckhardt – he made an appointment for us both to call on him the next morning – Sunday – at eleven o'clock.

At ten o'clock the next morning I was in Sybelstrasse, and spent an hour that seemed a lifetime strolling up and down before Number 12. About 11 o'clock it began. I started reciting to him without preliminaries: Shylock, Franz Moor, Belshazzar – I was excited and steamed like an oven. He looked at me, smiled at first – then he put his arm around me and said very encouraging things – something about temperament, instrument, feeling – and suddenly burst into roars of laughter. I was hurt – he saw it, stifled his laughter, and explained that I had "great talent," but – "the unfortunate German language!" And he laughed again, loudly and heartily as if at a great joke. Then he wiped his eyes and said seriously: "Language can be learned, but not the things you have," and he turned to Johanna Burckhardt, his pupil, who was to teach me German. He himself would give me two hours a week, which would cost me two hundred marks a month. I earned about sixty at my coffins, and I turned white and showed my disappointment.

He saw it and began to question me: how much did I earn? Didn't my parents send me any money? Why did I keep hiding my hand? I used to hide my hands because I felt that they were too big, and because at that time they were dark with stain and varnish. Nothing mattered any longer, so I told him exactly what my circumstances were. And behold, he seemed delighted!

"This is wonderful," he cried, "wonderful!" He opened a pair of sliding doors into another room – there sat a number of the gentlemen I had seen the evening before in his dressing room, among them the friendly priest.

And Professor Milan was telling them enthusiastically: "What magical power German art has, to attract these children from far away to come here and struggle and suffer polishing coffins" – he showed them my hands, eaten by stain and varnish. Everyone was excited and touched. "Very well, my Galician," he said, "you shall come to me as a free pupil, and you, Fräulein Burckhardt, will give him lessons for nothing too, I'm sure?"

And Fräulein Burckhardt said that she would. Everyone congratulated me and, drunk with my first great success, I left them and took a streetcar and went to share my happiness with my motherly friend.

The thermometer rose. I took a fresh start. New hopes filled my heart. I went to Fräulein Burckhardt's twice a week. Every Sunday I worked with Milan.

To me Emil Milan became a new, a German, a Christian Schimshale of Milnitz. He gave me not only lessons, but suits that he had no more use for, shoes, linen. He forbade me to see my countrymen; I must speak only German, and soon I began thinking and dreaming in my new language. Wherever I went, I was continually learning: words, poems, monologues, whole roles – by heart. He gave me a long list of classic and modern literature, and even the books themselves – I found that there were cheap editions, the little Reclam books, to be had too.

I went on polishing my coffins, and the workers liked me and called me the "Little Polack." But I did not mind that. Berliners call all foreigners "Polacks."

The foreman of the factory was named Lembke. He wore a reddish-brown beard, combed out on both sides. Once at noon hour he came over to my corner and saw me devouring my sandwiches along with one of Mephisto's speeches, sat down beside me, opened his lunch package, and said, "Well, Little Polack, always busy, eh? What are you studying all the time?"

When I had explained to him, he said: "Didn't I know it! I thought right away you were an artist! I'll tell you something," he muttered, chewing away, "you're working on medium-size coffins now. If you were on the big ones, you could do piecework and earn just as much in half a day as you do in a whole day now – and you'll have more time to study and you can let your hair grow even longer."

"Oh, Herr Lembke," I said, "you are like a father to me."

"Nothing doing, my boy – your hair's much too long for my taste," and he smiled, poked me in the ribs, and said: "Well then, Monday you start at the big coffins, on piecework." And the noon whistle blew a long amen into my ears.

Now I worked half days and earned almost as much as before. And at Aschinger's, for twenty-five pfennigs you could buy a couple of sausages with potato salad – and you could add oil and vinegar and mustard to your heart's content, and dunk as many rolls in the mixture as you wanted to – sometimes I managed to put away fifty at a sitting. And in Gormannstrasse there was a Jewish cooking school. There, for ten marks a month, a student could get two meals a day, and red-haired Rosa served endless portions of vegetables to boot.

The pea porridge with boiled onions was particularly tasty. Budding philosophers and poets and musicians ate there. We vied with one another in the number of portions of vegetables we could consume, and had a merry time. How the school could serve all that for ten marks a month is still a mystery to me.

Despite Milan's prohibition against talking with my countrymen, I could not break off with them entirely. With Milan and Fräulein Burckhardt I was meek and reserved – too meek and too reserved. But with my own kind I could let myself go – I was fresh, I swaggered. Naturally it tickled my vanity that I was beginning to grow beyond them, to soar above them. I led a sort of double life: with Milan and Fräulein Burckhardt, I was the recipient, I was given gifts, I was an inferior – so I needed something to balance that: my own kind. Besides, I was never what is called a taciturn person, a lone wolf, or a solitary. I always liked people – lots of people. I liked to go to large gatherings, to parade in demonstrations, to sit in the theater, in the movies, at the circus, at the races. Wherever people gathered in crowds, there I liked to be. People excited me more than performances or orators or actors. People in crowds excite me, stimulate me, make me happy, lift me out of myself, raise me to ecstasy. No, to live like Adam was not for me, especially since there was always an Eve running off somewhere and stealing apples. When I am in a crowd, my curiosity wakes, mobilizes. And curiosity is either my sixth sense or, after eating and loving, my third drive.

That was the period when I read everything at once pell-mell: Nietzsche and Hamsun, Kropotkin and Dostoevski, Artsibashev and Stirner, Gorki and Shalom Aleichem, Strindberg and Tolstoy, German classics, French novels. And I not only took seriously all that I read, I tried to live it: after I had swallowed Raskolnikov, no old woman, no old aunt, was safe from me. I am convinced that if my "watery-soup" aunt, who had suspected me of stealing, had come anywhere near me, we would both have perished – she by me, and I by the hangman. After I had read Max Stirner, I was "superman," and a peril and a terror to my friends.

My friend Schidlower had two sisters, who, like himself, could not adjust to life. But they were convinced that their little crooked brother was a genius. Such a genius that he would never become known or successful! Because only the "bad," and "pushers," the "superficial" achieved success – so their brother had taught them, and so they believed. Jealousy over my new start began to cloud our friendship. Nothing was said openly. Just a little dig here and there.

The older sister was very much "older" and a little withered. Her skin was neither yellow nor brown nor any other color, but a mixture of all colors, which produced a harmonious drabness. She also had false teeth, badly fitted by a bad dentist. When she spoke they shook, and when she was excited and flew into a rage – which often happened – her false teeth almost jumped out of her false mouth. She always knew everything better than anyone else. There was no theory, no subject, no topic about which she was not better informed, and on which she did not have the last word. There was only one thing she recognized – her brother. He was the genius of the family, that was clear, that was certain, about that they all agreed in the family. His lack of success she attributed to two things: his genius and his fat wife, who bore him a girl every year. Five squealing, happy creatures were already running around their two small rooms. Naturally the fat wife also believed that her feeble husband was something special, and already she could see signs of their great father in her children. The poor woman therefore worked hard and supported the entire family herself. But she was perfectly happy and confident, because she believed that the world would certainly recognize her husband's talents someday, or, if not his, their children's.

My friend's younger sister was shortsighted, wore glasses, and worshiped her brother; one corner of her mouth was perpetually drawn down in an ironical and self-satisfied smile. In conversation she expressed her assent in mysterious, half-ambiguous phrases. For example, when someone would remark searchingly, "The stars swirl through space from one eternal nothingness to another," she would smile understandingly and murmur, "Ah yes – so perfectly simple – from nothingness to nothingness – quite." Or when someone said of Raskolnikov that he had killed the old woman out of a profound sympathy, she remarked, "Exactly that – out of goodness – ah yes – quite," and sank into a meaningful silence of unrevealed, mysterious thoughts. She was a lingerie maker, sat all day at her sewing machine, had a white face, and smiled a faint, troubled smile like an old Chinese.

These two poor old maids did not like me, and the feeling was mutual. They were jealous of me for their brother's sake, they were forever taunting me, and I revenged myself by using them as guinea pigs for whatever I had just read.

In those days I was as soft and receptive as a cake of wax. Everything that I heard or saw or read, I tried out on those around me. After Stirner's *The Ego and His Own*, I tested his theories on the two old maids. I lorded it over them, said the most brutal things quite openly, and was generally rude – a vest-pocket "superman." But after Kropotkin's *Mutual Aid, a Factor of Evolution*, I became considerate and helpful. After Artsibashev's *Sanine*, I became dissolute, a little whoremaster. After *Werther*, nothing meant anything to me, I grew weary of the world and played with the idea of suicide. After an earthy story of Tolstoy's, I returned to my senses and became sociable. Whatever my mood, I succeeded in annoying the old maids. I knew perfectly well that I was putting on an act, but I annoyed them because I thought that they deserved to be punished for their secret jealousy.

Little by little I dropped my old circle of friends and grew gradually into my new milieu. I met pupils of Fräulein Burckhardt's and Emil Milan's, and we were at home in all the Berlin theater galleries and greeted our favorite players with loud applause and encores. At opening nights we shouted ourselves hoarse, until our idolized artists were forced to come out even after the fire curtain had descended, and beamed gratefully upon us.

Of the forty or fifty Berlin theaters, we concentrated on three: the Koenigliche Schauspielhaus, the Lessing Theater, and Max Reinhardt. After an opening we read the criticisms and did not always agree with the critics. We identified ourselves with our idols, wrote them comforting letters when they came off badly, and even wrote anonymous letters to the critics to tell them what we thought of them. When some theater put on a play that called for a crowd, we applied to the person in charge of supernumeraries and took part.

In those days Reinhardt was enthralling Berlin with his sensational production of *Oedipus* in the Schumann Circus, rank with art and horse droppings. Supernumeraries were needed to play the people – the Greeks. And we went to Plueschke, the assistant director, who hired us, and were allowed to sit around during rehearsals and, from a little distance, to admire our gods at work.

Reinhardt, small and slightly built, arrived at rehearsals like a general arriving on a battlefield. He had a little podium, which he mounted, and around him sat his staff: the set designer, lighting men, property men, and many, many assistant directors. Reinhardt gave his orders in a low tone, and his staff flew around and carried out his commands to the dot.

We were divided into groups, the groups were numbered, and, at a given signal, a particular group would rush from a particular direction to the great portal and cry, first softly, then louder, then in desperation: "Help us, King; King, help us; help us, Oedipus." Then more violently: "Help. Oedipus; King, help us, help, Oedipus!" Then, in a mighty outburst, with our arms outstretched: "Oedipus, Oedipus, Oedipus, Oedipus, Oedipus!"

And Moissi appeared and, in his musical Italian voice, which was both manly and sweet, said: "Children, why do you kneel before the door of my house?..."

We lacerated our knees throwing ourselves on the stage and clamored and wept real tears. We were despairing Greeks – for we felt the seriousness and were spellbound by the work of this man Reinhardt.

At the Koenigliche Schauspielhaus it was different. There the actors behaved with the self-importance of petty officials; everyone walked around as if he had on buskins and spoke beautifully – too beautifully to bear – and made gestures such as no one would ever make. I never got on the stage of the Lessing Theater – there were no openings for outsiders. But two of the actors who appeared there, we held to be the greatest in Berlin: Albert Bassermann and Oskar Sauer. Just as the Koenigliche Schauspielhaus actors were too unnatural, the Lessing Theater actors were too natural. They coughed and spat and scratched and made tremendous pauses – a performance there always looked as if you had accidentally found your way into a private house and were witnessing the most embarrassing of intimate discussions. The effect was somewhat painful. Reinhardt's theater was halfway between the two others. It was natural, yet nor ordinary – it was dignified, yet without any false emphasis – it was theater – romantic, poetic theater.

I had already been studying with Milan for two years, and burned to tread the boards. Many of my friends went to agents, auditioned, and were engaged to appear in small towns, where they played the parts we had seen our favorites perform in Berlin. I envied them and went to agents secretly myself. I had prepared a repertory of twenty roles – I recited my Franz Moor, my Mephisto, my Shylock, and many of the provincial directors wanted to hire me for such towns as Kottbus, Chemnitz, Beuthen. That gave me new hope. But I was afraid of making the decision: to accept an engagement, to simply run off without Milan's knowledge. I did not know what my capabilities at the time were; I only knew from my work with him how many faults I still had, how much I had still to learn. Yet I was on pins and needles to be on my own at last and to try out all the things I had learned for myself. I opened my heart to Fräulein Burckhardt. And, behold, she showed perfect understanding and she promised to speak to Milan for me!

So one day Milan let me recite for a whole morning without interrupting me or correcting me, and afterward he had a long and serious talk with me. "Yes," he said, grinning, "Fräulein Burckhardt has poured out your heart to me. Well, boy, I know very well that you are a wild Carpathian colt, a primitive comedian, and that you would like nothing better than to rave and roar to your heart's content in some barn in the provinces. Ordinarily, that is a very good thing, but in your case it is too dangerous. You would ruin your natural gift forever if you did it. You still need supervision. I am going on tour now for at least four months, but I want to keep my eye on you for a while longer. The best thing would be for me to send you to Max Reinhardt. You'll be in his theater school with other youngsters, and there you can sow your wild oats once and for all – and then we shall see. What do you think?"

What did I think! My face was on fire, my heart pounded – I stammered unintelligible words of thanks. Meanwhile he had picked up the telephone and was talking to someone at the Reinhardt Theater; there were to be auditions in three days, and I was given an appointment. "Well, my little Galician," he said, "don't disgrace me, and don't go getting a swelled head. That's a disease to which most actors succumb. And when they do, they are never anything but mediocrities. A man can achieve something great only by putting the thing he serves above his personal vanity. The thing he serves is always more important than the man himself. A man perishes, but what he served remains. What we serve is art, the poet's word, Shakespeare's word, Goethe's word – when you once experience the feeling of the word, you will be happy to serve it. And now – good luck! And think about all this," and he dismissed me.

I thought about it – did not my old teacher Schimshale from Milnitz talk about the holiness of the word back in little Horodenka? Yes, but he meant the words of the Bible. My new teacher, Emil Milan, in this great European world, meant the word in poetry, the word in the theater – I thought about it long and often. I am not through thinking about it yet.

27

There Is Something in a Name

When I entered the Reinhardt Theater, I found myself in a gathering of several hundred young people who were seeking to be admitted to the theater school. They stood together in groups, with shining, questioning, inquisitive eyes, dressed in their Sunday best, excited, talking, gesturing. Young people with dreams and ambitions, with the hope that the gates of art were about to open for them, that here they would cross the threshold into a new world, the world of the theater. But there in the lobby were the first barriers: the tables and chairs of the examining committee.

It was these strangers who were to decide who was worthy to enter the bright doors of the Muses and who was to be sent back into the grayness of the everyday world, among the million nonentities of the petty bourgeoisie, with their boring jobs. On Yom Kippur, the great Day of Atonement, life and death are weighed in heaven, it is decided who shall perish by fire, who by water, who by plague, and other terrors. But Yom Kippur comes every year – and, once every year of his life, each man gets his chance to pray for something "good." *But here it was only once in a lifetime!* Here sat human beings like you and me, with two hands and feet and eyes, and decided whether you had the right to dream, to hope, to strive, the right to that human activity, that human expression which they themselves exercised.

Around the table sat actors, directors, teachers – among them, Berthold Held, the director of the school, the diction teacher for the theater, and Reinhardt's assistant. Reinhardt himself was not present. The auditions went on for several days. Of the three or four hundred who were to recite, only a hundred would be accepted. Of those hundred, another sixty were dropped at the end of half a year, and the forty who were left attended the school for two years, paid twelve hundred marks a year, and emerged as full-fledged actors.

The auditionists themselves were a remarkable sight. Many young men and women write melting poems, or wild plays with murders in each scene, or paint and sketch – but more or less keep it to themselves. But many more want to get into the theater, and most of them are pretty strange birds. Most habitues of the theater galleries either become or want to become actors. What does an actor do? He speaks. And anyone – so they think – can speak. And many come to recite with that idea. There are the seasoned veterans of amateur societies – who consider themselves actors. There are the eternal, ancient students, who failed for a degree; army officers, cashiered for once breaking their word; playboys – they all seek refuge in the theater, because if you are in the theater you can get up late. There are daughters of good families, who always recite poems on birthdays and other family festivals and whom their aunts and cousins encourage and urge to take up the theater as a career, to become "artists." There are the usual "mother's boys," who are kowtowed to at home, who have never heard the word "no" in their lives – later they get used to hearing it. They think that art will say yes to them, like their families. There are others with pale faces and palpitating hearts, looking as if the trumpets of the Last Judgment were sounding within them. Very few come with any preparation, very few have done any work, either on what they are to recite or on themselves.

One young man declaimed a poem about a hangman. At the end he bent over in the chair and sobbed at intervals, heaving his shoulders most unnaturally, then straightened up coolly and said, "I can be funny too." "So we observed," said one of the committee, and everyone laughed. Yet another turned up his collar, lowered his head, rolled his eyes darkly and poured out Franz Moor's insanities in an exaggerated whisper. At one point he suddenly pulled a kitchen knife out of his pocket – the effect was very funny.

Out of the hundred, I was accepted as the only free pupil. A half year later would come the great "sorting," the great "winnowing" – the great and decisive audition before Reinhardt himself. The course of studies comprised voice training, gymnastics (principally fencing), make-up, diction, and the study of parts. I was a super in the evening besides and thereby earned thirty marks a month. Too much to die on, too little to live on.

Again my old trade stood me in good stead – I worked as a helper in a bakery once or twice a week and thus earned my keep. But it had to be kept a secret, for the other pupils were all from good bourgeois families. I had the feeling that I had smuggled myself into a fine company and might at any moment be discovered and recognized by my big hands and knock-knees and be cast out of those exalted circles to which I did not belong.

Furthermore, the director of the school did not like me. Herr Held was from Hungary, clearly from somewhere near my Galician homeland. He did not feel entirely at home in his position. He dressed as small-town gents imagine that fashionable gentlemen dress in Paris. He usually wore a cutaway, with white spats, light gloves, and a monocle which was forever falling out. He wore the monocle only when he was trying out some minor actor for a role, or when he lectured to us. But when he was with Reinhardt, he never wore his monocle and seldom his white spats, and he smiled submissively no matter what was said, and looked like a beaten dog. But no sooner did he return to the school – even if it was the same afternoon – than he put on his monocle and his white spats and his other expression, the lofty, superior one. And when he wanted to explain something, he used himself as an example. He was always telling us about himself.

He was a botched actor, an actor who never became an actor. He had been with Reinhardt in his early days in the provinces – that was how he had got his present position – everyone knew that. No one liked him as a teacher. We did not contradict him, we obeyed him, but he was not respected, he was not accepted, not loved! Of this he was not aware – he was far too taken with himself for that. Such teachers never know how they are watched by their students. Every wrong gesture, every stupid remark is registered. But he was the director of the school, and he could make or break us. So the students handled him with diplomacy and psychology instead of the other way around.

Being himself embittered, a man whose expectations had not been realized, he was particularly hard on the unrealized, the unsuccessful, in others. He never encouraged, he never praised what was positive. Instead he sought out what was negative. He made everything small and futile and ugly. I was particularly obnoxious to him. I still spoke with a foreign accent. And he imitated me, ridiculed me. If he had not been a Jew himself I should have supposed that he was an anti-Semite. He was really a Jewish anti-Semite. That is the worst kind, because, in their subconscious, they transfer their own personal inadequacy to their people, would fain desert in a servile attempt at assimilation, get stuck halfway, and then hate *themselves in their kind.*

Green-eyed Sonia Bogs, one of my fellow students, also contributed to the discord between Held and myself. Held used to work "privately" with his pupils. Now and again a girl would whisper tales out of school about this roué. Sonia had a fresh, Tartar face and liked to embarrass men. She explained to me that she did it only as a way of studying Wedekind's Lulu (the play was new then). We were friends and talked about everything together, naturally about Held too. So one day she told me that Held had given her an appointment. I was jealous, I suppose, and I scolded and warned her against him. The upshot of it was that he tried to be "nice" to her. She declined, saying, "So Granach was right after all!" She told me about it, so I was prepared for more trouble. And that afternoon Herr Held asked me, in front of the class, why I did not come to school better dressed. I was thrown into confusion, I blushed, and Wilhelm Murnau, a fellow student, who already had his doctorate and radiated authority, said, "But, Herr Held, perhaps he hasn't money enough."

"In that case," said Herr Held, "why does he insist on being an actor?"

"Because he has talent," Murnau answered, laughing in his face, and the whole class laughed too.

And Held, the teacher, felt that he was being whipped by his pupils.

"So-o-o-o!" Herr Held hissed, extending the syllable, in a furious temper at his own viciousness. "I don't think he has." He took his notebook out of his vest pocket and screwed his monocle into his eye. "In any case, he cannot recite for Max next week." He always spoke of Reinhardt as "Max" to emphasize their "friendship." "No, he is not far enough along for that yet – he has not yet learned enough from me, he has not talent enough yet."

At that I burst out myself, and, encouraged by the class and Murnau, shouted, "Herr Held, not to Germany and here to you did I come that I should learn talent, I came that I should learn technique, technique, technique!"

My answer was not only unidiomatic, it contained a plain grammatical error (I had said *"zu Sie"* instead of *"zu Ihnen"*).

The class roared with laughter, until Held, with his sour face, outroared them: "Not 'zu Sie' – 'zu Ihnen, zu Ihnen'!"

"Yes, of course, that is what I mean – *zu Sie, zu Ihnen* – you know exactly what I mean," I flung back at him, impudently, at the risk of being expelled from the school.

The incident spread through the theater like wildfire. The other directors and teachers, who did not like Held, said that it was right for me to defend myself. They called me "Technique" and smiled at me. Baron von Gersdorff, teacher in the school and social adviser for the theater, took me aside one day and had a long talk with me. I opened my heart to him, and he said, "Let me attend to this matter – you shall recite for Herr Reinhardt next week."

My outburst had had the effect of drawing attention to me. Directors, actors, and particularly the pupils in the school were suddenly much nicer to me. Among them were Conrad Veidt, Wilhelm Murnau, Lothar Muetel, Walter Storm, and others who later became famous.

Walter Storm invited me to dine at his parents' house the following Sunday. I lived in a little attic room for which I paid twelve marks a month, and the neighbors complained about my "studying" roles. It was far too loud for them. I always envied my fellow students, who lived in fine houses where there were plush sofas and soft armchairs and people "resided" so comfortably. Now Walter was taking me to just such a fine house for Sunday dinner.

I arrived there about eleven. They lived somewhere in the "West" – a fourteen-room apartment. First we sat in his study; then it was time to go to dinner. The many rooms with their red-plush sofas and flowered armchairs bewildered me. Yes, I envied Walter deeply for living in such a fine house, having such small hands and no knock-knees. He was beautifully dressed too, wore spats, and frequently screwed a monocle into his eye. He said that an actor had to play officers and barons and counts and must accustom himself to fine things.

Around the table were his prosperous father, head of the firm of Storm & Company, his mother, older and younger brothers and sisters, his father's business partner with his family, and uncles and aunts – lots and lots of aunts. The conversation opened over the hors d'oeuvres with a discussion of Schildkraut's Shylock; when the soup was brought in, there was a gradual transition to Moissi's Oedipus and his other roles; over the vegetables, they proceeded to Wegener's Mephisto, over the roast to Bassermann's King Philip, and during dessert there was general laughter over Arnold's comic Thisbe in *Midsummer Night's Dream*.

When the good dinner was finished, the gentlemen stuck large cigars into their faces, and everyone rose and wandered into the big living room with the red-plush sofas and flowered armchairs. Here we were urged to display our art. We let loose, blared out our repertory – monologue after monologue, poem after poem. They could not have enough of it. Finally we gave the pact scene from *Faust* – Walter as Faust, I as Mephisto.

When it was all over, coffee and cakes were served, and everyone began to talk most professionally about the theater. The aunts especially let loose. One of them, Aunt Emma, the most talkative, dominated the conversation. She was so fat that she could hardly squeeze into one of the big armchairs. The armchair looked as if it were overflowing with her. She had a roll of fat under her chin, which waggled, bright red cheeks, and a voluntary-involuntary lock of blond hair that kept falling into her face over her nose, and at every second or third sentence she blew the lock up and it disappeared for a while but always returned to the same place again. She had on a low-necked purple dress that allowed you to see rather more than the beginning of her white breasts, which heaved up and down and stood out from her body like two large cow's udders.

She talked about actors and the theater in an intimate, sensual voice; you would have thought she was talking about some rich dish. Why, she knew simply everything about Moissi: what he thought of during a performance, how he slept, what he liked to eat, his love affairs. She knew Bassermann's entire pedigree – that his ancestors had owned a vineyard, she knew about his fondness for horses and music and his great romance with Elsa Schiff. She knew that Reinhardt had married and that they were already expecting the stork. Yes, indeed, she was personally acquainted with one of Wegener's divorced wives, who had told her such intimate things about stage people – but of course they were most of them things that could not be repeated in mixed company.

And now she started on us! Dear Walter – oh yes, when he was still a child he had such expressive eyes that she had always known he would be an artist. "Only," she said suddenly, turning to him, "you see, Walter dear, you are really good. But look at the way Herr Granach is always tossing his hair and how full of temperament he is – that is artistic! You ought – how shall I put it? – you ought to let yourself go more and toss your hair sometimes – you should copy Herr Granach a little – you are always so cool, so indifferent – you ought to get a little more excited." And all the while she was beaming at me, and she gazed at me with a moist glow in her eyes, and I was bewildered by the look and by her heaving bosom.

Walter's mother threw her a hostile glance and hissed, "But Emma, I beg of you…"

Aunt Emma sank into an offended silence, her bosom heaved sulkily. The younger members of the family laughed. An uncle told a joke about two traveling salesmen. Everyone laughed heartily, but more at Aunt Emma than at the stupid joke.

Walter and I took our leave, and we went to my twelve-mark garret, and there he opened his heart to me. How he suffered from his family, how hard all that made his life for him. Then, for the first time, I understood how revolting a family, with all its plush furniture and bedbug sofas, could be. Every cushion a stumbling block, every overstuffed aunt a brake. I had no aunts and no family connections, no one helped me – but no one got in my way either.

Yes, sometimes it was difficult. I led a hard existence in my narrow attic room. But that attic room meant freedom, independence, and Walter with his spats and his monocle and his aunts and his sofas was in prison. This compensatory justice made me feel good. A couple of sausages at Aschinger's on

Sunday, with the potato salad that you could stretch with oil and vinegar and mustard, and all the rolls you wanted for twenty-five pfennigs – the five courses served in Walter's home were not to be compared with that. But even had the five courses tasted a thousand times better, those uncles and aunts were a catastrophe, a peril to one's very life. Beware! Keep away!

Came the great day on which Reinhardt was to audition. I was not on the list, but Gersdorff told me to come. I stood in the lobby and watched Reinhardt and his staff, among whom was his brother Edmund, the business manager, who ran the theater. As the students passed in review one after another, I suddenly saw Gersdorff bend over and whisper something in Reinhardt's ear, then they both looked at me. Then Gersdorff called me over, introduced me, and, after a short conversation, I was told to recite. I gave Franz Moor, then the First Player from *Hamlet*. I was asked to continue, I saw encouraging smiles. Only Held looked me up and down with cold contempt – he had put on his most disgusted expression. I began Shylock's speech. I saw and thought of nothing but Held, and when I came to the words,

> "If you prick us, do we not bleed? If you tickle us, do we not laugh? If you poison us, do we not die?"

I looked straight at him; the outburst was meant for him, was aimed at him, and the whole thing became personal, full of grief and despair, and tears ran down my face. I was really unhappy and cried my grief to the world and forgot everything else, and when it was over I felt a little ashamed. And there was Reinhardt coming up to me, speaking kind, appreciative words in that strangely friendly voice of his; then he asked me where I came from. When I told him, he said to his staff, "Naturally – a fellow countryman of Bogumil Davidsohn's," shook my hand and laughed heartily; then, turning to Edmund, "We'll give him a five-year contract," and Edmund told me to come to his office that same afternoon. The staff congratulated me, and Held said, "Luck is a swine, and goes to its own kind."

But his remark could not trouble the happiest hour of my life. For I had never thought I would get a five-year contract when I left the school – that went beyond all my expectations. That same day I signed the five-year contract: 75 marks a month the first year, 125 the second, 250 the third, 350 the fourth, and 500 the fifth. I was introduced to Ottomar Keindl, secretary of the theater, and I was given a few small parts in plays which were already scheduled.

When the rehearsals for Tolstoy's *The Living Corpse* began, I was given the part of a waiter in the ninth scene who has to say, "I know nothing about it." "I know nothing about it," ran through my head all day, all week. I chewed the words, the syllables – the words, the very letters, danced through my brain in my dreams. I soon saw that this waiter, with his single line, "I know nothing about it," was the most important part in the play. For, in that scene, the desperate Fedia (Moissi) is lonely, forsaken, at the lowest ebb of his fortune, the police spy trying to give him the finishing stroke; he calls me in as a witness – but I know nothing about it. *I* know nothing about it – I *know* nothing about it – I know *nothing* about it! I am Fedia's only salvation – I love him, I find it horrible to be called as a witness against him. I must "act" that, with love and anger, with sympathy and protest – yes, it was a terribly difficult job.

Rehearsal time came. I sat in a corner and watched how Reinhardt worked with the actors, how every little gesture, every least intonation was discussed and settled, how the rehearsals suddenly warmed and were finer than real performances! How Reinhardt listened, how his mobile face reflected the actors' expressions – how he kindled one passage, quenched another. How the great actors listened to him like little children, studied his expression, hung on his words, looked into his eyes for help. How this mutual give-and-take created a climate, an atmosphere in which time and space were forgotten; how everyone felt the intoxication, the joy of the dramatist's thoughts and words and situations – and I felt: I am here too – I am breathing the same air that they are – and they are those of whom I dreamed, whom I honored and loved – those whose movements and gestures and voices I drank in from the gallery! That is really Moissi, with his musical Italian voice, the man of the South with his big brown eyes and that lyric-melancholy turn of the head. Here, in real life, his voice is just as lovable and fiery as it is in his Romeo, just as melodious and thoughtful as it is in his Hamlet. That is really Papa Schildkraut, with his forever kindly, forever tender, forever fatherly great eyes. That is really Bassermann with his slightly husky voice, with that unique South German tone color, Bassermann's tone color, Bassermann's technique, with the body of a straight young poplar and those sunny, blue, shining eyes! That is really Wegener, chock-full of vigor and vitality, with the same impudent, aggressive humor in real life too!

There was tremendous activity – *The Miracle* was being rehearsed in the arena of the circus, one of Strindberg's plays at the Kammerspiele, and *The Living Corpse* at the Deutsches Theater. It was spring, they were standing in groups in the court, the unforgettable, imperishable court of the Deutsches Theater. The rehearsals had not yet begun. They were talking, holding private conversations – I slipped among them, to overhear what they could say about their to me so sacred calling. I heard – I could not believe my ears – they talked just like anyone else. Wegener, clicking his tongue, was saying: "So, last night, I found an old bottle of burgundy in my cellar that my grandfather must have kept hidden somewhere. I, nothing loath, knocked off its head. And, children, I tell you..." And he seemed to smell the aroma over again in his imagination. Bassermann had on riding clothes and spurs, and he was giving an enthusiastic account of the manners of his three-year-old mare, Lisa. Gertrude Eisoldt was talking to Moissi: "So, Alexander, remember that the first radishes come right after the lilies of the valley and they taste unearthly – but there is nothing better in spring than the first new potatoes with oil and cottage cheese." Schildkraut remarked: "Cottage cheese is cottage cheese. There is nothing more wonderful in the world than a good piece of boiled beef with dill sauce."

The stage manager rang the bell, and the rehearsals began, and little by little Lisa, the mare, vanished, along with the radishes; the burgundy and the boiled beef with dill sauce were forgotten; the new potatoes with oil and cottage cheese disappeared. And Goethe was speaking, and then Tolstoy and Strindberg. Poetic thoughts and emotions filled the house, sought expression, strove to put on flesh and blood. Actors and directors wrestled with their material, like Jacob with the angel: "I will not let thee go until thou hast blessed me."

There lay Reinhardt's director's book, full of accurate sketches and plans; everything had been prepared, planned in advance – but he took inspiration from the actors too. Schildkraut, the most emotional, the most touching of all actors, brought tears to his eyes. When the scene was finished, he inspired the others to enter into the mood that had been created. Bassermann came all prepared, every detail fixed and polished, even for the first rehearsal. Reinhardt beamed, was delighted. But his best instrument was Moissi. He played like Paganini on his Moissi-violin.

Now *The Living Corpse* was being rehearsed. The entire cast was present, photographs from Moscow were handed around – Stanislavski was putting on the same play at the same time. The rehearsals proceeded, time became more and more precious. Assistants worked with smaller groups, with single actors – things became more and more intense. The framework was already raised, there was hammering and polishing and painting and cleaning up still to be done – nowhere in the world is time so precious as in the theater before an opening. Reinhardt and the actors were completely wrapped up in each other. He worked with them singly too, and no one was allowed to be present. Only Murnau and I lay on the floor of the stage box and watched and listened and learned how Reinhardt worked with his actors. Everything was taken apart and unscrewed, as a master mechanic takes apart the works of a clock: every least spring, every tiniest screw, every wheel is examined and brushed and polished. So every least idea, every smallest emotion, every intonation was examined, felt, explained, discussed, soldered, and then, piece, by piece, put back in place, until everything fitted together again and was a clock, a performance; and so Moissi's great speech rang out again – that shattering speech, at once defense and indictment, came to birth before the examining magistrate. Lisa's outbursts of feeling were quieted, Mascha the gypsy was inflamed. So each character was kneaded, shaped, fused into the whole. Reinhardt was the great potter, and all were clay in his hands.

And so the great day of the opening arrived, and the posters were put up, and there stood my name with all the others. Not as it is today, when the stars have their names in gigantic electric letters and the good actors are almost not mentioned. No. There the parts were listed just as they stood in the book, except that the actors' names were added. My very small part was listed exactly like the leading man's, in the same small, ordinary type. There it was: "A waiter, Jessaja Granach." I was very, very happy. I could hardly grasp it!

Then, a few days later, my name was changed: Hermann Granach. I did not like it. I went to the secretary and protested – I did not want to be called Hermann.

"Very well," said the secretary, "but Jessaja won't do either. It sounds too Jewish for the German stage."

"All right," I said, "but I don't like Hermann. I won't be called Hermann. It doesn't suit me."

"But my dear young man," the diplomatic secretary soothed me, "you take it all too seriously. Believe me, a name is nothing. What's in a name?"

"A great deal, to me," I answered.

"Well then, what name would you like?"

"Stefan," I said.

He considered for a moment and said, "No, that won't do either. Stefan is too Hungarian. What do you think of Alexander? Alexander Granach – there's a name with four *a*'s for you, and Alexander Moissi only has two! Agreed?"

"Agreed."

And the next day I read my new name on the billboards, my new name with the four *a*'s. It warmed my heart many more than four times. Little by little I grew accustomed to my new name – it was a part of the new life I had begun, of my vocation, of the theater. I have looked after it to the best of my ability. A name is something very important, and not, as the secretary implied, nothing but sound. No, the old saying is wrong.

There is something in a name!

28

And the Crooked Shall Be Straight

In those days the path of a young actor in Germany led, after a theatrical school or "private" teaching, to some little hole in the provinces or to a traveling company, known as "hams." There you served up a new, full-blown part every night – or every second or third night – until you had the luck to reach a somewhat larger town, where you worked more slowly and carefully – a new play every four or five days, or only every week.

After a long spell of this hamming around, if hope and strength and talent survived the process, you were "discovered" by a manager and went to Nuremberg, Dresden, Koenigsberg, Stuttgart, Munich, Hamburg, or even Frankfurt-am-Main.

In these cities there were distinguished dramatic institutions, theaters subsidized by the state or the city, companies with a stamp of their own. And in these cities you could be "discovered" for Berlin. Berlin, the hottest, most alive theater town in Europe, the ultimate aim and the final hope of every German actor.

A few actors, exceptions, had succeeded in being discovered in Berlin, without a "detour" through the "provinces." In Berlin there were two possibilities for young actors: The theaters gave cheap performances Sunday afternoons – these, the great actors usually managed to avoid; it was really too much for them to play Franz Moor in the afternoon and Lear in the evening. Here a young actor had a chance to show himself.

Another form in which opportunity presented itself was: An actor in a leading role fell ill and canceled his appearance at the last minute. Then someone had to "jump in" and take his place. Each youngster had his favorite among the great masters, whom he tried to imitate, whom he especially loved and revered, whom he regarded as his model and teacher – and it was precisely this favorite who the young actor hoped would have a slight illness, at least a sore throat.

I was especially fond of Rudolf Schildkraut and Albert Bassermann. I loved and honored them, as I loved and honored my father and my teacher Schimshale from Milnitz. It had never entered my head to wish my father or my teacher Schimshale any evil. But here I stood in the wings every evening, admired the actor's "genius," his "greatness," studied his movements and gestures and intonations – what some little sigh or some little motion of the hand could bring out of a sentence, how a pause, a cry, a silence revealed a thought, made a feeling live. I compared their expressions, weighed them against each other, and thought to myself that it was all wonderful, but still it could be expressed differently. I found places where I could have cried out, or wept, or been silent differently – yes, but when, when? I caught myself thinking horrible but wonderful thoughts: It would be glorious if one evening, five minutes before a performance, one of those two gods whom I loved so dearly and deeply were to find himself hoarse, too hoarse to speak. The performance would have to be canceled! And, suddenly, like a shot from a pistol, I would "jump in"! Stand on the stage! "Save the performance"! Be accepted! For that is what it would come to – being accepted, being "let in." Somehow the door must open for a man. He must be given an opportunity.

And so it befell, one Sunday afternoon, that the cleverest of character actors was hoarse, the "sneakiest well poisoner," the "tiptoeingest murderer" in the company, the "keenest incendiary" and "eye roller" in the theater, Friedrich Kuehne, was hoarse as a post, and I jumped in to replace him as Lucianus in *Hamlet*. Kuehne had never done me any harm – but I thanked God for making him ill, for making him hoarse for my sake. I would have wished cats and rats into the throats of the two actors whom I most honored and revered if that would have made them go home or stay in bed, so that I could "jump in," "save the performance," "knock off" Mephisto or Franz Moor or Shylock. I had wish-dreams about it, of how by once "jumping in" I leaped overnight from the darkness of obscurity to the light of fame. But even in my dearest dreams and imaginings I saw the great stumbling block: my crooked baker's legs, my knock-knees! And now it had come true, and that Sunday afternoon Kuehne had a rat in his throat, and I had my Lucianus.

> *"Thoughts black, hands apt, drrrugs fit, and time agrrreeing;*
> *Confederrrate season, else no crrreaturrre seeing;*
> *Thou mixturrre rrrank, of midnight weeds collected,*
> *With Hecate's ban thrrrice blasted, thrrrice infected,*
> *Thy naturrral magic and dirrre prrroperrrty*
> *On wholesome life usurrrp immediately!"*

Every word had five *r*'s, a curved red mustache stuck up in front of the dead-white make-up on my cheeks. The *r*'s rolled on my tongue, my eyes rolled, my hands were clenched for murder! The poison dripped into the ear of the sleeping king, the crown was set on my brow – the real king called for lights, the court was in panic – Hamlet triumphed!

My part was finished. I was trembling with excitement. Into those few sentences I put as much intensity and strength and ecstasy as a mature actor would use in playing Lear twenty times. I stood in my dressing room before the big mirror – it all went on echoing in me: my hands still stretched out tensely to seize the crown, my lips muttered over the words with the many *r*'s, my eyes rolled, evilly, planning murder – it was all much easier, righter, better than it had been on the stage. The echo is always better – as the best answers always come to you *after* an argument.

Suddenly I glanced down at my clinging tights. All was forgotten – there was my obstacle! There they were, knee pressing against knee, my crooked baker's legs! What use experience, when two such crooked witnesses were there to betray me to the world? To tell the world that I did not belong there! With that warrant out against me, I could go no further! That was reality, that was clear. And that clear reality was my clear and real despair.

The performance was over. Most of my young colleagues congratulated me, were nice to me. I alone knew that it was impossible, but I could not tell anyone why. They all hurried away. I remained alone in the dressing room, for the evening performance.

The old wardrobe man, Haltschke, came in. He was the young actors' banker. He was a usurer. He lent a mark and charged twenty-five pfennigs for it. Haltschke was little and toothless – long dirty hairs grew out of his nostrils and ears. He had evil, blinking eyes and a mournful, croaking voice. He would always put up for a sandwich and beer. He fleeced us, Haltschke did. On payday he stood next to the cashier, and the young actors always owed him more than half their salary. He turned every pfennig over five times before he would let it out of his hand. He held every penny up to his bleary eyes, the usurer. But he was a help in times of need.

Now he came in, bringing me a sandwich, a schnapps, and a beer. I swallowed my meal, stretched out on the sofa, and dozed off. I began to see things, disconnectedly – then settled gradually into a long dream. I saw myself as Hamlet, on a stage which, at the same time, was a bakery. And my black silk costume was full of flour – the audience was whispering that I ought to let the wardrobe man brush me off. And Haltschke called from the wings in his croaking voice, "I can't do it, I can't help him, he owes me money already." And the rolls in the oven were burned, and my knock-knees were tied together, and I could not stir from the spot. And there was a hospital there too, and I rang at the door. And my father stood there and said, "Go on ringing, they'll make you straight – all that is crooked can be made straight," and he pressed the bell button himself, and I heard it ring, a very long time, and then again, and I opened my eyes slowly, and I was awake and I knew that the stage manager was ringing for the evening performance. What did I want in the hospital? What did my dead father want? He looked so friendly and rang the bell for me.

The play that evening was *The Living Corpse*. I acted the gypsy father. My wife in the play was a beginner too, a deeply tanned girl, radiant with health. Her name was Salka Steuermann. She came from my homeland. When we had finished our scene, I asked her if she believed in dreams.

"Yes," said Salka.

"My dead father came to me this afternoon."

"Did he give you any advice?"

"Yes," I said.

"Then don't talk about it to anyone, and follow it."

I took her advice and till now I have never told my dream. I stood every night on the finest stage in Germany with the best actors in the country, but I stood there on my crooked baker's legs. Everyone could see what I myself had seen that day in the mirror. But what did my father want? It was the first time since his death that I had seen him in a dream. He brought me a message. "Tell no one, simply obey it," said my clever young countrywoman.

That evening it became clear to me that I must overcome this last obstacle. My crooked legs must be straightened. "All that is crooked can be made straight."

The following day I went to hospitals and clinics. I rang. I went to the hospital near the Reinhardt Theater. I saw doctors there. I told them my problem. They listened with interest, spoke of a risk, of courage, and of money. I was willing to take the risk, courage I had – but money I had not. As I was leaving, a young doctor followed me and made an appointment to see me at his private hospital, the Nollendorf Sanatorium.

I went there the next day. Dr. Heimann and three other young doctors received me. They made me tell them my story, examined me, consulted together, and after a long while they said that the operation could be performed. But I must sign a statement that I would accept the risk myself, and then the operation would cost me nothing. Only, after the operation, I would have to lie in a plaster cast in the sanatorium for two months, and that cost twelve marks a day, and the money for that I must somehow scrape together. I had been offered a good buy, a bargain.

I went to Baron von Gersdorff, who in the course of time had become my patron, and explained the whole matter to him. Gersdorff was a confirmed bachelor who had once been an officer in the Guards. He came of an old Prussian family who for many generations had belonged to the officers' corps, the oldest Prussian nobility. Gersdorff heard me out, took the name of the doctor and the sanatorium, and asked me to give him time to think it over.

A few days later he invited me home with him after a performance and, among other things, said: "See here, my friend, you come from the East and I from the West. You are descended from a long line of pious Jews, I from a long line of pious Prussians. You were a baker, I was an officer. And yet we have something in common: we both love the theater. With this difference, that you have a great deal of talent for acting and I none. Now you want to stake everything on one card. I understand that very well. There was a time when I staked everything on a real card, and I lost my position in society by it, which I did not want to do. But you are gambling with your eyes open, on purpose, to escape from your social position. So I have talked to Dr. Heimann. It is a difficult operation, but he is anxious to perform it. You see, everyone is ambitious in his own profession. However, he explained to me that it was a fifty-fifty chance. In your place, I should think that over very thoroughly. I have also talked with a well-to-do friend of mine, who will undertake to pay the sanatorium charges. If you ever earn a lot of money, you can simply pay it back. There is no need for you to feel that you are accepting charity."

I made my decision right there, and it remained a secret between Gersdorff and myself. The season was over. I received six weeks' wages to cover the vacation period. The first thing I bought was a revolver, in case the fifty-fifty chance should turn up the wrong fifty. No one else knew it; I did not even tell Gersdorff – it was my own private decision, and I did not intend to burden anyone else with it. I was gambling with my life on my own responsibility.

The time came. Gersdorff took me to the clinic, put his library at my disposal, together with a very convenient reading board, which you could adjust with screws and springs so that, no matter in what position you lay, you could always have your book before your eyes.

After two days I was brought into the operating room. Dr. Heimann was there, with the three young doctors who were to assist him. They talked to me cheerfully about the theater, the last opening, Reinhardt's performances in the circus, my favorite parts – they even urged me to recite something for them.

I was in good spirits – my old curiosity kept me intensely interested in the proceedings. The feeling that, here and now, something was going to happen, that the last obstacle to my self-chosen career was going to be removed, banished, raised my spirits, excited me. Everything ran through my head: all the scenes of my life flitted by, up to the time I went to the theater, up to today, up to that moment.

Meanwhile I declaimed speeches from various roles.

The doctors were excited and stimulated too. They looked at me as hungry soldiers look at a tasty, smoking roast after a long march, or as ambitious actors look at a fat part. They were delighted with their declaiming patient, who now sat up straight while they stuck him in the small of the back with a long, thin needle and injected some liquid. Then they stood around and did nothing – they seemed to be waiting for something – they kept asking questions, and I chattered away and acted quite unconcerned. But neither they nor I had our hearts in the conversation – it was merely mechanical conversation – in the background a cold tension lurked.

Then after a little they began to feel my legs. I was surprised – I saw them moving my legs, and I felt nothing. They smiled and assured me that from now on I would feel nothing, absolutely nothing. They told me to take hold of my legs myself – funny, I took hold of something that was a part of me – it was in the same place, I saw *my* legs, I grasped them, and felt nothing. My body from the waist down was without feeling, dead. They began to shave off the hair on one knee. I felt nothing.

Now they were very busy. Instruments were produced: chisel, hammer, knife. The chief surgeon made a long cut on the outer side of one knee, a strange knee. I felt nothing – only a sort of dull scraping, as if I myself were cutting open a carton. No blood flowed, the open place looked reddish – it all reminded me of a butcher shop. Then they took the hammer and chisel and struck hard, very hard – how tough a human bone is! They worked hard, oh yes, they exerted themselves to the utmost, they forgot me – and it did not hurt. Suddenly they stopped. They had gone through the bone, it was broken.

Then they suddenly remembered that it was actually my bone – they looked at me, asked how I was feeling, and urged me to recite some more. But I had no desire to recite, and I declined. I felt cold drops of sweat on my forehead and a touch of loneliness around my heart.

"Well," said the chief surgeon, the flesh cutter and bone breaker, "that's done it." He lifted my dead leg and bent it in all directions, like a strange bone in a butcher's shop. "How would you like to have it now – bowed a little as a change from the old knock-kneed effect?" And his assistants smiled their applause to his charming joke.

"Just make it nice and straight," I said, falling in with the gentleman's humor.

And my leg was carefully pulled and laid out straight and wrapped in damp plaster-soaked bandages and put in a straight splint and covered with much more plaster. Then a weight was fastened to the end of my foot and a weight on the outside of my knee, so that the bone would surely knit straight. Then I asked them to go ahead and do the other leg. They laughed, and the chief surgeon said, "No, my friend, we shall give you that pleasure five days hence."

Then I was taken down to the ward, where I lay with three other patients. The operation had lasted almost four hours. I was brought food, but I could not touch it. I tried to read, and could not – I tried to sleep, and could not. I could think of nothing but what had just happened. I thought of the way those four men had worked over me. Suddenly there was a peace and a quiet within me such as I had not felt for years. I thought of my native village and of "Little Pity" and "Thank God," I thought of old Jus Fedorkiw and my father, I thought of Horodenka and wondered whether the two bricks were still missing from the dome of the little church. I remembered Riffkele and Malka, the gallery of the theater in Lemberg, and my running away. I thought of Emil Milan and Gersdorff, and still the four men in white stood before me – then I thought of my revolver, which lay beneath my pillow, wrapped in a white handkerchief, hidden under the mattress. I reached for it with my tired hand, touched the place – yes, it was there. God be thanked!

...Many slow hours went by. Suddenly I felt an itching in my knee, something was scraping me there, shaving me – odd! Then I felt a painful cutting, then a thrust, then a blow, a hammer blow, and another and another – I cried out. It hurt horribly. I began to groan and scream. My leg was waking from the injection. It was beginning to live and to hurt insanely. Every blow of the hammer, which, before, I had seen and not felt, I now felt, without seeing it. My bones rebelled in pain.

Night came and brought chills and fever to rack me. My soft-eyed nurse, Maria, gave me something quieting and comforted me. But her sympathy only made me more wretched. The other patients awoke and were annoyed at the disturbance. I controlled myself, and they went back to sleep. Maria kept watch at my bedside and praised me for keeping hold of myself. She caressed me and whispered into my ear: "What you did was a very brave thing. Now you must grit your teeth and not give in. It's done, and it will soon be over." She gave me another pill, and it really quieted me.

The next morning the doctors came, were very charming, and praised me. Gersdorff came. They told him how humorously I had taken the operation. Gersdorff pressed my hand, asked me to tell him all about it, and I felt better and said, "Oh well, there's no such thing as physical pain."

"It's a good thing you think so, you healthy Carpathian horse! You romanticist! You are really both," he laughed, "a romanticist and a horse, a romantic Carpathian horse!"

I began to eat and to read again – only one thing troubled me: I could not get up, I could not walk, I could only half sit. I could not go to the toilet. But the nurse was so tactful and kind that I soon got over being ashamed of even those most private necessities.

The four days were over. The fifth came. I was taken to the operating room once more. This time the doctors were much calmer, and I much more nervous. It was all far more businesslike. They again asked me to recite something – much as I wanted to, I could not do it. I tried to oblige them and began to recite "To be or not to be" half aloud; I thought of the revolver under my mattress and felt gloomy. This time I shut my eyes too – I did not want to see them working on me. I was much weakened, and a cold sweat soaked my body.

A nurse attended me, took my pulse, and gave me something to drink and something to sniff.

This time it all went much faster – but to me it seemed to take much longer. And now my other leg was broken and swathed in bandages and plaster and put in a splint and hung with weights, just like the first time.

I was brought back to the ward and felt a strange, weary emptiness around my heart. I literally felt time passing – I felt that I was growing older – I felt something changing in me – I felt that I had become serious and mature. I felt my veins, the blood in them, and every nerve in my body. Maria came and wiped the cold sweat off my forehead and gave me quiet, kind attentions, and a look that was far beyond what her duty demanded. I asked her to arrange the desk for me and began to read.

It was Dostoevski's *The Brothers Karamazov*. I read slowly and quietly, so that the people in the book stood visibly before me. When I came to the passage where Ivan, the son, beats his own father, creeps into a barn and opens his desperate heart to his youngest brother, Alyosha, and then asks him, "What is the use of it all? What is the use of it all?" – I stopped reading, for the stupor had left my body – my body came back to life, and the cutting and the hammering of the operation were living things. In my bones and in my brain hammered, "What is the use of it all? What is the use of it all?" My pulses raced, my heart pounded loudly.

Sister Maria brought supper and took my book away. I took a spoonful of soup and then another, and the hammering in my leg and my head stormed: What is the use of it all? What is the use of it all? And I spat out the soup, and I shivered and shook, and tears choked me, and everything became dark around me, and my fears and my fever cried out: What is the use of it all, what is the use of it all, what is the use of it all?

It lasted only a few minutes – my roommates, who before had been impatient with me, looked at me quietly and sympathetically. I was bathed in a stream of sweat, my excitement died away, and I became quiet. Maria was sitting by my bed; she stroked me tenderly – I closed my eyes and felt ashamed before the others and before myself. But the feeling of oppression had really become less, as if I had lost a burden – I felt better and quieter and pretended to doze and then dropped off into a real sleep.

At night I woke, a different man – I opened my eyes slowly. Maria was still sitting there. It was her turn for night duty. She looked at me, smiling softly, and whispered, "Do you feel better?"

"Yes," I said.

"I knew it," said she, and without any ceremony bent over and kissed me on the forehead.

I stretched out my arms, drew her to me, and said softly, "Kiss me, Maria, kiss me."

She did not resist, she only looked around to see if the others were asleep and whispered, "If you will promise me to go back to sleep..." And she kissed me like a girl, like a real woman, and I drank my fill of her warmth and her mouth – long, very long, until I was filled with her kisses and her tenderness; and it left me with a long, sweet aftertaste, and she tucked me in carefully and tenderly, and I fell asleep like a babe at the breast.

Next day, Gersdorff came and said, " You are pale, Louise, like lemonade.'"

"Yes," I said, "I must take it back – there *is* such a thing as physical pain."

He told me that he had already talked with the doctor, who had assured him that the operation had been a hundred per cent successful, and that I was the best patient he could have asked for.

Weeks passed – I began to recover and to feel bored. Gersdorff set me a task: I was to write him a synopsis of each book that I read – it would keep me occupied and give me practice in German. But it did not suffice. I became impatient and bored.

One of my neighbors in the ward was a young man, somewhat crippled, a wise-cracking know-it-all. With him I discussed the theater. Or rather: we had regular quarrels – besides which, we had a mutual dislike for each other. He was also jealous because Maria paid more attention to me than to him. One day he made a dirty crack about "love." I insulted him, and he reported me to the head nurse, Agathe – me and Sister Maria.

Agathe was an officer's widow who had seen "better days." She was old and hard and stiff as a broomstick. She had a thin, cross-looking mouth, was self-righteous, and was always in a bad humor. She came in one day when Maria was bending over me, about to kiss me – she discharged Maria on the spot. Then she made a scene with me – not over Maria, but because she found an ink spot on my coverlet.

"You'll pay for that coverlet," she screamed. "I shall send Baron von Gersdorff the bill – let him know, too, how you behave here."

While she was scolding me, I took the ink bottle, slowly opened it and poured it quietly, drop by drop, onto my coverlet, glu glu glu glu glu, until it was empty and the coverlet had a gay pied pattern all over it. "I can do what I like with my own coverlet!"

She telephoned to Gersdorff, who came at once and flatly sided with me.

Thin-lipped Head Nurse Agathe hated me. I did all that I could to nourish her hatred. One day I tied a soupspoon to the head of my bed with a piece of string, and whenever she came in I picked up the spoon as if it were a telephone and pretended to talk over it: "Hello," I called into the soup-spoon-telephone, "The Nollendorf Insane Asylum speaking. No, not sanatorium – insane asylum. What? Head Nurse Agathe? Oh, she is a sweet, kind person – oh no. What? On the contrary! She is very nice to the patients, particularly to me! When my inkwell accidentally spilled over my bed the other day she didn't say a word. On the contrary, she comforted me – I was very unhappy about it."

She called the head doctor, who heard her out, laughed, winked at me and said: "Can't you see he is an actor? And he has to practice his profession. You mustn't be offended at that! After all, it was his legs I broke, not yours. Let him amuse himself a little...."

Soon the two months were over. The splints were taken off, the plaster removed – suddenly, freed from their bandages, I saw, instead of two crooked knock-kneed legs, two straight, pale things that looked like two thin sticks. They were stiff, I could not use them. They could not yet carry my body. I was taken to a suburb of Berlin, where my knees were given a course of massage that hurt even more than the operation had.

But soon I was able to stand, to stand on my own legs, but with the help of crutches. When I made my first attempt to walk, Gersdorff came again and confessed that he had been very uneasy. It had really been extremely dangerous. The doctors had warned him most earnestly. "Well," he said, "what would you really have done if the operation had failed?"

I pulled the loaded revolver, still wrapped in a white handkerchief, from its hiding place and handed it to him without a word. And he put it in his pocket quite casually and said: "It's a good thing you gave me that piece of junk. I'm sure you haven't a license for it. I'll give it to the police lost-and-found office. You stupid Carpathian horse!"

Within three months I could get around very well with canes; when half a year had passed, I went back to the theater, without them! Just as before! Only now my legs were straight! The last sign of my past had been removed. The last hindrance to my new profession had vanished.

My friends congratulated me and said they had never noticed that my legs were crooked. Well, possibly! But I had noticed it. And I believed that my crooked knock-knees stood in my way. I could not forget the beggar woman in Zaleszczyki who had reproached me with my big hands and my baker's legs – and compared them to her little son's small hands and feet. In every young colleague I saw a little son with small hands and straight legs. My hands had not troubled me so far – but my legs! Now they had been broken and were straight!" All that is crooked can be made straight," my father said to me in my dream before the operation. I obeyed him.

The revolver was gone. The obstacle was gone. I felt a great, quiet joy in my heart. "And the crooked shall be straight." Now I knew that nothing more stood in my way. I believed it fully and wholly, and my heart filled with self-confidence and happiness. The last obstacle was overcome. The way was open.

And the crooked was straight.

29

Alas for a Beautiful World!

With my legs straightened, I returned to the theater, which looked like a ripe wheat field bearing a bumper crop in my faraway, flat Galician homeland. It was the season of 1913–14, the harvest time of the Reinhardt Theater, the high point in the development of that great artist. The previous years had already brought productions that were like great theatrical festivals. After the *Oedipus* in the Schumann Circus, both parts of *Faust* came to the main stage. The second part of *Faust* took Berlin by storm. The performance began at five-thirty in the afternoon and ended at twelve-thirty at night. From eight to nine there was an intermission, and the audience went out to dinner. And the Kaiser's chancellor, Bethmann-Hollweg, came to the theater in the afternoon in a frock coat and after the intermission he reappeared in full dress. Not only the actors, the audience too changed their costumes. The leading parts were prepared by two or even three actors. As at the races, if anything happened to one horse there was another ready to continue in his place. The papers were full of theatrical news and greenroom gossip. Then *The Miracle* returned to the circus, and after it, the *Oresteia*. Orestes (Moissi) was hunted therein by the Furies of Greek mythology with strongly plastic, alfresco-like gestures, supported by a powerful speaking chorus which made the five thousand spectators shudder.

In the afternoons children and grownups were intoxicated by Maeterlinck's *Blue Bird* with music by Humperdinck: Bread and Sugar and Fire and Cat and Dog talked like human beings and escorted the children through their dreams. Sugar, the sweet thing, broke off one of its fingers, and good, faithful Bread cut a slice out of its belly, to feed the children on their wanderings.

In the other corner of the court, on the small stage, new playwrights were getting a hearing: Strindberg and Wedekind. In Strindberg's work, the sexes, man and woman, fought in a suppressed, stifled speech. The hero was Suspicion. Bourgeois society, so prone to be lulled into the illusory sleep of bluebird romanticism, was pilloried. The false relations of society were analyzed in a new, hard language, their filthy roots exposed. When the curtain fell after Sheet Lightning, the respectable audience sat there shocked and racked for minutes, unable to applaud.

Here Wedekind had his first performances. He himself blared the leading roles of his plays across the footlights. He raved over the stage like a fanatical prophet and shot his accusing speeches at a curious, shocked audience. In his *Franziska* there were two roles, named "Swine-dog." The actors were tied back to back by their arms; one wore a pig mask, the other a dog's head. They were the censorship and the critics. "Swine-dog" grunted and barked, outraged by beauty, which came on the stage in the form of a naked girl. The play was banned. There was a play called *Hydalla*, in which a certain "Dwarf-giant" who fights for truth and beauty is exploited and abused by his friends and society and is finally so persecuted and driven into a corner that he hangs himself with a rope without having time to soap it. There was *King Nikolo* too – his enemies dethrone and exile him, but he returns to his country as a wandering comedian, and, as such, sobs out his own story in the market place so sincerely and genuinely that he is pronounced the best of clowns. His successor, the erstwhile master butcher, does him the honor to hire him as court jester.

At the same time Reinhardt was producing his Shakespeare cycle on the big stage: *Lear and Hamlet* and the comedies and the historical plays. A wealth, a harvest of theater, on which several generations were able afterward to live. At least a hundred of the best actors of the period had been brought together – at their head were Bassermann and Schildkraut, Moissi and Viktor Arnold, Wassermann and Abel, and, among the women Else Heims, Gertrude Eisoldt, Tilla Durieux, Lucie Hoeflich, Camilla Eibenschuetz, and many others. The younger generation were represented by Ernst Lubitsch, Wilhelm Murnau, Fritz Kortner, Joseph Schildkraut, Conrad Veidt, young Danneggers, and many, many more.

We, the young, stood in the wings and watched the rehearsals, filled with enthusiasm and shyness and solemn devotion. But we were not alone in revering Reinhardt so greatly. The public, the people of Berlin in those days of the Kaiser, honored him more than they did their Kaiser. Who wanted to talk about Lehmann – as Kaiser, with his pointed, turned-up mustaches, was called? But not to talk about Reinhardt was to be uneducated. We young people were very proud to be members of his company. Yes, it was illusionistic theater, holiday theater, pleasure theater, in contrast to the later political and problem theater.

It was the great era of development, of culture, in Germany – there were already many socialists in the Parliament – workers and intellectuals had already founded the Volksbuehne, where new social plays were produced. The poet of the poor had already been discovered: Gerhard Hauptmann. The Silesian weavers rebelled on the stage, the Kaiser had given up his box, a wind of progress was stirring the air. The theater was the center of the epoch.

In the old Café des Westens sat artists, philosophers, politicians, painters, bohemians, young and old together, and they attacked and criticized the "common enemy," the slumbering Philistines, the empty-headed petit bourgeoisie. Franz Pfemfert brought out his aggressive, independent newspaper,

Die Aktion. He wrote his bold leading articles full of political attacks and printed new writers: Franz Werfel, Paul Boldt, Ernst Blass, Franz Blei, Richard Dehmel, Maxim Gorki, August Strindberg, and many more. Groups sat around the tables at the Café des Westens and discussed new trends in politics, and everyone knew that a great change must come.

I had a feeling of satisfaction – it had been worth while! This was a different world from standing by the trough or the oven in a bakery. When I wore tights now, I saw my straight legs and was pleased by them. I was pleased by my decision to have them operated on, I was pleased by the successful operation, I was pleased by my growing self-confidence, and I knew that henceforth I should go forward unchecked. I had but touched the hem of my ambition, yet I was already filled with happiness. To stand on the stage was for me what serving God was for my father – except that it was more joyful!

Life in the theater is not only colorful and rich in variation, it is long. You live far longer than ordinary mortals. How short and monotonous an ordinary human life in comparison with the life of an actor! If a man has the luck not to die early of measles, smallpox, scarlet fever, diphtheria, typhoid, pneumonia, or plain hunger – he reaches seventy. Out of his birth, he gets nothing – the pleasure is all his father's. Baptism, falling in love, getting engaged, getting married – birthdays, silver wedding, golden wedding – the grave! Nothing in the funeral for him either: the baked meats are eaten by his friends. But an actor – first of all he has opening nights! Those are high holidays! The discovery of a new playwright, of a new play, or even finding something new in old Goethe or old Shakespeare – and then, the many years that an actor can live in his parts. For example, consider the ages of these characters:

	Age:
Lear	112
Mephisto	50
Hamlet	30

Franz Moor	25
Shylock	60
Othello	40

These add up to 317 years, which, as a good actor, you can live in exactly one year. So if you act for thirty years, you live 9,510 rich years, instead of a pitiful seventy. The Chinese reckoning goes back five thousand years. So an actor can be twice as old as the Chinese reckoning and five times as old as the Christian. What does it matter when, to gain 9,510 joyful years, you stake but a wretched seventy! I had gambled on the operation, and now a 10,000-year realm beckoned me. I had every reason to be happy.

When the historic theatrical season of 1913–14 came to an end, I decided to take a walking trip through Germany, for two reasons: first, to try out my new legs, second, to become acquainted with the country and the people. To study these new countrymen of mine, whom, in the course of time, I should have to act on the stage.

I set out in the direction of Kassel – I just had money enough to get there. In Kassel my money came to an end. As a traveling journeyman baker, I used to go to bakeries, speak my password, and always received help from my fellow bakers. Here I went to call on my new colleagues and was disillusioned. They were stiff and haughty. In my new trade there are only the "great," who are glad to be worshiped, and the "small," who are glad to serve. No baker's warmth, no solidarity. A wonderful, a magnificent profession – but full of envy and jealousy and poison.

From Kassel I took to the highroad, which is a world in itself. It was summer, you could sleep in the hay and there were shelters, you spent the night and went on. I began to go "on the bum." And it satisfied my curiosity and it was fun, for I knew that I should be getting my salary again in August. In the first village near Giessen I went into the village inn and asked if I could have something to eat without paying for it.

"Why, yes," said the hard-worked hostess, "here is some bread and drippings."

"I'd like to have something to put on it, too," I said good-naturedly. "Haven't got it," was the answer.

"Then good-by," and with a "Thank you," I left the inn.

The few peasants who were sitting there over their beer grinned. When I had got outside, one of them knocked on the window, called me back, and bought me a thick ham sandwich and a glass of beer. After a little conversation he said: "Just so you won't go home and say that a German village lets a man go by hungry…" I promised to make a true report.

One night I came to a little town, ran into a policeman, and asked him where I could spend the night. He said that the nearest shelter was in the next town, three hours' walk away. I was tired, and it was already midnight. I asked him to arrest me, so that I could go to sleep.

"Well," said the bemustached guardian of the law, "I can't do that. It's against the regulations. Of course, if you committed a crime or attacked me, I'd be obliged to arrest you!"

Whereupon I let out a loud yell and made a grab for his saber.

"You fresh guy, come along, you're under arrest." He led me into a cell in the town jail. I went to sleep at once, and about seven o'clock in the morning he brought me a pot of black coffee and a chunk of bread and wished me luck on the road.

In Bad Nauheim there was air that you could not only breathe, you could take hold of it. Take hold of it, touch it, with nose and face and eyes. It smelled of all sorts of flowers and foliage and roots. Close hedges, beautiful gardens, avenues of shady old trees – it was eleven o'clock in the morning. I stood in front of the great Kurhaus, with its garden restaurant; the tables were set, a direct invitation to eat. My belly was hungry and my eyes were hungry. My mouth watered with hunger. I was ready to do anything for food. Such a wonderful odor, such a lovely landscape, and such an empty belly – funny, I was starved to death and in good spirits at the same time.

I saw a big, stout gentleman in a cutaway with a rosy, freshly shaved face and a thick, turned-up Wilhelm mustache, giving orders to the waiters. There were no guests about. I went up to him. "You wish – ?" asked the gentleman. I looked him in the eye and told him my life history in three sentences: actor, the operation, traveling to study, hunger!

He called a waiter and ordered a five-course lunch. The waiter asked whether I would prefer beer or wine, and, if wine, whether white or red. I chose wine, red wine, it goes without saying! A feast! When I had finished, I went to the man in the cutaway to tender my thanks. "Oh, just send me a couple of passes some time – I'm glad you enjoyed it!"

I wandered on to Lindau on the Swiss border, then turned back; on the road I encountered carpenters from Hamburg, young apprentices – others again who spend their lives on the road and despise us who wander only seasonally, the runaway sonny boys and various sorts of wanderers. There were homosexuals on the road too, and they always had the addresses of fine gentlemen in various places.

I joined a group of carpenters who were heading for Bavaria. When I arrived in Munich, suddenly the placards announced the murder of the Austrian Archduke in Serbia. Austria declared war. The old Emperor said: "I am spared nothing." The town seethed with excitement. Every half-hour there was a new extra. Notes were published; the kings and kaisers of Europe sent telegrams beseeching one another not to declare war. One could not make head or tail of it. No one wanted war, and everyone plunged into it.

I went to a theater and found some actors there whom I had known in Berlin. They bought me a ticket back.

Berlin was drunk with war enthusiasm. Students and soldiers entering the Army, half of them in civilian clothes, sang songs. The Kaiser shouted in the palace square: "I know no more parties, only Germans! And now we shall thrash them. I did not want this war!" I understood nothing of it all.

I went to the theater. Everything was in confusion. Some of the actors were already in uniform. My best friend, Wangenheim, was one of them, and when I parted from him in the evening he asked me suspiciously whether I was not really a spy. Suddenly I was a foreigner. My best friend no longer trusted me. Rehearsals were interrupted – it looked as if the stream of life had stopped running – as if the whole of life had suddenly come to an end.

I went to the Austrian consulate, where I was accepted for military service. I was given orders to join the Austrian Army and a free railway ticket home.

Berlin suddenly swarmed with all sorts of news, gossip, rumors, spy scares. Two "nuns" were arrested – but they were not nuns, they were two disguised Russian officers who were trying to kill the Kaiser. The poor Kaiser! Every minute there were new extras, new decrees. Suddenly we heard that Belgium intended to betray Germany. But the German armies were already there. The fortress of Luettich (Liége) was stormed single-handed by General Emmich. The papers praised the general in verses:

> *Up then spoke Emmich:*
> *"By God, I'll take it!"*

There were other funny poems in the papers:

> *Every blow a Frenchman,*
> *Every shot a Russian*
> *Serbs must die-ie-ie.**

Ha, ha, ha, how funny! I was ready to leave and went to the theater to say good-by. My patron, Gersdorff, had fallen at Liége. I was deeply affected. Many actors were already in uniform. Reinhardt was at a rehearsal, serious and preoccupied. Suddenly the comedian Viktor Arnold appeared. The

---

*These verses have a humorous rhyme in the original German.

short, stout, whimsical man who, as Georges Dandin, wept real tears with his audience – he wept for grief, while his audience wept with joy and laughter; the eternal actor with the clown-mask of genius. He rushed on the stage, threw himself at Reinhardt's feet, and wept desperately: "Herr Reinhardt, what now, what next? The world is destroyed, is going to ruin, this beautiful world, the deluge, the end of the world!"

Arnold the comedian sobbed and wept, no one could quiet him. He was taken home. When he was alone again, he broke a windowpane, cut his throat with a splinter of glass, and bled to death.

The kings and the kaisers lied when they said that they did not want the war! They had prepared it and created it and sent their people out to mutual slaughter. Here was a comedian, an artist, a man who felt in his heart the destructiveness of war. *He* had *really* not wanted it! He really could not bear it, the war, and he preferred death to living in a world in which men who believed in God, who had the Scriptures, who were the heirs of the great spiritual treasures of culture, could find no other way out but to shoot bullets into one another's skulls and stick bayonets into one another's bellies.

The greathearted actor, the comedian who, laughing himself, made others laugh, Viktor Arnold, left such a world of his own free will. Alas for the artist Viktor Arnold, and alas for a beautiful world!

30

Almost a Stranger in My Native Land

With my heart pounding I left Berlin, bound eastward from the same Schlesische Bahnhof by which I had entered it years before. Much had happened in that time, and alas that it had all to be broken off!

The trains were packed. We met troop trains with the famous cattle cars, forty men or eight horses, open cars loaded with canvas-covered cannon and scrawled with comic inscriptions and caricatures at which no one laughed. At the station similar troop trains overtook us – and there we were fed too. At every little town at which we stopped there were committees: ladies served sandwiches, cake, coffee, beer. People sang out optimistic remarks, everyone was a prophet, a Lord of Hosts, all-wise, and an armchair strategist. Every civilian and soldier had detailed information about everything, how and where and when we would be victorious, would fight the enemy, how Germany would soon have the Russians, the French, the English – whom God wanted to "punish" anyway – in her pocket, and be *"ueber alles."*

I was an ally, an Austrian. I was accepted and nicknamed "Comrade Laced-boots," an allusion to the drawing-room elegance of Austrian officers.

Germany was drunk with war and with conquest. The papers were full of pictures – the Kaiser's, the princes', the generals'.

Everyone was convinced that the campaign would be a "pushover," that the enemy would be done for in six weeks, and that every German would have a fat goose in his pot for Christmas and a "bed of laurels" on which to rest after fighting.

When I reached the Austrian border, the picture suddenly changed. The enemy armies, known as the Russian steam roller, had already broken through in the east. We had already begun to make "strategic retreats." Refugees had already been driven from house and home. There was no war enthusiasm. Soldiers and the civilian population spoke Czech, Polish, Ukrainian, Hungarian, Slovenian, German – a babel of different languages. People did not understand one another as they did in Germany; there was mutual suspicion. It was said that the Czech women in Prague had pulled their soldier husbands out of the trains, that the soldiers had thrown away their arms and had been shot – yes, the Czechs and Slovaks suddenly did not want to die for the nice old Emperor, yet he himself had said that he had been spared nothing.

Here, in Austria, all would have been happy if they had been spared this war. You already saw wounded from the Russian and Serbian fronts. The latter said that the Serbs had given them a far from friendly reception. Women had even poured boiling oil on them from the houses, and old men and "malicious children" had fallen on them from ambushes. "Malicious children" – yes, there were those, too. The soldiers admitted, however, that the Serbs were extraordinarily brave.

At the induction centers the procedure was as follows: You were asked whether you had already served in the Army or not. Those who had served were given railroad tickets to join their regiments, and they had to make their own way to regimental headquarters. Those who had not served were sent to a reception camp for training, and thus at once began the "merry" life of a soldier.

I saw that I was in a fix. To be a soldier, to go to the front, eventually to fall – for that I was ready (for even here my curiosity tickled me) – after all, there were millions headed for the same fate. But first I wanted to go home – to see little Mama, the village, the town – I had been away from home fourteen years – were the two bricks still missing from the dome of the little church?

And I had not "served," poor I! Why not tell a little lie? They did not want this war; well, I didn't want it either. One little lie more or less obviously didn't matter.

All this ran through my head as I stood in line outside the despatching office. Suddenly a well-fed sergeant major was asking me, "Have you served?"

"Yes, Sergeant, sir," was the answer.

"Where?"

"Twenty-fourth Infantry Regiment, Kolomea."

And there I was with a railroad ticket to Kolomea, and I was free to set out.

I went to the railroad station and took the route through Prague. I wanted to see what the Czechs were doing. But no one was rebelling there. They shouted *"Nazdar"* and handed out food. I was fed free at the stations, I was a free man, with free transportation, who, before he went to die for his old Emperor, wanted to see his home once more. I was much excited.

The farther east I traveled, the sadder everything became. I reached Lemberg. Three of my brothers were already soldiers. Two already at the front and one, Schabse, with whom I had gone to school, had just been called up. I visited him at the barracks. He had just gone to sleep when I arrived; he jumped up and looked at me, half sleepily, half reproachfully, just as he always did when we were still at school, in case I had something up my sleeve. "So there you are! Where have you been all this time?" Then he suddenly cried and said, "I have two of the sweetest little girls – they're with my wife in Kolomea. I don't know how they can get along without me. It's only for them I'm sorry."

Then we went with my other sister-in-law and my elder brother and his grown children to the cemetery, to visit the grave of our father, who had died from an operation during my absence. I saw the piece of ground where my father lay, and I could not grasp it, and I would so gladly have looked into his kind, honest eyes and told him everything! It was denied me. He whom I most loved was there no longer.

After that I went on to Kolomea, where my regiment was. But I did not leave the train there. I went on to Horodenka, my town. Home.

None of the Germans I knew in Berlin had had a good word for Galicia. Rumania, Bulgaria, Hungary, Serbia, Montenegro – no one took offense when these Balkan countries were mentioned. But mention the word "Galicia," and everyone turned up his nose. From the slow-moving local train I looked now at that fat, sleepy earth. I devoured the beauty of those green, green hills, of those little winding streams, those lakes, those dreamy woods. It was all much more beautiful than I remembered – and the people in the train! They had a broad calm, and curiosity at the sight of a stranger. How pleasantly the homely Ukrainian of the villagers, the Yiddish of the townsmen, fell on my ear!

They questioned me, and I told them about Berlin. They wanted to know everything – what such a faraway world looks like, what the people live on, what sort of soil you find there, and prices, and whether the Kaiser ever quarrels with his wife, and what the royal family has to eat on Sunday.

Broad-hipped, full-breasted girls with downcast, burning eyes, and complexions like the native rye dough – they were certainly still children when I left home – smiled at me interrogatively. There was Okno, the last station before Horodenka. Soon the first peasant houses were visible, then, far off, the Romaschkamm estate – we were there! Horodenka-Mjasto: The town of Horodenka! Home!

The little station looked even smaller. Koppale Zankie was waiting with his one-horse rig, with which he drove people into town for five kreuzer. Just as he did years ago, when I left town for the first time. There were white streaks now in his reddish-brown beard.

The conveyance was already full, and he was the first to recognize me. Suddenly I was surrounded, everyone was shaking my hand. None of my relatives was there. I had sent no word. Koppale embraced me like a brother and called to his passengers, "Children, you must all get out. I must drive him into town alone. Alone, on the back seat."

And we started, and Koppale went on, "Just let them see you in the upper streets, just let banker Jungermann see you – let them all see that the lower streets produce great men too!"

I wanted to sit beside him and drive the chestnut mare.

"Oh no," he said, "you must sit up there by yourself, like a real gentleman, and it won't cost you anything either. I'll take you to your mama – that's a good deed I've been waiting a long time to do. Yes, yes, we've heard about you, you're a famous man in the wide world – oh yes, a distinguished visitor," and he cracked his whip so the people turned to look, and he winked and shouted: "Do you know who that is? It's Aaron's Isaiah, the Granach from Germany – he's traveled all over the world."

I was trembling; it was all I could do to restrain my emotion. "Did you remember to tell them that we Horodenkans are nice people too?"

Horodenka! We had reached the broad avenue of chestnuts, the market place; the first thing I looked at was the gay little onion-domed church – and there, yes, thank heaven, the two bricks were still missing! Lord, how those two missing bricks, where the owls had nested, had stayed with me all the time I was abroad! Home! Home, with the two missing bricks!

Koppale drove me to my uncle's – Mother had married again, and he did not want to bring me straight to see the man who had taken my father's place. I was grateful to him for that. I did not want to see him either.

My uncle's house was soon packed – vodka and herring and black bread went round. It was gay; I was plied with questions. I, nothing loath, discoursed upon everything that I knew as well as upon everything that I didn't know.

Then little Mama came running, still wiping her hands on her apron, as she had always done; she did not look at me, she threw her arms around me and kissed me and held me so for a long time – then, like a little girl showing off her big brother, she looked round and accepted the congratulations and banter of the company.

"Riffke, he's taller than you are."

She laughed: "All my sons are taller than I am."

"How many does that make that you've given the Kaiser?" asked another.

"Are you a soldier?" she asked. "Then he's the fourth, God be praised!"

And she drank a vodka and chattered and laughed, and everyone talked at once and kept asking more questions, and so perhaps half an hour passed, and she still had me in her arms, and then she looked into my eyes and became still and sad, and two tears rolled down her face, and she began to sob softly, then louder and louder until she was weeping really desperately. I could hardly quiet her. "Mama, Mama, you were so gay – what's happened to you?"

"My child, my little son," she sobbed, "I don't recognize you. Again I don't recognize you!" And she cried softly. What did she mean by "again"?

I was given a bed in my aunt's kitchen. Her daughter Anna I still liked. When her mother had gone to sleep, Anna came to me and suddenly said, intimately: "You know I have always been fond of you. You can tell me all about it. I'll be as silent as the grave. I won't tell a soul! Give you my word of honor. Just between us. Tell me the truth: Was it you, or wasn't it?" Whereupon I learned the following story:

Three years previous a circus had come to town, and one of the young performers looked like me. My little sister Matele hung around the circus all day looking at him. Needless to say, he looked at her too – she was very pretty, just fourteen years old, and he was seventeen. So all day long they looked at each other and smiled and looked, until one day my little sister asked him, "Please tell me, aren't you my brother Isaiah, maybe?"

"Why, of course I'm your brother Isaiah," the boy answered.

My little sister ran straight home and told Mother that I was in the circus, but didn't want people to recognize me; but I had finally admitted to her that I was her brother.

"Doesn't want to be recognized?" cried my brave little mother in great agitation, and hurried off to see her perfidious son. She raised a tumult – neighbors, relatives, young fellows who had gone to school with me followed her. A vast crowd besieged the circus. Little Mama wept and shrieked, the crowd backed her up and yelled: "What baseness, what perfidy, what heartlessness! A son who won't let his own mother know him!"

My schoolmates wanted to refresh my memory with a beating. The young performer was white as chalk. No, he wasn't her son, he had only been joking, he absolutely wasn't, he cried.

"Look, these breasts gave you suck!" cried little Mama in desperation.

The police came, arrested the false son together with the director, who produced before the burgomaster in person papers which showed that he had taken the boy ten years before from an orphanage in a distant part of Hungary. So the matter ended.

But when the circus left Horodenka, the whole town became firmly convinced that it had really been I, and so it remained.

And now, when I assured my cousin on my word of honor that it had not been I, she said: "All right, I won't ask you again. I expected you to tell me the truth. I know it was you. Otherwise you wouldn't keep on lying about it."

Mama too believed that it had really been I. For when I went to the village to visit my eldest brother, she saw me off and made me an earnest, motherly discourse: "Well, my child, I won't urge any more. You are grown up now, and you must know what you are doing. But the other boys who leave Horodenka come back one after another, and marry, and settle down. Even Edziu Gruenberg, the smith's son, the wildest of them all, who has traveled all over the world – he even went to Czernowitz – came home and married, and he has two sweet children. And you? Someday – God forbid! – you'll fall off one of those horses and hurt yourself, and then what will you have? At least promise me to give up this circus business after the war and settle down and marry and raise children. I should so love to have grandchildren in your house." I promised her all that she asked.

And I returned to visit my native village, where my eldest brother was living just as my father had lived before him. His wife, in the meantime, had also borne him a houseful of children, and he himself looked just like Father and had an eldest son who looked just as he had in the old days. And his son managed the household, just as, in our house, he himself had been my father's deputy.

The first evening the parlor was filled with peasants. I was plied with questions and again told long, long stories. The next day I had ceased to be a guest and fell to work as though I had been a member of the household for years. I kneaded black earth and water and straw with my feet and helped to repair the stable.

The children were around me all day and assailed me with questions about my new, fabulous profession, and I explained to them in detail what the theater was, with examples and summaries of various plays, and they understood it all and were enthralled. They liked best the story of the Moor of Venice; their sympathies wavered back and forth between Othello and Desdemona.

That night we all sat in the parlor, and my sister-in-law said: "You've been telling the children about your theater all day. I'm not the stupidest person in the world, you might tell me one of your stories – or even show me one of your tricks – anyone can tell stories, show me, let me see what it's like!"

I took a sharp knife in my right hand, shut my eyes, muttered to myself, held up my left hand, and began to explain: "Look at the palm of my left hand. Do you see a hole in it?"

"No," she said, half amused and yet interested, "there's no hole in it."

"Now then," I continued, "I shall count three, then I shall stick the knife through my hand, then it will fly through my left eye, then through the window, then it will come in quietly by the door and lay itself on the table. Hocus-pocus, comgalamora, contrawango, tschinda, dagor, one, two, three — "

"Stop, no, no!" she cried, fearfully excited. "I don't want to see it, I don't want it done, above all not in my house."

The others began to laugh, but she kept looking at me suspiciously, as though I were some strange wizard and conjuror. It amused me to pass as such in her eyes, and I said equivocally, "Well, I'm rather tired today and I'd rather sleep in the hay in the barn tonight."

I saw from her look that in any case she would not have slept under the same roof with me.

So, about three o'clock in the morning, when I was sound asleep, someone cautiously waked me. It was little Donia, twelve years old and radiant with health. She rode a horse better than her eldest brother.

"What is it, child?"

"Oh, Uncle, I couldn't sleep, and because you're leaving in the morning I wanted to ask you one more thing."

My eyes became accustomed to the half-darkness, and Donia said, "Please, Uncle, tell me the truth: if Mama hadn't stopped you, would the knife really have flown through your hand and then through your left eye and then through the window and then come back through the door like a person and laid itself on the table?"

"What do you think would have happened, Donia?"

"That's just why I couldn't get to sleep. I just can't imagine it."

"Then you're right, my child; between ourselves, I can't imagine it either."

"You were just teasing Mama because she doesn't like you?"

"Yes, because this noon, she slipped your big brother half a glass of vodka and didn't give me any."

"Shall I bring you one now, with a piece of honey cake?"

"So you want to buy my friendship, eh? Bribe me so that I won't hoodwink you like that?"

"Yes, and because I like you, Uncle, really like you."

And she vanished. I am sure that, if it had not been dark, I should have seen her blush – her voice sounded as if there were a blush on her face.

She came straight back with a large glass of vodka and honey cakes, and we sat there, talking merrily, and it began to dawn. My brother rose to milk the cow, and Donia told him the whole story of the conjuration, and he milked the cow and laughed aloud until the cow turned her head and stared in big-eyed wonder at the laughing milker. But we could not explain it to the cow, for she would have understood it no better than her sister, my brother's wife.

So the next day I set off, and left behind a good, clever niece and an unpleasant, stupid sister-in-law, who has never yet found out what the theater is, poor thing!

I arrived in Kolomea, where I was to join my Twenty-fourth Infantry Regiment. But the regiment had just left. Russian patrols had been seen in the nearby villages. The Austrian Army was in retreat. Every hour brought new, sensational rumors. The prosperous section of the community had long ago fled to the interior of Austria. The next day word went around: The enemy is coming. But no one came.

The following day artillery fire and rifle shots could be heard, but far off. Soon smoke was seen rising from the nearby villages. A part of the suburbs was afire, and the railway station.

I went to the market, near the town hall, and crept along slowly close to the walls – my old curiosity at work. No one to be seen anywhere. Suddenly, on the sidewalk, as if he had sprung out of the earth, a sweating Cossack on horseback – he had stopped, and with his carbine pointed at me asked in a frightened voice, "Are there any soldiers here?"

"No," said I, very friendly and courteous. He looked just like Paul Wegener, the actor, as Holofernes.

He galloped away, and I ran into the nearest house and peered through a window into the market place. The same Cossack returned with four others, slowly, watching the sidewalks, the walls of the houses. Then from another direction came a similar group. And a group from the left, and one from the right – soon a good-sized detachment galloped through the town into the market place. A white flag was slowly raised on the town hall. A few of the Cossacks jumped from their horses and went into the town hall – the Russian flag was hauled up. Then gradually other bodies of troops appeared. The town was occupied. I was in enemy territory. It was September 1914.

I lived in the house of my sister-in-law, the wife of the brother whom I had visited in the barracks at Lemberg. We soon grew accustomed to the Russians, but not to being hungry. As if for fun, I went to my baker neighbors and remarked that I was still good at my old trade. I went to work and thus supported my brother's wife and two children and myself.

I now knew that the war had not only interrupted Reinhardt's theatrical harvest, but my development as well. I need hardly have gone through having my legs straightened just for this! However, I thought, every day thousands of soldiers are killed and many are wounded and crippled – I should be happy that I am not one of them. Meanwhile, I'm alive, and someday when it is all over I'll go on. Yes, the chief thing is to be alive! The living have hopes and plans. A dead soldier has neither.

So I decided to live, and wait until the time should come when I could resume my career. What a good thing it was that I had my old trade! It was a sort of capital. After all, my excursion into the theater was an adventure. But when naked life takes you by the throat, it is good to be able to resist, to have a reserve. My trade as a baker was my reserve, my capital. A world at war, armies withdrawing, others entering, generals making plans, towns changing masters – but everyone needing bread. I baked bread, provided food for others and for myself, and bided my time – almost a stranger now in my native land.

31

The Prospect for the Common Man

The front shifted farther and farther west. The Russians reached Lemberg, Przemysl was besieged. We were behind the Russian line. The same girls who had smiled at Austrian officers on the sidewalks now smiled at Russian officers. Life bloomed again. Some lines of business even had a boom: restaurants, cafés, and especially brothels were packed. The bakeries also worked at full speed. They supplied bread to the Russian Army and did a good business.

Life was restricted, of course – there was curfew, there were harsh edicts, now and then a Jew was flogged or hanged for alleged espionage, there were heavy taxes – but life went on.

Winter came. The Galician winter, when the earth puts on a thick white cloak to protect her trees and her seeds from the bitter east wind. The children went coasting and sliding as in other years. The air was cuttingly cold, the snow crunched under your feet – in such weather it is almost a pleasure to work in a bakery.

One morning the baker waked me – I was to go with him to collect a payment of several hundred rubles from a Cossack regiment. The sergeant paymaster had been drunk and had thrown him out, and he could not go to an officer because he spoke neither Russian nor German. He promised me a share of the money if I succeeded in obtaining payment for the bread he had furnished.

We entered the sergeant's office – and found ourselves in an unroarious carousal. We were received with drunken jibes and thrown out.

Going home, the baker said, "Well, I'll have to charge it to overhead. We've already made plenty of money out of them. It's not as bad as it might be."

In me the incident awakened a kind of sporting curiosity – I decided to take the battle of the unpaid bread into my own hands. I went back to the barracks alone, without telling anyone. The drunken soldiers poured vodka over me and drove me out with their nagaikas, giving me a few lashes on my skull and back.

Crossing the barracks yard, I ran straight into the arms of an old colonel to whom another officer was just reporting that the troop was ready to march. I had on a short leather jacket and puttees, so my appearance was half military. I drew myself up smartly and told the old officer the circumstances in German. The old soldier liked my story. He seemed impressed, too, by my speaking German, because he answered me fluently in that language: "Very well, my son – you shall be paid for your bread."

In less time than it takes to tell it, the disconcerted sergeant came running. The colonel bawled him out, not omitting to mention his drunken condition, and I was given 540 rubles on the spot. Beaming, I thanked the colonel and vanished.

I went home with a pocketful of money and conflicting thoughts. Crossing the market place, I encountered the baker, and we went to drink vodka to celebrate our defeat.

"They seem to be withdrawing," he said; "before long, our troops will come in, and then you and I will be soldiers."

"And we'll refuse to pay some baker for his bread," I philosophized and ordered another vodka, and we both laughed thoughtfully.

"How much would you have given me if I had collected the money for you?" I asked my drinking companion and employer.

"Half," he said and emptied his glass.

I ordered a third vodka and said: "Prosit! Is that all? Catch me risking my precious actor's life for your dirty money!"

Suddenly we were both in fine spirits. He was doubtless thinking of the many thousands he had made; I was thinking of the money in my pocket. "Well," he said, turning the glass in his fingers, "simply because you're an artist and the money is as good as lost anyway" – for now, out the window, we could see the Cossacks marching off – "well, that being the case, I would have given you four hundred, or even five hundred."

And we began to sip our fourth vodka.

"Is that a bargain," I said, "or are you just talking?"

"Here's my hand on it," he answered. And the vodka laughed inside us, and I took forty rubles from my pocket, laid them on the table before him, and was an honest man. He was dumfounded and looked at me in astonishment – but he had given his hand and his word – it had been a clear agreement, business is business.

Now I had honest money all of a sudden; I rented an empty bakery, bought flour, and started a business of my own with my sister-in-law.

One day the word went round that our troops were returning, and the same scene was played over again: the suburbs began to smoke, the thunder of cannon became more and more audible, then rifle fire – one morning the Russians had gone. Then suddenly the Austrian advance guard appeared, and the army followed immediately. The Russian flag was burned on the balcony of the town hall, everyone kissed the soldiers, there was dancing in the streets. The following days brought only one visible change: The Russians had hanged Jews as Austrian spies, and the Austrians began hanging Ukrainians as Russian spies and called them Russophiles. Whichever army came, men were hanged.

Placards soon appeared, ordering those liable to military service to present themselves. I went, and at once became a soldier. No one asked or cared where we came from, where we had been all this time. They were simply glad to get new cannon fodder.

We went to a receiving camp. Then we were loaded into the cars with famous markings, forty men or eight horses, and shipped to the interior of Austria. First we came to the Salzkammergut, then to Steiermark, Mitterndorf.

On a rainy and snowy March day of 1915 we marched into the little town. The population received us as unkindly as the weather.

We were the Twenty-fourth Infantry Regiment from Kolomea, made up of Jews and Ukrainians. There was not a village in East Galicia where the Austrian Army had not hanged a few peasants.

The men, particularly the intelligent ones, were in a bad frame of mind. I made friends with a student, Babiuk, the son of poor peasants from a village near Kolomea. The population of Steiermark was worse than unfriendly to us, and as we came through the little market place a group of well-fed townsmen stood watching us, and one of them said: "Look at that bunch of louts – they've been with us all this time and haven't yet got rid of their lice. We could really do without them!" Babiuk said to me: "Do you hear what they are saying about us? But we're good enough to croak for them!"

That was the state of mind of the Austrian Army: The Czechs hated the Austrians, the Austrians hated the Czechs, the Ukrainians, the Croats, the Slovaks, the Poles, the Jews! The Hungarians hated them all indiscriminately. There was no friendship among these peoples. A mixture, a jumble, even among the officers. No common cause, no common ideal.

We were put into uniform, and our training began. Our commander was an officer in active service, First Lieutenant Steinitz. When he heard that I was an actor he sent for me, talked with me about the theater, actors, literature. He was an intellectually alive, cultivated man, transferred from the reserve, and he had no great enthusiasm for the war. He gave orders that I was to be issued a new uniform and invited me to the officers' mess in the evening.

After the good food I performed and entertained the company. Many of the gentlemen had their wives with them. It was very pleasant. They were all very decent to me, and Steinitz doted on me.

The next day he ordered me to report and had me petition for the artist's right to one year's officers' training. To obtain it, I had to take an examination at the Academy of Music and Dramatic Art in Vienna. It was long before the answer came. In the meanwhile he made me an instructor – I became a lance corporal, then a corporal. Then I went to Vienna, took the examination, became an officer candidate, a one-year volunteer. Why volunteer? In any case, I had a wonderful life!

Our cadre went to Hungary. The battalion command set up an independent detachment of one-year volunteers for officers' training, with Steinitz as commandant.

There I began to enjoy the privileges of the upper classes: better quarters, better food, better treatment – quite different from the plain army soldiers, who after six weeks of hard labor, called training, were sent straight into the field. A few of them resisted, managed, by various tricks, to wriggle out of being sent to the front so quickly.

Especially favored was the trick of the gypsy women, who lived outside the town. There, for only one krone, you could get a wonderful case of gonorrhea, which sent you to the hospital in Nagyvarad for four weeks. For two kroner, a soft chancre, which kept you in the hospital for at least six weeks. But if you were willing to spend money, you could get a real case of syphilis – the "hero's death" being thereby indefinitely postponed.

One day the command was changed, the one-year volunteers' detachment was disbanded, and we all went to Freudenthal in Austrian Silesia. There I was put into a line company, given field equipment, and at the beginning of 1916 I went to the Italian front. Steinitz had protected me for almost a year, denied me the hero's death.

With me, of his own free will, went Jurko Slezak, a young Ukrainian from the Carpathians. He said that since he would be sent to the front in four weeks anyway, he might as well go a little earlier in order to be with me, for we liked each other a lot. Slezak had already been wounded three times; he had lost one thumb, but he was indestructible. He was big and strong. He towered above our column like a giant – a Carpathian peasant, a *"huzul,"* as they are called there, well grown and solid like their old beeches. Yet Slezak had a sly smile, like a little boy. Like every good soldier, he hated mechanical drilling, and I always gave him "barracks duty" so that he could stay home. The detachment had understood it, because he was the only one of us who had been "out there." He was so touched by my sense of justice that he voluntarily went to the front with me, and I, on my side, was so touched by his decision that I felt as close to him as to a big brother.

We went into the Tirol, back of Innsbruck, in reserve. The maneuvers became harder and harder and our provisions worse and worse. The bread was particularly inedible. It was composed of a mixture impossible to define. It fell to pieces; we had to put it quickly into our caps. It crumbled and was clammy and tasted like sawdust.

We might go into the trenches any day, the maneuvers were hard, and the soldiers were hungry. A man from Galicia with sawdust bread is a man in despair. Every soldier also had an "iron ration" in his pack which he was to save. It was some sort of dry biscuit and canned meat, and it was checked every few days. One day the "iron rations" were gone. In their desperation the men had devoured them. That was on a Saturday.

On Sunday came the order that, instead of going to church, the whole platoon was to be "tied up."

"Tying up" was a famous punishment in the Austrian Army, and this was what it looked like: the victim was stood on a block or a stool against a stake or a tree, on which his arms were drawn backward and tied together, with a cord, very high. The block or stool was then kicked out from under his feet; his toes barely touched the ground. There he hung, a symbol of human suffering. Tying up was reckoned by hours. But the strongest man, after an hour or half an hour, began to bleed at the nose and mouth and lost consciousness. Medical personnel stood by, took the bleeding and fainting man down, threw water in his face, and as soon as he came to, the sergeant had the procedure continued. That was how they wanted to win the war! Every soldier hoped to get to the front as soon as possible, so that he could sneak over to the enemy with a white handkerchief and finally escape such treatment.

That, already in 1916, was the state of mind in my regiment. Not even a dog remains faithful to a master who gives him nothing to eat and beats him regularly into the bargain.

One day we had a visit from a shaky old man in a general's uniform – he looked as if he had come out of moth balls. The battalion stood to attention, and the little old man made a speech that was a mixture of patriotism and senility. Among other things he said: "The father of our country, the kindly Kaiser, sleeps neither day nor night in his anxiety for you, his children. Yes, he prays for you continually, and he expects that when you catch an Italian you'll give him a neat stab in the belly with your bayonet and twist it round a few times for good measure."

"And then be tied up, you stupid arse!" broke out an old soldier who had fainted three times while hanging from the stake and was still trembling with agitation.

"What did he say?" asked the little man from the moth balls.

"If it please Your Excellency, he was cheering His Majesty," quickly answered our captain, a rather fat reserve officer named Weigel who was a lawyer in civil life, and so he saved the unfortunate situation.

"Bravo, bravo, His Majesty, the all-highest war lord, hurrah, hurrah, hurrah!" And the battalion gave three laughing cheers, and the inspection was over.

The Tirolese population regarded us as we in Kolomea had regarded the Russians: we were foreigners to them, invading troops. And many of us were already trying to desert into Switzerland, were caught, court-martialed, and shot or sent to the front under guard.

One day marching orders came; we were to be sent in. We reached the right wing of the Italian front, near a mountain called Monte Lemerle. The Italians held the mountain, and we were to "take" it – we were to thrust our bayonets in their bellies and turn them – but one regiment after another was bled white there.

We formed in a wood, and there were handed over to a Captain Czerny. He was a short, robust man, with several medals; he spoke with a Czech accent and was notorious in the entire regiment as a torturer and tyrant. He had the platoon commanders and officers come forward at once and delivered a strong, rather drunken speech, made the platoon commanders give some rifle drill to demonstrate their ability and show him the quality of the men.

A Lieutenant Schalk, from Gratz, who had been in the trenches since the beginning of the war – his mind was weakened and he had a perpetual tired smile – could not give his commands loudly enough. Captain Czerny bawled him out before the men, calling him "dung heap," "milksop," and "shirker." Another officer with a Jewish name he called "Lieutenant Matzoth" and had the bugler play reveille in his ear to wake him up, because, in the captain's opinion, the man was still asleep.

Then when my turn came and I gave a couple of commands – it is true that I did it a little theatrically, I acted a little; in those days I went at everything as if it were a role – he instantly asked, "Hey, you latrine-platoon leader, what are you in civil life?"

"With your permission, Captain, I am an actor."

"What are you? An actor, a Mr. Mimic, a clown, a stage fool?" he bellowed, as if I had murdered his only child. He doesn't seem to care much for the theater and actors, I thought. He bellowed on, "You barnstormer, you – in civil life you make fun of the Army, you play a colonel with a red nose – and here you want to be a reserve officer? You'll be a turd as long as I'm captain!"

He yelled and bellowed, and I stood stiffly before him, looked obediently into his little, dancing, impudent eyes and thought, There's a part, there's a part – boy, boy, if I could only play you!

Suddenly some shrapnel burst over our heads – an artillery shell hit not far from us, directly upon a sitting group, and another and another. The wood had been found by the enemy artillery. The noise of the guns was uninterrupted, and columns of smoke kept rising into the air. Men screamed, crawled into hiding. But Captain Czerny was still cursing the theater. We were the only ones left standing. He scrutinized me sharply; I stood stiffly and did not stir. I would show him that an actor and a Jew was no coward. "Dismissed!" he yelled and disappeared himself.

I ran to a moaning man from my platoon who was calling my name desperately. There he lay, behind a rock, covered with blood and dirt, one hand pressed to his side, gasping, "Help, help me!" I undid his coat – a shell splinter had torn him open on one side; bloody, clammy things were falling out of his body, and I tried to hold them back with my bare hand. They gushed over.

I yelled for stretcher-bearers. The shells kept landing. Not far from us a small donkey carrying two stew kettles was lifted into the air by the pressure of an exploding shell and was buried, the shattered bones together with the soldiers' soup, under a heap of rubble. I still kept my hand against the open, damp place in the warm body that was already dead.

After a while the firing stopped. Stretcher-bearers came and laid a heap of flesh and bones with glazed eyes on a stretcher. The stretcher was bloody and dirty too. They took off his identification tag. An hour ago this thing on the stretcher had been a healthy, living man. I could not take hold of anything with my hand for weeks.

That was our first day at the front, before we had even seen the enemy, to say nothing of turning our bayonets round in his guts as the shaky general from the moth balls had told us the old Kaiser wanted us to. It had begun. While our own captain was cursing and reviling us as if we were patricides and infanticides, the enemy was killing us from the other side. We were in the middle. It was a fine prospect for the common man!

32

Let People See What People Are Like!

Suddenly, at Monte Lemarle, the command was "Forward!" No one knew where. We dragged ourselves along, trudged, trotted like cattle; it was chaos and night. Stinking mounds lay there – dead horses; wounded lay groaning for help – they could neither die nor move; you trod on something, a soft mass that once had been a man. Groups came toward us, a few wounded and prisoners.

The nearer we got to the line, the fewer officers we saw. They always hid in caves, the non-commissioned officers were the commanders.

Early in the morning we were in a place on the slope of the mountain, and it looked as if the inhabitants had left their houses at the last minute. In one house the table was still set with an unfinished meal; in the bedroom were soft beds with silk sheets. My friend Jurko Slezak cried, "Look, look at the fine things there are in this world!" and took down his trousers and made use of one of the fine, silk-covered beds. Later he found a watch shop and filled his pack.

But soon the place was under artillery fire again, and the order came, "Retreat!" We ran in wild disorder and mixed with another regiment, the Forty-first, from Czernowitz. I knew that my youngest brother was serving in it.

Suddenly there was the chatter of machine-gun fire on our flanks, salvos in the center; we flung ourselves in the dirt and crawled rearward on our bellies as well as we could.

Then Czerny's voice. He was cursing and raving as if he were at maneuvers: "You cowardly bunch of polenta eaters! *Huzuls*, dumb Carpathian oxen, may lightning strike you! Shoot, shoot, you dogs! Where are the milksops, the matzoth lieutenants, that clown platoon leader?"

"Here, Captain," I shouted and tried to find him. We could not see each other. I only heard his voice going on: "You swine, you dirty Jew, you want to shoot me, do you? You'll croak twenty times over before you can do that!"

I kept perfectly quiet and looked for him. He had given me a marvelous idea. Go on and shoot him, something inside me said, shoot him, he is your real enemy. What has any Italian ever done to you? You've never even seen one. But this man is your enemy and the enemy of your people.

A detonation interrupted this logic, and another, and another.

"Back, back," everyone cried in confusion, and we rolled and crawled and ran as best we could.

And some hours later we were outside the line of fire, and yet we had not seen the enemy. Only, here and there, stray groups of prisoners.

We assembled again somewhere in the vicinity of the wood whence we had set out a few days before. Slezak opened his pack and sold watches at bargain prices – to be paid later. He gave me the finest as a present. That was the only light moment, for we had been reduced by half. But Czerny had been preserved for us.

The men got dysentery – you ran wherever you happened to be. At first the others laughed, then it spread like a panic. Aside from dysentery, I acquired an abscess in my right armpit.

Finally, days later, the commissary came up, with written orders for the captain, who was now leading our battalion. We presently heard that we were to go to another sector of the front.

As soon as it grew dark we set out. Captain Czerny and the bugler, who was also the estafette, had horses and rode at our head. Slezak marched beside me. I had the miserable abscess, which seemed to draw the blood from my whole body into itself and pained terribly. I could no longer carry my pack and my rifle, and Slezak took them from me and carried them to the baggage wagon.

We marched for two, three nights. We heard that we were going to Isonzo, on the left wing of the front. We named ourselves the "K. and K. Kakregiment" (Royal and Imperial Shit Regiment), for that was what we did unceasingly. Our morale was of the same sort. We marched on, sweating, panting, leaning on one another, and learned to sleep while moving forward.

My abscess brought on fever; I collapsed, was unable to rise, and lay there. Slezak worked over me, talked to me, and begged me like a mother not to lie there – because that would be the end. He got a few men together. They sat me on a rifle and dragged me, feverish as I was, with them. Soon the whole platoon took turns carrying me. I had lost all my strength, had come to the end of my rope. I would have liked best to lie there and croak.

Suddenly we were ordered to halt. The captain sent for the platoon commanders, and as well as I could I went up with the others. It was beginning to dawn, and Czerny cursed out his company and platoon commanders: "More sense of your rank, gentlemen! These Galician peasants and Jew swine have to be handled quite another way! They are plain shirkers, traitors, and Russophiles. Just drill a hole in one of the swine when he goes soft. You'll see how the others will run!" Suddenly he looked at me and paused a moment. "Barnstormer Platoon Leader, forward!"

I stepped slowly forward.

"Where is your equipment, you swine?"

"On the baggage wagon, Captain."

"'I respectfully inform you,' you filth."

"I respectfully inform you, Captain, it is on the baggage wagon."

"Bugler, bring him his equipment at once." The bugler trotted away.

"Why did you relieve yourself of your equipment, you dirty Jew?"

"I respectfully inform you, Captain, that I am ill," boiled out of me.

"You are what? Ill? That's something new," he laughed evilly. "You shirker, you swindler, you clown. If you were ill, you'd be lying in the hospital. People aren't sick here."

He unbuttoned his revolver holster, took out his revolver with an evil smile, and went on in a self-satisfied way: "Gentlemen, I shall now show you how to make an example." And, turning to me again: "How are you holding your hand, you offal? Stand at attention when I speak to you," he bellowed, now completely hysterical. On account of the abscess in my armpit I was holding my right hand away from my body. "Hands at your trouser seams, you swine, or I'll shoot you down," and he aimed at me.

Everyone stood in suspense, looking now at the captain, now at me. But I clenched my right hand, made a strong effort, my arm came down, and my hand was at my trouser seam. The abscess in my armpit burst as a consequence, and a warm juice ran down my body.

"You see, gentlemen," our captain went on in triumph, "you have only to take energetic measures, keep a firm hand, and all goes well."

The bugler now brought up my equipment and hung it around me.

"Dismissed, and resume your march," our captain ordered.

When I returned to my platoon, the Czech officer candidate, Hanusch, had a good idea: he emptied my pack, divided the contents among the men, and filled it with hay. Now I was carrying something light, and it went better. That morning Hanusch, who was an engineer in civil life and always smoked a pipe, said to me, "You know, you mustn't think that all Czechs are like Czerny."

A few days later we were in Udine. On the right was the Doberdò, on the left Monfalcone. There we halted for the first time and camped. There we soon got hot soup too, tents were put up and latrines dug. So we sat, anywhere from twenty-four to thirty of us in a latrine at once, and there we discussed all our problems. I once went in and heard a discussion that sounded like a court-martial. What would you do with Captain Czerny if you could catch him after the war? Sentence him to death. Yes, but what kind of death? That was the great subject of debate. Everything was enumerated, from slow hanging to swift shooting, and no agreement could be reached. Then my friend Slezak made a proposal that was unanimously accepted. When Czerny was caught after the war, he was to be sentenced to the following death: his battalion would form and dig a big latrine, lay Czerny, in full parade uniform with all his medals, down in it, and then the whole battalion would sit down and slowly cover him with shit. Then a monument was to be erected with an inscription explaining why the battalion had executed this sentence upon its captain.

We were ordered to open a second line of trenches behind Monfalcone. The place was under constant artillery fire. We went at night. First the officers stayed behind, and then even the sergeants. It was worse than being in the trenches, where there was at least shelter. No one could work. We crawled into hiding behind cliffs and rocks, remained there for the prescribed time, and then returned with heavy losses, without having touched a shovel.

On the way home the officers and the sergeant would suddenly be with us, and no one said anything about it.

One morning a detachment with yellow facings came toward us.

"Is that the Forty-first?" I asked.

"Right," was the answer.

"Haven't you a private named Granach with you?"

A soldier jumped out of the ranks and cried: "At your service, Platoon Leader," and my youngest brother Charles stood before me.

We stood there as if nailed to the spot, unable to put out our hands. I knew that he was going into hell. I explained to him what to do, and we parted.

When we got back we learned that we were to march again. We were to be sent in at the Isonzo.

Two days later we were somewhere in a hot, unfriendly, rocky Alpine terrain. We passed the night in a great cave in a mountain. Above us, the same night, the Italians were withdrawing. We knew it and were wary – perhaps they knew it too. In the morning the coast was clear.

We heard that a volunteer patrol was to be sent out to Hill 412, near a mill that had been bombarded. I volunteered, in order to get away from Czerny for a while. With me went Hanusch, who was a specialist in map reading, a private, and Jurko Slezak, who was always at my side and never left me, faithful fellow.

We went through the desolate Alpine terrain, which was full of the traces of war. There lay a dead, bloated horse, rifles thrown away, wrecked wagons, barbed-wire entanglements, a putrefying body, old wreckage. Soon we saw in the distance something like a series of trench traverses and, off to the left, the ruined mill. We crawled warily through chevaux-de-frise, heavy wire entanglements – all was still, far and wide not a living soul. We were soon in a trench, which the Italians had undoubtedly left that night. We sat down, each devoured a can of concentrated rations and smoked a cigarette.

Hanusch went back with the private to show the troop the way, and Slezak and I stayed there. Night fell, Slezak went to sleep, and I looked toward my right at Goertz (Gorizia), which was under fire. It was quite far away, however. You could not hear the explosions; only here and there little columns of smoke rose.

Soon after, the troop came up – as if into a dwelling. Everyone was happy to be in a trench at last. Everyone was looking for his platoon, his detachment, one crawled over another, all cursing.

Slezak was still sleeping; someone stepped on his face. He woke and let loose his best Ukrainian curses. He called the fellow who had stepped on his face – him and his father and his mother – the juiciest names in his native language. The soldier was a corporal and let Slezak have a couple. I gave the corporal two much harder ones back.

"How dare you hit me?" the fellow bellowed.

"How dare you hit that man?"

"I'm a corporal."

"And I'm a platoon leader. Get along now and complain if you want to."

We did not have peace in the trench for long: on the same road by which we had come, Italians suddenly appeared, whom we received with rifle fire. It lasted a few hours, then there was quiet again.

The next morning we saw the enemy before us, behind his barbed wire. It was the first time. He had already dug in, and was looking over at us through chevaux-de-frise. You could hear him, and even see him here and there. Then one fired, then ten, then thirty, then there was steady firing for several hours, after which things calmed down again.

During the day it was fairly quiet. But with the coming of darkness star rockets went up on both sides, then firing and shouting, which increased to the point of hysteria. The Italians tried again and again to storm our trenches and were "repulsed" again and again.

So we lay there – food and water becoming scarcer – our mouths swelled with thirst. It was the beginning of August 1916 and very hot. Anmunition was running out too; we had to "economize" on cartridges. I suddenly was very wide-awake – my natural curiosity had mobilized all my faculties. I kept my platoon together, the men liked me, we talked everything over like friends. I was a good soldier.

Little by little the Italian artillery fire found us. Many traverses were simply swept away. We now lay concealed in foxholes, and soon there were no more officers to be seen.

I was tempted to find Captain Czerny now and report the situation in full. I knew that his staff was in a cave to the left of the rear trench. I went, creeping along with my friend Slezak.

There he sat with his officers in a snug cavern. I saw a heap of all sorts of canned provisions. The staff looked the worse for liquor and depressed.

I reported: "Captain, I respectfully report – three days without provisions, no water, and our ammunition is running out."

He gave me a pale look and grasped the situation. He was a good soldier himself. He had understood that I had come to show him that I was no coward, for the road to the cave was extremely dangerous. He greeted me spiritedly, though his tongue was somewhat heavy, "So, it's the actor" – it was the first time he had addressed me without a curse. "Well, the Italians aren't going to eat you. Here's a sack of ammunition, and there's a bottle of cognac."

"Thank you, Captain. With your permission, I don't drink," I retorted.

Slezak and I took the sack of ammunition from the corner and crawled back. So, I thought, crawling home to my foxhole, now I have shown him how an actor and a Jew behaves when it comes right down to it. And that gave me a quiet feeling of satisfaction, and I chuckled to myself.

Slezak told the men how I had acted, and they said I was right. It was a pity about the cognac, someone ventured, but what was one bottle for a whole company? For it was a whole company that I was now responsible for. The bigwigs were lying in the cave.

That night I saw the enemy eye to eye for the first time, and this is how it came about. There were two Rumanians in my platoon, and whenever the battle began to rage and everyone on both sides was shooting and shouting, these two knelt down and prayed. The Italians came closer to the barbed wire, shouted and shot and tried to take the trench again. A lot we cared about the trench! But we knew that, before they took it, when they got closer, they would first throw in their accursed "potatoes," their hand grenades, and of those we were afraid. We were willing to be captured, but not to be within range of grenades! We didn't want to be croaked by their croaking potatoes! That was also the real reason why the men fired so desperately. Just keep them out of range!

But my Rumanians, whenever anything started, knelt down, folded their hands, and prayed. I caught them at it several times. The others were disgusted by it too.

And again that night, when hell broke loose – I looked to the left – there they were, down on their knees, with their hands folded, praying, praying again! In my excitement, I slapped one of them. "Shoot, you hound. You can pray later on, when God has saved us. Shoot!"

And they shot, and I shot, the whole trench banged away for two hours in a devilish symphony, and then it was quiet again. The Italians had been driven back once more. The assault had been "repulsed." We fired a star rocket. They had gone, a few lay dead outside the wire, the others were back in their trench.

I looked through my loophole. There – right by my face, a soft whistle, "tiuhh" and a warm breath of air. Someone was shooting at me from very near by. I ducked down, electrically charged with awareness. There it was again, tiuhh! Right past my mouth!

Still crouching, I tried to think who it could be. It came from my left. Yes, of course! The Rumanians. I had slapped one of them. They must surely hate me as I hated Czerny. I crept over to them. They were praying. "Listen, you louts, you've shot at me twice! Say 'yes' and I won't do anything to you. But if you lie and say 'no,' you're dead men."

"My Lord Platoon Leader," said one of them with tears in his eyes, "I swear by God Almighty that I did not shoot at you. God preserve me from such thoughts!" And he crossed himself.

No, he had not shot at me, thought I; no one can lie as honestly as that.

I went back to my station and peered through the loophole again. Suddenly I heard a rustling, a crawling, and then silence again, a rustling, close by. Suddenly a man was standing over my traverse. An Italian, life-size and fully equipped. With a cloth gas mask over his face and his rifle in both hands. In a fraction of a second my rifle was at his belly. Our eyes held each other. "Don't move, or I'll fire."

My rifle against his belly, I held my finger on the trigger; slowly I freed my left hand, pulled at his coat: "Come on, jump!"

And he was in the trench, on his knees, speaking Italian. I could not understand a word, but I knew that he was begging for his life. He was still clutching his rifle, the soldier's bride. I knocked it out of his hands and calmed him – the tension ended. He emptied his pockets, gave me his gas mask, cans of rations, a comb, a pencil, Italian money – everything that he had he put in a pile in front of me. I offered him my hand; we shook hands heartily. A great relief for both of us.

We had made peace. He wanted to kiss me – he knew that now he would not be shot.

I sent him back, with Slezak, to the battalion command; from there he was sent to the rear with other prisoners. Czerny cursed and gave me to understand that you don't take single prisoners – there was a superstition about it. For every single prisoner you take, you lose a whole platoon.

And so I had looked the enemy in the eye. But what eyes a man has when Death stands before him and then lets him off! It is something that cannot be described. It is something that can only be "performed."

There are two new roles I want to play after this war, I thought, that night: Czerny, hysterical, cursing, with his sharp, dancing eyes; and my enemy, with his velvet-soft look, with those eyes marked for death and granted life. Two magnificent roles, that someone must write, and I perform on the stage. Then let people see what people are like!

33

"We'll March Right into Sunny Italy!"

We had no communications with the main body of the Army. The front was somewhere behind us now. The Italians had made a big band on either side of our entrenchment and pushed their line on far behind us. We lay there, cut off, without food, without water, and with little ammunition. All we had was swollen faces and lice. Now not only the Italian artillery was pounding at us, our own was firing on us too – the Austrian artillery always fired short. The trench traverses were soon swept away, and the big dying began.

"Mama! Mama!" – you heard it constantly. The last farewell of the dying soldier. They cried "Mama!" and their hands clutched the stony soil, as if they wanted to hold onto the earth longer before they went. "Mama," in all languages. One of the praying Rumanians fell and cried "Mama," a Pole cried "Mama," a Ukrainian cried "Mama," a Jew cried "Mama," a Czech, the Italians in the barbed wire; they all took their leave of this world with that one word. Only one young Italian officer, who was caught in front of our wire, cried out "Venezia" and died so, with the name of his native city on his lips.

We had only a limited supply of cartridges now and did not return their fire. One morning at dawn, after a fairly quiet night, Slezak sat down with me and we discussed what we could do. We were so hungry that we felt nothing any more, not even hunger. We were already apathetic. The Italians showed themselves in front of our shot-torn barbed wire – half-length figures. They mended their trenches, dug themselves in, they were good targets – but none of us fired a shot.

Slezak and I were watching a bearded Italian – he seemed to be an elderly man; he must have come in with their relief. We saw him take off his pack and lay it down on what had been the traverse; then he began to dig. The pack was full and fat, like a fine calf. We began to discuss and argue about what could possibly be in that fat pack. Now and again the Italian glanced over at us too. We were not twenty paces away. Slezak was sure there was canned food and bread in the pack, perhaps polenta too, because they ate polenta just like ourselves; and, I added, perhaps wine too. We could taste the contents on our tongues. The more we thought and talked about it, the more the pack attracted us. It looked straight into our eyes and hypnotized us, that pack!

"Well, Platoon Leader," said Slezak finally, "you are a marksman and I have long arms. We could try it." "Good." I saw it perfectly.

I quietly checked over my loaded rifle, and we crawled slowly out, lay down and kept still, waited; we had plenty of time. Then we noved forward on our bellies, not merely like soldiers, but like thieves! Inch by inch we crept on and stopped, crept on and stopped, Slezak in the direction of the pack and I, to cover him, straight toward the man, the owner of the pack – I never took my eyes off him.

The Italian stopped working and looked at us as if petrified. He knew it – felt it; I had the bead on him. The slightest movement, and I would pull the trigger.

We stopped; we were five paces from the pack. Slezak pushed himsellf slowly forward between the shot-torn chevaux-de-frise. The Italian, I could see now, had gray hairs in his beard – a father, I thought, a good, quiet soldier.

Slezak's long arm reached out; he touched a corner of the pack – he put out his other hand and grasped it.

The Italian looked quietly into my eyes – yes, he understood what we were up to; he was almost amused.

Slezak had wound the strap of the pack around his right hand and was drawing it back, at the same time using it as cover for his head. The pack caught in the wire, but it kept coming back. "Forward" is not the only fine word; "back" is often just as good.

Slezak was now well behind me, and I began to crawl backward too. Several Italians were watching us now; none of them fired. Back, back we went, faster now. I heard Slezak tumble into the trench. I had veered off a little to the right. Slezak soon had me by the leg and pulled, helped me, and there we were in our foxhole again! Home again! Home from a long, long journey!

Slezak crossed himself. We wiped the sweat from our faces and looked at the pack. Neither of us spoke. Only then did we begin to feel excited. For we had a rich booty.

It appeared that our whole detachment had been watching us and trembling for us. The news sped down the trench in both directions. The old Italian soldier, the rightful owner of the pack, called out, *"Bravo, bravissimo, Austriaco,"* and a few others joined him. We had been watched from both sides.

In the pack we found a regular shop: soap even, and shirts and coffee and sugar and socks and handkerchiefs and writing paper and ink and cans, cans of macaroni as thick as your thumb and full of meat! We had a real banquet. We devoured with relish our last meal in the Austrian Army.

For the next day we were prisoners. And this is how it happened:

From four o'clock the next night until about seven, the firing was deafening and incessant – pure hell. By morning there were many casualties, dead or wounded.

The Italians were now standing fully exposed in their trenches and in front of the barbed wire, shouting and beckoning. *"Olà qua, Austriaco, vieni qua. Pane, aqua, vino, bella*

Italia! Vieni qua, vieni qua." They shouted this for hours on end, and we wanted to go, but did not dare.

Then Slezak took the shirt he had found in the Italian's pack the day before and fixed it on his rifle and planted it in front of our trench, and another stuck his rags of shoes on his rifle and did likewise, a third a handkerchief, a fourth a bit of canvas, a fifth a pair of dirty socks, a sixth an empty pack, a seventh his underdrawers. And in two minutes the whole battered trench, as far as you could see on either side, was decorated with these grotesque, comic flags, which only soldiers in their deepest need could have thought up.

The Italians yelled, "*Bravo, bravissimo, Austriaco,*" and laughed and beckoned and shouted again and again, "Come on, come on – *vieni qua, vieni qua, Austriaco,*" and began to throw things, and we ducked and were terrified. But they were not hand grenades. They were cans of food! Canteens of water! And bread – the enemy threw us real bread! We could not believe our eyes.

The men were suddenly alive; all their weariness had vanished. Both trenches shouted long explanations to each other in strange tongues. Our Rumanian shouted back in Italian and translated: "They say we have nothing to fear and want us to come over." What an importance he suddenly attained among us! He became our interpreter, our mouthpiece, our leading man! Yes, everyone gets his big moment.

He stood up fully exposed, kicked aside a cheval-de-frise, and started off; a few others went with him. To left and right men did likewise. Some of them still clutched their rifles. The Italians knocked the rifles out of their hands and were just as frightened and excited as we were. And we all shouted at once, and we all threw our weapons away and held up our hands. But the Italians did the same. Then we all ran toward their rear together and suddenly slid down a rocky hill.

There a detachment of Italians was encamped, several hundred soldiers. They jumped up, thought they had been surprised by the enemy, and yelled and ran with us. They ran with their hands in the air, alongside of us. Thousands of men, Italians and Austrians, were running with their hands up, frightened to death. A huge mob, an Austrian and Italian army, ran, panic-stricken, up and down the hills of that desolate rocky country. And no one knew who had captured whom!

Slezak was at my side. The Italians were afraid of him because he looked so big and strong. Several of them fell upon him. I shouted for help in German.

An Italian sergeant appeared, quieted the men, and, running over to our side, said in German, "Do you speak German?"

"Yes," I said.

"My name is Stern from Naples. We have a brewery."

"My name is Granach, from Berlin – I'm an actor."

We introduced ourselves as if we were in a drawing room or traveling on a train, all the while running for our lives!

Then we ran into some Italian reserves. You could see wagon trains. Italian officers yelled and cursed, fired their revolvers into the air, stopped the racing herd, explained that it was we, the Austrians, who were prisoners. The hordes began to calm down, and Stern from Naples, whose father had a brewery because he had married the daughter of a brewer from Munich – for which reason he, an Italian sergeant, had been able to tell me all this in German – Stern took leave of me now with these words: "Well, congratulations! You have the stink behind you! I still have to take all that offal in the face."

We were now separated from the Italians and got into formation and were taken still farther toward the rear.

On the way we saw a familiar sight. An Italian company stood in a field. An officer gave the command in Italian: "Helmets off for prayers." An army chaplain blessed them, just as we had been blessed before we were sent in. For their weapons and for our weapons, prayers went up to the same God! What a dilemma!

"Even God has a hard time during a war," said Slezak. "Who is He to help now?"

The Austrian artillery suddenly remembered that there was a war on and fired on us. We suffered casualties from our own shrapnel bursting over our heads.

We came to a farm wrecked by shell fire. A stray shot landed, the roof of a barn rose up and slowly lay down on its side. Then there was quiet.

We were each given a concentrated ration and a loaf of bread, white bread, such as we had not seen for years. Slezak fondled the bread and kissed it, as a big brother fondles and kisses his little sister after a long absence. The big fellow wept for joy. We first devoured the bread with our eyes, then it rapidly disappeared down our throats. There was even a stand where you could buy cheese, salami, and wine – Chianti.

Neither Slezak nor I had any money. While we ran, we had been searched for trophies and our pockets had been emptied. Each of us went off in a different direction to find friends and raise something.

There were eight or ten thousand of us there from different regiments. The corporal, whom I had once slapped for Slezak's sake, saw me.

"There you are, you son of a whore," he shouted, and instantly several of his friends joined him.

"That's the tramp, the gangster who hit me."

I had to laugh – he, the Ukrainian, the Christian, consoling me about my own people! He winked one eye and laughed with me.

We spent the night there, and the next morning we were all roused at four and given more bread and black coffee, and soon a huge column of us was marching through a broad plain into the interior of Italy. I marched with Slezak in the first double file. We wanted to be the first to see Italy!

Our column was accompanied by a cavalry escort, riding on either side, and a very young officer rode at our head. He sat on his horse, dressed with the greatest elegance, slender and girlish, wearing patent-leather boots, and gloves, and a high brown fur shako with a patent-leather strap that went under his chin. When we came to a crossroads, our drawing-room war lord halted the column, turned his chestnut horse, profoundly studied a map, which was rolled up in a fine leather case, took his opera glass which hung at his side, and thoroughly examined the terrain. Then, giving us a smile which disclosed two rows of large white teeth under his thin, elegant mustache, he took his reins with his right hand, and with his small left hand made a gesture to the right, in which direction we set off. I had never seen such an elegant gesture! Who could play him? I thought – only Bassermann! He smiled just like that when he played Percy Hotspur in *Henry IV*. And he was made up to look just as tanned, he had the same slender, lithe figure, as our cavalry officer.

While I was puzzling over casting this "role," we arrived at a field railroad station, and there we were loaded into cattle cars just like the ones at home and rode for a day and a night to the interior of Italy. We traveled slowly, being frequently shunted into freight stations – no one knew where we were headed. Now we would hear that it was for Sicily, now for Sardinia. We went through Naples, soon afterward Salerno, then rode a few hours more and were unloaded and marched to an old monastery: Certosa di Padula, Provincia Salerno.

In our detachment of officer candidates we used to sing a gay soldier's song that told of the booty we should capture in various countries:

> *Brother, if it's bacon that we seek*
> *We'll cut a slice from a Russian's arsecheek.*
> *The hussars are riding, their sabers are flashing,*
> *The Hessians are storming, the Jaeger are storming,*
> *Follow brave Radetsky,*
> *Who won the battle at Santa Lucia.*
> *Patriot, stride him dead*

*Put the ax to his neck,
The* couillon *Napoleon.
Brother, if there's no wine for you and me,
We'll march right into sunny Italy…[and so forth]*

Yes, we had marched into Italy, but not the way it said in the song! We marched as war prisoners, *prigioneri di guerra!*

And, although it was not in the manner foreseen by the song, not one Austrian soldier was unhappy about it. The men really had not wanted the war. The one thing they wanted and wished for with all their hearts was to survive it!

Here, as prisoners in an enemy country, we had the best possible chance of surviving.

So it was good to march into Italy, even in this fashion.

34

Roads Always Lead Somewhere

Certosa di Padula, Provincia Salerno, was a monastery built in the fourteenth century, with a great main building that had an inner court, with many loggias and cloisters, with cellars and catacombs, with a heavy main gate barring the outer world and an inner gate leading to a great domain. This domain was miles wide, with old cypress avenues and olive hedges, and a space in the middle where sixty barracks were built, and the whole was surrounded with thick old walls as high as a house, on the walls the guardhouses, from which Italian sentries watched us, had been built.

In each barracks were three hundred beds. In the middle there were two rows of two-story cages and on either side by the windows were single beds. We had straw mattresses and hay pillows, two sheets and even two linen towels, which were changed every four weeks. The ranking non-commissioned officer was commandant of the barracks and responsible to the Italians for order.

You could volunteer for work, too, for which you were paid a small sum each week. The money was deposited with the Italian authorities, and we were given camp money for a part of the amount; with that we could buy cheese, salami, sardines, fruit, and wine in the canteen. The camp was really a little town, in which, as time went on, clearly defined patterns of behavior, good and bad, developed.

The kitchens were managed by our own non-commissioned officers. In the morning we got black coffee and a small loaf of bread, at noon macaroni and bacon, and at night rice and bacon, or the other way around.

The commandant of the camp was an old retired general. There were eighteen thousand of us prisoners and two thousand Italian guards, a gigantic setup. The treatment we received was perfectly friendly and humane. But there was no communication with the outer world.

At headquarters, where the Italians lived, our officers were also accommodated in old monks' cells and had their own officers' mess, better food, and higher pay. Rank remains rank even among prisoners and continues to have privileges!

At first I was simply hungry. The other prisoners, who had been there for some time, had lost their trench hunger. They gave us their bread, or bartered it for pencils, knives, watches, whatever we had. I found a countryman, a young fellow from my Horodenka, who had an ambition to learn to read and write. He was an old inmate of the camp and had eaten his fill and had some money. I became his teacher, in return for which he gave me from six to eight loaves of bread a day, which I then devoured with my friend Slezak – and still we were always hungry.

For the bread, I dictated letters to my pupil three or four hours a day. An enormous fictitious correspondence developed between parents and children, lover and sweetheart, friend and friend. I found it so exciting that I did nothing day or night but think of the problems that kept arising between these people. Now the parents were in despair over lost children; now the lovers quarreled; now the friends betrayed each other. Then the parents found their children again; the lovers were reconciled and swore to be faithful forever; soon the friends cleared up their misunderstanding and were again "true as steel."

The life of these eighteen thousand Austrian soldiers of all nationalities acquired a pattern of its own. The real lords among us were the Bosnians. They were big, fine-looking men. They wore red fezzes and spoke Italian fluently. Next came the Dalmatians, who were always in good spirits, drank wine, and also spoke Italian fluently.

The Czechs dissociated themselves from the rest of us completely, wore their Sokol emblems, and talked openly about the fall of Austria and national liberation. It was 1917. Then there were the South Slavs: Slovenians, Serbians, Croats. They cursed the monarchy and spoke against it and called the old Kaiser a blockhead. And when the news of his death reached the camp they were drunk with joy and said: "The Old Man has croaked."

This was painful for me to hear, because I had been brought up to respect the old gentleman, whose welfare was prayed for in synagogues and churches, and whose picture was in every house, the symbol of earthly order and security. But at the same time I began to feel a revulsion. We heard that Karl, the young grandnephew of the dead Franz Josef and nephew of the murdered Archduke Ferdinand, was to be kaiser, the same Karl who, as a young lieutenant stationed in Kolomea, was at home in every brothel! The whole district had talked about it – a scion of the royal house going around with whores!

A young soldier who is a prisoner becomes thoughtful. To die the death of a hero for an old, white-haired anointed gentleman – yes! But for a kid who went to whorehouses like any soldier – no! He could never be an anointed!

"Die for that one too?" said Slezak, who had been a pious peasant all his life. "Not likely! Did we find our lives on a dung heap?"

Thus even loyal subjects became thoughtful.

In the course of time we got our fill of sleep and food, and other problems arose: first boredom, then sex, homesickness. Some went to work. In that way you often got out of the camp among civilians and could look at the walls from the outside for a while; those who went always brought back fantastic tales. Others carved figures and cigarette cases out of fine wood, and children's toys. The Italians brought them the material and then bought the product. Others opened coffee stalls. For that you had to contact an Italian guard too, who provided the coffee and sugar. Early in the morning these coffee dealers made good coffee – not like the weak stuff we were given – and brought a small can of it to your bedside for two centesimi; and the same in the afternoon.

Groups formed which were friendly, others which quarreled, there were liars and swindlers and tellers of stories. As long as their tall stories were interesting, they had an audience. But when the storyteller went too far, his listeners began counting their buttons, brushing their clothes off with their hands, scratching behind the ears. The storyteller soon saw that he was being laughed at, slunk away, or joined in the laughter. Soon all knew one another inside and out, and we got on one another's nerves and stopped talking to one another, and the best friends quarreled over nothing.

Nine o'clock was bedtime, but we did not strictly follow the regulations. And the Italians themselves winked at infractions of the rule.

There now developed friendships between men which were like marriages. Normal men, who had wives and children at home, began to have "relations" with each other. Almost everyone masturbated. Toward evening couples would disappear into various corners of the domain, and wild rumors spread.

Once it was rumored that a woman, a real woman in a soldier's uniform, had been smuggled into the camp. It ran through the camp like wildfire. Something in the nature of a panic broke out. "A woman, a woman," men whispered to each other. We ran from barracks to barracks, and to whichever one we came, we heard that she had just gone to another. No one could sleep. We ran around the camp sniffing like dogs when they smell a bitch. The guards were mobilized, the prisoners were forced back to their barracks. A drunken woman in uniform was really found and driven out like a bitch. At the gate she screamed at the Italian officer: "Yes, I'm a whore. If you'd give us back our men, we wouldn't have to be!"

Then came an edict: the death penalty for any prisoner who touched an Italian woman. So eighteen thousand men were thrown back upon each other and upon themselves.

In the meantime our macaroni and rice got thinner and thinner, until finally nothing was served but a thin, watery soup, in which you had to fish around to find a piece of macaroni or a grain of rice – to say nothing of bacon.

We soon discovered that our sergeants – keeping up the old Austrian sergeants' tradition – had begun to steal here too. They sold our provisions, had elegant parade uniforms made for themselves, ate good salami, and drank wine – all at our expense. They were leading a marvelous life!

Discontented groups talked it over in the different barracks. They then all consulted together, and we decided to go to the commandant of the camp and complain.

The commandant, the retired general, a kind, friendly man, who went from barracks to barracks with his staff on Christmas Eve, wishing us a merry Christmas and saying that he hoped the next year we would be home with our families, received our complaint understandingly and asked us in a fatherly way what would be practical for him to do for us. We asked him to dismiss the sergeants from the management of the kitchen and to allow us to feed ourselves with the same rations. The next day we had full plates heaped with macaroni and bacon as never before. Likewise that evening with the rice, and the following days as well! The sergeants were shown up; they had lost the war in camp too! They were now ignored and scorned, while we ate our good meals every day. I was kept busy all day supervising the kitchens, in the course of which I came to be a good cook myself, and it was a lot of fun.

One day a deputation of Americans from the Young Men's Christian Association appeared. They were shown around the camp and inquired what they could do to make life pleasanter for us. I was the speaker on this occasion too and asked them to arrange to have one of the barracks set aside as a theater for us so that we could get up performances. They gave money to have a barracks with a stage built in the middle of the camp, and in a short time I had got together a stage-struck troupe. We went to work.

For plays we took what we could lay hands on – we had very little choice. So, pell-mell, we played Roderich Benedix's farces, Shakespeare's *Othello*, Strindberg's *Vikings*, the play-acting scene from *Midsummer Night's Dream*, a play about a lighthouse keeper with a father-and-son problem. But our biggest success was Erckmann-Chatrian's great melodrama, *The Polish Jew*, which played to full houses for a long time.

Soon we had a Czech, a Jewish, and a Hungarian company, and we were the sensation of the camp. The Italian officers came to our performances regularly and were delighted.

It goes without saying that the women's parts were taken by men, and we had two real prima donnas: Hirschfeld, a Viennese mechanic, played the leading ladies, but the ingénues went to Domenega, a seventeen-year-old Italian boy from Trieste, who had somehow gotten into our army. He had no beard yet, and he was always blushing with embarrassment like a real girl.

Occasionally one of the men would get a civilian coat made out of a blanket, and for the women's parts the best tailors in the camp sewed bed sheets so artistically that they served now as long nightgowns, now as skirts and blouses such as fine ladies wore. Naturally everything was white. For footgear, everyone had the same Austrian mountaineering boots studded with nails, and when the leading man whispered something to his lady about her pretty feet, and the "lady" put up her nail-studded boot, there was always instant applause. Hirschfeld could swing his hips coquettishly and played most of the time with his back to the audience, to their great delight. The Italian officers came backstage during the intermission and made the ladies pull up their dresses, thus convincing themselves that the ladies were not real ladies.

The prices were eight centesimi for the best seats, five for the next best, and three for the rest. The receipts were divided, and I, as producer, director, and leading actor, received three shares and so became a wealthy man.

The Bosnians always reserved the front rows and sat there every night in their red fezzes, and when the performance was over they would put one or two pails of Chianti on the stage, and actors and Maecenases and the other friends of the theater celebrated in this fashion every night. They also gave the ladies little presents and held Don Juanish conversations with them.

The stage, depending upon the character of the play, was hung either with dark blankets or with white linen, and the window frames were cut out of paper and fastened to these backgrounds with pins. The electric-light globes were wrapped in red or green paper, depending upon the mood to be induced. In our poverty we had, without knowing it, a stylized, expressionistic theater, and everything went wonderfully.

Until one day the Hungarian company upset all our plans.

They put on a folk play with a big garden fete, and in their desire to go us one better they cut down twenty olive trees and built a real, live garden on the stage. The Italians came to the performance, saw the real olive trees with their olives, which were just ripe, and forbade all further play-acting! Neither prayers nor entreaties were of any avail. The Hungarians had cut down twenty of the finest olive trees and spoiled the hedge! As an old artistic people, the Italians were against such realism. And boredom descended upon the camp once more.

But handsome Domenega, our young ingénue, who had never seen a play in his life, remained the prima donna and the center of the camp. He was very grateful to me for his privileged position and came to my bedside every morning to drink coffee and sat by my bed every night before bedtime. It was obvious that he loved me – and I loved him. But I saw the way the men paired off in the camp, and every night before I slept and every morning when I waked I prayed: "O God, don't let me become a homosexual!" God heard my prayer.

Occasionally a prisoner would go mad and disappear. About that time, one suddenly dashed through the camp naked, dancing and shouting and laughing – he was caught and taken to the first-aid station; then we heard that he had been sent to Florence. In Florence there was a clearinghouse for prisoners who had gone insane. They were exchanged through the Red Cross and sent to a sanatorium in Switzerland.

I had been in the camp ten months, and a great restlessness and yearning came over me. Eight months at the front, ten months in camp – I had not seen a woman for eighteen months! I had wild dreams and abscesses, and, as if that were not enough, there was always Domenega with his rounded girlish figure and his coquettish child's eyes! No! No! No! Something had to happen!

Slezak was still constantly with me. He was now extremely proud of me, ever since he had seen me on the stage. Of all the men in the camp, he remained the friend with whom I shared my secrets. One day I went for a walk with him and unfolded a brand new plan: I would go mad one night! Whatever happened, he would be the only one to know that it was not real insanity. All I wanted was to be sent to Florence, and from there, through the Red Cross, to Switzerland. Once in Switzerland, I would simply jump off the train, confess that I had played a trick, and be a free man – able to act again, to follow my old profession, see women, instead of vegetating here.

Slezak was depressed over parting from me at first, but the plan was so wonderful, and he was so proud that I had entrusted no one else with my secret, that he promised to keep it to himself.

I began by speaking to no one. Domenega was hurt and stopped coming to visit me. When anyone spoke to me, I looked away and gave some senseless answer. I did not shave, sat by myself and shammed. I began falling down.

The men looked at me suspiciously. Slezak came, full of anxiety. He told me that people were already whispering jokes about me, kept asking him what had come over me. "Good, Slezak! You know nothing. Tonight I'm off. Don't betray me. Now scram!"

That night about two o'clock, when everyone was in a deep sleep, I commenced to scream fearsomely. I began by demolishing my bed, throwing things around, tore off my shirt like Paul Wegener as FranztMoor.

"The graves give up their ghosts," I yelled.

Everyone woke, men tried to quiet me. I hit anyone who came within reach. They grabbed me. I resisted with all my strength, was finally overpowered and tied.

Suddenly I was really screaming and crying. I no longer knew whether I was acting or had really gone insane. Really crazy, flashed through my mind; you're really crazy, something within me said, a normal man doesn't think such things. You're crazy, my boy, the voice within me said. I began to feel horribly sorry for myself, completely miserable.

The stretcher-bearers came with a stretcher and carried me to the first-aid station. It was daylight now. Slezak stood by, weeping with me. Neither he nor I knew whether I was acting or really crazy. However that might be, I was certainly ill.

The doctor came, nodded as he read the report, remarked that mine was the eighth case that year, wrote down the particulars. I was shaking with real anxiety. When everything had been attended to, and he had even signed a railway pass to Salerno for me, he asked, "What is his occupation in civil life?"

"The theater – actor," said Slezak proudly.

"What, an actor?" the doctor burst out, looked me in the eye as one horse thief looks at another, and went on: *"Commediante! Povero misero!* You're not crazy! Really clever of you to think this up! Untie him! Let him go!"

I was taken by surprise, got confused, stepped out of my role, and begged, "But, Doctor, really, I *am* crazy, I am insane!"

Whereupon the whole room burst out laughing with the doctor, and the latter triumphantly explained: "There you are! A really insane person always insists that he is perfectly normal. Take him away!"

He gave me a kick in the behind, and I was back in the camp courtyard, so ashamed of my defeat that I got a real case of melancholia.

But for a few days I was the sensation of the camp. Everyone came to congratulate me on the performance I had put on for the men that night. Everything would have gone perfectly if my profession had not betrayed me. On the other hand, if I had not been an actor, I could not even have made the attempt. Even the Italians laughed about it, and called me *"Grande Atore"* (Grand Actor).

But I was now even more obsessed with the idea of getting away. I had a brown jacket made out of a blanket, wig hair and make-up left from our theater. I could disguise myself and go out as a civilian! But how far would I get? We were in southern Italy.

One day a notice appeared on the bulletin board: six hundred men could sign up for road building in northern Italy. Northern Italy, I thought; that is the French border, the Swiss border. Slezak and I signed up at once, and we left the camp. Only to get out! Out of the desert solitude of camp life into a new, unknown place with unknown possibilities! I had my brown jacket with my wig hair with me, and a plan, a definite intention, to escape. This war, I thought, can go on for many, many years, until I am an old man. A man must always have plans. Why shouldn't they work this time? You must try and try; nothing is brought to you on a silver platter.

So, once again, I had a hope and a plan to drive me on. Once again I was full of something!

And, with that, we went north, to build roads. Roads always lead somewhere! We shall see where.

Granach (right), Berlin 1930s

In Berlin, 1929

Granach practicing his golf swing for the newspapers,
Grunewald, Berlin 1930

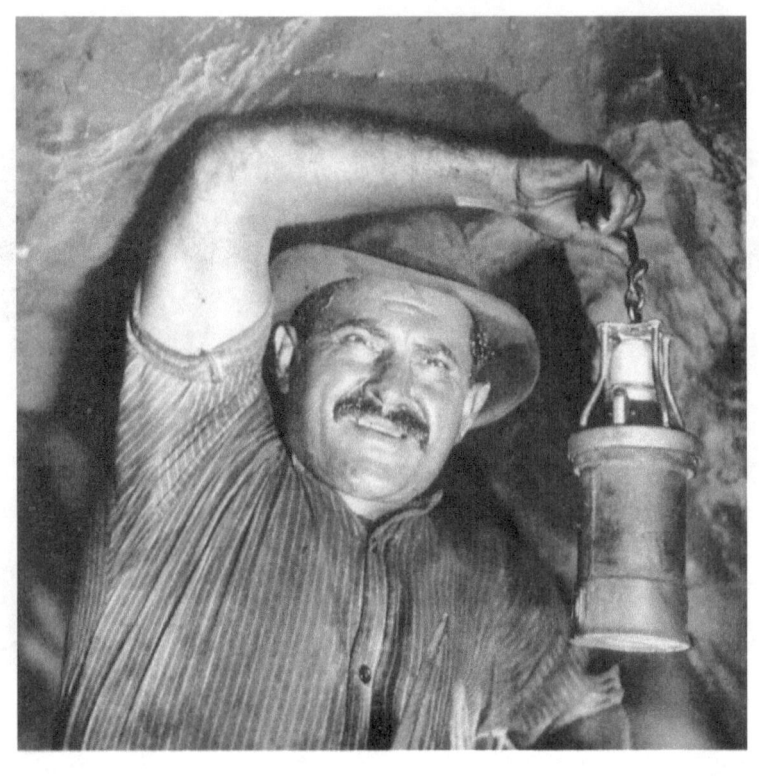

Alexander Granach in G. W. Pabst's *Kameradschaft*, 1931

Aboard the *Bremen* during Granach's first voyage to America, summer 1931

In the role of a legionnaire. Written on the back: "With all my heart, your old father 10/01/34"

Granach (left) with Greta Garbo in *Ninotchka*, directed by Ernst Lubitsch, MGM Studios lot, Culver City 1934

With the daughter of fellow Galician actor and director
Leonard Steckel, Zurich 1938

On the beach in San Francisco with rabbi and author
Emil Bernhard Cohn, circa 1940

Granach with director and friend Leopold Lindtberg,
Zurich 1938

35

Life Comes to Meet You Halfway

Now we – we, the refuse, the ballast, the most worthless freight of the war, we, the war prisoners – were journeying from southern to northern Italy. At first our route lay along the coast. In the distance we could see people in bathing suits playing and swimming, gay umbrellas and baskets – all that was still going on!

The incident happened in Pisa, Pisa with the leaning tower, of which there was a perfect view from the railway station. There, as at other stations, people were standing along the barrier, talking to us. We could speak Italian now. A plump woman stood there, a mother in her forties, with large, kind dark eyes, full of tears, sympathizing with us: "No letters from home, oh, poor, poor *prigioneri di guerra!* Away from home so long! So long parted from your *maminos* and brides and sisters and wives!" – so an Italian mother sympathized with us and pitied us.

Near me stood a young woman in her early twenties, dressed in black, neat, with an olive-colored, transparent, delicate complexion, black hair drawn straight back into a knot, and two big gray, questioning eyes with long black lashes such as all the movie actresses in the world would like to have.

And there was a boy, a street urchin, barefoot and ragged, running back and forth to buy something for a prisoner. He disappeared and came back, and ran off again and came back again, bringing bread and cheese and salami and a wicker flask of Chianti, earning a couple of centesimi each time; he was sweating with excitement and rushed off and came back, and the guards turned a blind eye to it.

I had my last two lire. I said, "Here, boy, bring me a flask of Chianti too, and a piece of cheese and bread out of the change."

And the boy ran off, but this time he was gone longer, and the engine whistled, and the doors were shut, and the girl with the gray eyes and the long lashes looked up warmly, and the mother wept and sobbed and wiped her nose with her apron, and the train started.

The girl with the drawn-back hair slowly raised her small hand and waved and smiled, almost guiltily, for the first time, so that you could see two rows of dazzling teeth. We were moving faster, and the mother was weeping heartbrokenly, as though we were her own sons she was seeing off. The long-lashed beauty smiled at us seductively, but the boy with the wine and bread and cheese had not come back!

We were deeply impressed by the three generations: sympathetic mothers, exotic beauties, and impudent street urchins. Is this typically Italian? Couldn't it take place in my own town too? Yes, of course! It is the same all over the world.

The others, to whom the boy had brought what they had paid for, gave us a swallow of wine for consolation and a mouthful of cheese, and then teased us in return.

We traveled on, day and night, always northward, until one night we were unloaded in the town of Aosta, in the valley of Aosta, the valley that divides Italy from Switzerland and France. You could see the Valpelline mountaintops, with their eternal snows. They could be the gateway to freedom!

We were handed over to a troop of guards, and taken to stay in Cogne, a place near Aosta, there to make roads for the newly discovered mines. An Italian sergeant was with us as interpreter. He spoke German fluently. But as our detachment was composed of Ukrainians, Poles, Croats, and Slovenes, I was given the job of interpreting for the interpreter.

Presently we were marching together along a narrow mountain road toward our destination, and we had a stimulating conversation. The Italian interpreter was Sergeant Ludovico Merlo, a reservist, who owned two hotels in Aosta, Hotel della Posta and Hotel della Corona. He was a short, slightly built man in his forties, with good-natured, intelligent blue eyes and a neat pointed beard. He spoke animatedly, as if he were delivering a lecture, and seemed to be glad to air his German again – he had learned it in Germany.

"What do you think about the war?" asked the "enemy" sergeant and interpreter, with whom I had instantly become as intimate as though I had known him for years.

"The war – I? I've known better ways of spending my time! I think a lot of Shakespeare, but nothing of a war that forces me to kill or be killed, instead of following a profession that amuses me and other people as well."

"Yes," said Merlo, "if we had met in the trenches, we would have shot at each other, and here we are, having a useful conversation. The thing is, we ordinary people were never asked what we wanted. Always these great lords! They not only drink our best wine, sleep with our prettiest women, and live in palaces, they simply send us off to die whenever they please. Look at my men who are guarding you, and at your men, marching there. If you asked them, they would certainly all want to go home to their jobs and their farms; every one of them has a family, a trade, a home, where they did useful work. But one day it was drop everything and go and kill or be killed! When two neighbors come to blows, they go before a judge, who fines the one that started it. But when these prime ministers and diplomats can't agree to do business, they go to war, arrange mass murder. When some hungry devil steals a loaf of bread, he is locked up; when a drunkard breaks a window, he is fined; when someone commits a murder, he is hanged – but when these big shots commit hundreds, thousands, millions of murders, they call it war, and it's all right and legal. These warmakers ought to be properly punished! Isn't it shameful that mature men can't find any way out except to smash things to pieces every twenty or thirty years – smash everything that has been painfully built up? Not to mention the orphans and widows!" Thus spoke the "enemy" an Italian sergeant who was set to guard me. I never heard an Austrian sergeant talk like that.

Then he asked me, "How do you like Italy?"

And I told him about my experience with the weeping mother and the boy who disappeared with my two lire and the beauty with the tight-drawn hair and the gray eyes and long eyelashes, the loveliest eyes on earth.

"Yes, yes," Ludovico smiled with satisfaction, then he shook his head. "Ah," he said, "every mother in the world is weeping over this war. What you lost through the boy will be made up to you here. You'll get plenty of wine to drink, and plenty to eat too, because I run the kitchen for the officers and the engineers, and you will have to help me. But as for the prettiest eyes in the world," he said dreamily, "you're wrong there. You see, I worked a good many years in Berlin as a waiter, and there I had an Anna. Lord yes, my Anna!" And at that he broke off suddenly and seemed to search deeply into himself, as in a dream: "Anna! What eyes she had! Of course our Italian women have beautiful eyes. But eyes like my Anna's in Berlin – there aren't any, even in Italy."

So talking, we marched over bad narrow roads through a defile into the mountains, and after several hours we reached Cogne, where a camp had been set up for us.

The next day we were divided into working parties. I was assigned to Merlo as interpreter and assistant cook in his officers' kitchen. The first days he took me with him everywhere; later I could go about almost as I pleased. The men's diet was much better here than it had been in the camp at Padula. There were various workshops, in which some went to work at once. The others built roads. We were well paid, because we were working for a private enterprise.

I was with Ludovico all day, helping him with the shopping and in the kitchen. We cooked for some ten gentlemen, who assembled for dinner at eleven o'clock and sat at table until two. They began with trifles: anchovies, tuna fish, sardines, various salads, salami, cold ham, wine, then a rich soup, which was not a soup at all! To make this soup, fat marrow bones were boiled the day before, then the bones were taken out, and the liquid allowed to stand overnight to chill, until it formed a real jelly. Then slices of bread were toasted and rubbed with garlic, then raw green stuff was cut up fine with onions and mixed, and a lot of Parmesan cheese grated; then all these ingredients were put in layers into a big iron pot – a layer of jelly, a layer of bread, a layer of greens, a layer of Parmesan. The pot was filled to the brim layer by layer and set in the oven. And the soup was not a soup, but it tasted better than soup and vegetables and meat together! After the soup there were various roasts or chickens or geese or game, then puddings, then a dish of assorted cheeses, then coffee and cognacs and pastries. Such a meal lasted three happy hours.

And when the gentlemen left, we cleared the table, set it again for ourselves, and spent just as long a time over food just as good or perhaps better. Because we put the best bits aside for ourselves.

In this fashion I was kept busy all day, and I became more and more friendly with Merlo. The best thing of all was those dinners. For we sat over them until we were really drunk. We ate and drank, and discussed all the world's problems, as if the two of us were alone responsible for them and as if the two of us alone could solve them.

Merlo had his hotels in Aosta and knew the region thoroughly. I asked him about outings into France and Switzerland. I learned from him that the easiest way into Switzerland was over the Valpellines, the next easiest over the Great St. Bernard. Often he even showed me maps, and I plunged into profound study. For those mountains seemed to look at me and beckon me: Come, come on, here I am, my son, over my back you can climb into free Switzerland – to freedom.

I kept my pack hidden in a corner by the bed in which I slept, carefully covered with a blanket. For weeks I had been taking provisions from the kitchen. I reckoned that an escape over the Valpellines or the St. Bernard would take two weeks, for I had learned from Merlo that a trip under normal conditions took only four or five days. I reckoned on fourteen, because I would not travel much by day, but would stay in hiding, and travel at night with the polestar to guide me on my right and Mont Blanc on my left.

So I should need provisions for two weeks. First I got together crusts to serve as biscuit, then sardines in oil, anchovies, tuna fish, salami, and cheese. In a few weeks my pack was as full as a cow before she calves. I had also made a sketch of the valley of Aosta, with which, in conjunction with the polestar, I could orient myself.

The main problem now was, how to escape from the camp and the district where the men worked in groups under guard. Here chance gave me a broad hint: every few days an Italian peasant from the neighborhood came to camp to collect scraps of bread for his goats. He was my height and had a lame leg, a pointed beard, and a thick turned-up mustache. He would limp into camp with an empty knapsack and limp out again with it full. I resolved to disguise myself as him. I still had my civilian jacket left from our theater in Padula, and make-up and wig hair.

To this plan I adhered. I observed the man as often as he came. In my spare time I had made the right kind of a beard and mustache; I needed only to fasten them on with mastic.

I considered taking Slezak with me – but there were two reasons why it was out of the question. In the first place there were heavy punishments provided for attempts to escape. One man had just been given forty days on bread and water. But prisoners who were caught at the border, were, according to the latest orders, simply shot on the spot as spies! And Slezak was a giant of a fellow whose height always attracted attention. Not only did I decide not to take Slezak with me this time, but also tell him nothing about it.

But what about Merlo? We were real friends by now. Could I simply run away without saying a word to him? No, that I could not do.

Then the day came. My knapsack was so full that there was no room for even a pin in it. My jacket was ready; my beard and mustache in the pages of a book, needing only to be put on; canteen, drinking cup, towels, soap, even tableware and cooking pots were not forgotten. I had only to set off.

The officers and engineers got up from dinner – we set the tables for ourselves, and now I knew that I was eating my last meal with Merlo. I was extremely excited, could not look him in the eye, drank glass after glass of Chianti, and considered how to break the news to him, how to make my confession. But each time I tried to open my mouth, the words stuck in my throat, and I washed them quickly down with another glass of Chianti and became gloomy and melancholy and was on the verge of tears.

Merlo noticed it and asked me solicitously why I was so unhappy.

"Ludovico," I sobbed out, "we are eating our last meal together today. I can't stand it any longer! I am sick, I shall go crazy if I don't make a run for it."

Ludovico turned white, swallowed a full glass of wine, and I went on:

"We belong to enemy armies, you are guarding me, but we are friends, and I have to confess to you, I have to tell you, so that you won't think I played you false."

Ludovico, my "enemy," was deeply affected; there were tears in his eyes as he filled our glasses again and said: "But, man, I've known all the time that was what you wanted to do. I kept buying more canned goods than we needed. I knew you were cutting crusts of the bread. I saw through your questions about outings. But I hoped that you would not actually tell me, so that after you were gone I could truthfully swear that I knew nothing about it. However, I'm tired and feeling dull and I'm going to sleep." He put his arms around me and kissed me like a big brother, laid fifty lire on the table, and vanished.

I hurried back to my barracks in the camp. The men had already gone to work. I put on my civilian jacket, strapped on my knapsack, went to the toilet, gummed on the beard and mustache I had prepared, looked at myself in my pocket mirror, and a real actor's delight came over me at my likeness to the Italian who came to get scraps for his goats. "Spit three times and don't forget the lame leg!" I reminded myself. And I limped cheerfully out.

If they catch me, I thought, I'll put on a show, pretend it was all a joke.

And when I reached the gate, there stood Fiorello, the engineer, and Tenente (Lieutenant) Caliacci arguing. I had waited on them at table every day for the last six weeks. They did not even look at me. Well limped, my boy! I congratulated myself, proud and excited.

Now I was in the village, I, the poor Italian, who had collected such a full knapsack for his goats that day. I limped through the village, a little faster that day than usual, and soon it was behind me.

At the end of the village, just where I had to turn off, a group was working, my tall friend Slezak towering among them. I turned before I reached them and went straight across the meadows. There! Slezak had noticed something. He stared after me and recognized me. He slipped away from the working party, followed me, sank down into the grass, and called in a whisper, "Granach, God help you! What are you doing?"

"Don't look at me. Go back and keep your mouth shut," I answered between my teeth, without looking at him.

He crawled away. I could hear him behind me muttering, "May God be with you!"

I bore sharply to the right and got into the woods. I could still see the working party, but they could not see me. I went faster and faster up the steep slope, following a mountain brook. It grew steeper and steeper, and suddenly I could go neither forward nor back. A real wall rose above me. I lay there, holding fast to a cliff, cold sweat breaking out on me; my stick slipped out of my hand and fell straight down – I heard it strike a number of times, then all was still. I was still too and considered my next move.

I slid carefully to one side and thus got out of my uncomfortable situation. And now I worked my way slowly forward in zigzags, alone in a gloomy mountain forest. I was still ascending; it was getting quite dark. Soon I saw the wall of a hut. I felt half at home, half afraid that someone might be inside. So I sat slowly down, with my back to the wall, and rested and waited.

Have they missed me in camp yet? I wondered. Of course! I had been climbing for at least five or six hours. It was completely dark now; the sky was full of huge diamonds with a silver-dusty path through them. Full of a crying stillness. And a howling silence!

Theater, I thought. And I took off my beard and mustache. I am acting a drama, with a real forest and mountains and sky and stars for a setting. With lots of action and no text, nothing but imagined words and the wind. Winds from far away whistled in the treetops, gossiping gaily to themselves, telling all they had experienced on their distant journeys, and I understood not a word. I felt alone and strange, sat leaning against the wall as if paralyzed, and was afraid to move. Soon I fell asleep and dreamed a wild, confused dream.

I saw Reinhardt and his whole staff putting on an extraordinarily big show. The whole valley of Aosta was the stage. And the Valpelline mountains and the Great St. Bernard and Mont Blanc were the set. Bassermann, Schildkraut, Wegener, and Moissi wore such gigantic heel pads that their heads were as high as the mountains. And the scripts for their roles were so big that it took two men to turn the pages. Yes, and the entire Austrian and Italian armies were camped about as supernumeraries, and Ludovico Merlo was the stage manager. He rode around on horseback and called to me, "When I sound the gong, you go to the back of the set and climb over it – then the curtain falls!" But first I had to be auditioned with orchestral accompaniment. And I was not prepared! And the orchestra played and sang and piped; I slowly woke, it was still playing! No, it was singing! A huge orchestra of birds. And the first rays of the sun broke through the trees. It grew light. It was day.

I continued to sit there, mulling over the last scraps of my dream; then I stood up slowly and sneaked cautiously around the hut. It was old and partly ruined; not only the door but a whole wall was missing. It had certainly been long abandoned!

I went on up the slope until, after some hours, the forest became thinner, and there stood a tall cross marking the summit, with the altitude inscribed upon it. There was a spring too, hedged in by a natural circle of rocks and stones, and a pleasant morning stillness hung around me.

I seated myself comfortably, stripped to the waist, washed in the cold spring water, spread a towel on a rock, set the table for myself as if I were entertaining an honored guest, and served myself my first meal! With tuna fish and cheese, I drank the clear, fresh, spring water. I took out my sketch. Everything corresponded. I saw Mont Blanc and the adjoining Great St. Bernard and the Valpellines. I decided to go on until about noon.

Soon I saw the whole valley of Aosta spread before me – it looked near enough to touch. I glanced at my map. I had only to cross the river in the valley of Aosta, then on to Mount Valpelline, whose back was the Swiss border itself. Yes! It was all so simple on the map.

How did the reality look? Quite different, of course. Here I was on a plateau, from which I could see into the valley. I soon found a trodden path and discovered another little brook, which doubtless came from the place where I had breakfasted. Here was the place for me to stop. From here I could set off by night without having to wander around.

It was already noon, and warm. It was the middle of August, just a year since I had been taken prisoner. I sat down beside the spring, took off my shoes and had a foot bath. I reflected, did some figuring, struck a balance: Three years of war, of these eight months at the front and one year as a prisoner. So this was the first time in twenty months that I was doing what I wanted and going where I wanted. I was glad I had fled – for the first time in twenty months I was enjoying freedom. I was proud of myself for having made it possible to be taking that foot bath so quietly and peacefully.

I thought of the camp, of Slezak, of Tenente Caliacci, the Italian commander of our work group, that pale-faced young member of the upper ten thousand, whose haughty nose had not yet smelled powder.

His war service, because he belonged to a noble family and had good connections, consisted in guarding prisoners.

Tenente Caliacci la Savoia always wanted to know what we prisoners were saying and what we thought about the war.

Every day after work, the men gathered in my barracks to hear the news. I related the scraps I had picked up while waiting on the gentlemen at table, and added something to them. The men knew very well that I was a storyteller, but it amused them. One night we discussed who made the best soldiers in the war. Among us there were many Serbs, Slovenes, Croats, Dalmatians, Ukrainians, and Poles. We agreed that the Serbian soldiers were the best, then came the French, the Germans, and the Russians – English and American soldiers we knew nothing about.

Suddenly our *tenente* joined the conversation, and, to annoy him, we said that after the Russians there was no one for a long while, and then came the Italian soldiers last of all. The *tenente* blazed with anger and precipitated the following scene with me:

He: "Caporal Maggiore, someday it will be a great pleasure to me to lock you up on bread and water for the impudent things you say and the insulting opinions you express."

I: "Signor Tenente, in the first place, prisoners are not forbidden to talk to each other. And when we do you the honor not to deceive you and to speak out as soldier to soldier, it's the opposite of an insult."

He: "But you talk too much, Caporal Maggiore, and you are impudent. A while in the lockup will do you good."

I: "Signor Tenente" – I laughed at him, and the bystanders with me – "if you lock me up for nothing, I'll run away."

He: "If you run away, Caporal Maggiore, I shall shoot you down."

I: "How will you be able to shoot me down, Signor Tenente, when I've run away! You'll have nothing to shoot at but my soul." The men roared with laughter, and the milk-white face turned blood red, and he screamed hysterically.

He: "You – you haven't got a soul! The most you have is a fart, Caporal Maggiore. That is your soul."

I: "Wonderful, Signor Tenente. You'll have to shoot at that then. But your aim must be good, they're notoriously invisible...."

I thought of this conversation, as the clear cold water of the mountain brook gushed over my feet. Meanwhile I looked at myself in my pocket mirror and thought, Tenente Caliacci certainly doesn't look as pleased as you do.

Suddenly I heard bells and running footsteps. They came nearer and nearer, sounding like a crowd of boys and girls talking excitedly. It was sheep! Dear, good sheep, come to the brook to drink. A whole flock. In my pocket mirror I saw a young man behind me, the shepherd. I saw him look at me in amazement. I got up slowly, but he ran off. I ran too, in the opposite direction. When we were about a hundred paces apart; we both stopped, looked round, and ran from each other again – we have not met to this day! A pity – he was doubtless a nice fellow.

Looking into the mirror once more, I knew why he had run. I looked like a whole corporation of murderers. Patricide, matricide, and infanticide seemed blazoned on my unshaven, sweating face, yet in my heart there was nothing but peace and friendliness!

I soon found a safe spot in a thick clump of trees and lay down and slept. Toward evening I began to descend into the valley, and soon saw that I had underestimated the distance. Everything looked so near! But you don't travel through the air, you travel over the earth! And the earth forces you to accommodate yourself to her contours and has her highways and byways, and more especially her detours. It was not until the second morning that I got into the valley.

On my sketch a thin line ran through the valley, but here the line was a broad roaring stream, impossible to cross. My plan was to circle the town of Aosta at a distance. When you are escaping you can't go running into people's arms! So I wandered along the stream a whole day and then another day, and nowhere did I find a bridge. It goes without saying that I avoided people.

But finally one morning I asked a lonely little farmer where one could cross the stream. He spoke cheerfully about the bad times and the war's lasting so long, and I also learned from him that the stream got wider and wider toward the west and that the only bridge in the valley was the bridge of Aosta, which led straight into the town of Aosta. Nothing could be clearer.

I remained in the vicinity for the rest of the day, and at night began slowly working my way toward the town. About six o'clock in the morning more and more people passed, with goats and donkeys, with carts full of vegetables and milk, and I was soon among them and crossed the bridge, and there stood a sentry on each side, and I strolled on casually, humming an old song that I had learned in camp from the Italians:

Addio, mammina,
Mammina mia,
Andiamo, partiamo,
Andiamo, partiamo,
Addio, mammina,
Mammina mia,
Andiamo, partiamo,
La libertà.

Singing it, I walked by the two sentries. One of them only shook his head. Doubtless he thought what all soldiers think when they see a healthy civilian in such a good humor in wartime: Look at him, will you! The swine is still in civvies, and he's singing. And I have to mount guard! What a shirker, what a smart peasant! So thinks, thought I, the sentry.

And I was in Aosta! First I passed a parade ground, overflowing with soldiers. They were drilling in large and small formations.

Soon the town began. There were shops. There was the Hotel della Corona, belonging to my friend Ludovico Merlo. I was tempted to go in and deliver greetings from him. You don't say so! Instead I went into a small shop and bought three pairs of socks, and so got change for the fifty lire my friend had given me. Then I bought three loaves of fresh bread, and three more in another bakery, in order not to attract attention. Then I tried to go through the vineyards instead of by the street, and attracted more attention than I had in the thronged highway. I swung back to the highroad, and at the end of the town there was a little wine shop standing by itself, and there I bought a big flask of Chianti and went merrily on.

Soldiers, alone and in groups, met me and overtook me. I fell in with a leisurely donkey driver, from whom I learned – what I knew already – that the highroad led to the village of Valpelline on the slope of the mountains of the same name, which I knew to be the Swiss border.

My companion was very talkative. He was proud too that he had at once recognized me as a Neapolitan, from my accent. Our guards in Certosa di Padula were from Naples, and we spoke their dialect. Here the people had rather a French accent. He took me for an Italian and asked me if I had relatives in the neighborhood, and how I happened still to be in civvies, and whether I believed that the war would last much longer.

But I did not know whether he was well disposed toward me or whether he would hand me over to the next *carabiniere* we met. And I sat down to rest and let him go on, and after a while I disappeared into the woods again, and the first thing I did was to lie down and sleep, so that I could think over the rest of my journey with a clear head.

To judge from the number of soldiers on the highway, it was clear that Valpelline was a garrison town and heavily guarded. It was the border, too. So the thing to do was to make a wide detour around the town. But first get some sleep and some rest.

My knapsack was still full. I found an inviting spot where a clear shallow brook flowed. There was a flat stone there too; I laid out my towel on it and spread a friendly table with a friendly meal. I divided myself into two people; one served, talking in friendly fashion the while, and the other was touched by this hospitality and grateful. The whole procedure begot a pleasant frame of mind.

After my meal, and after a good sleep, the brook waked me, suddenly becoming louder and wider, and I set off. Following the polestar and making a circle through the woods around the town of Valpelline, I walked on until at last the sun rose, and I was tired again and rested again and slept again and another day was over; and I rested and slept and went on, always cheerful, and ate and slept and walked, and there was no end to it.

On the third day I suddenly saw a towel! My towel on a flat stone! And a shallow brook and a Chianti flask and an empty sardine can! *I had wandered for three days in a circle!*

Sweat sprang out all over me. I was terrified. My cheerfulness vanished! I lay down on the ground and gave myself up to the shock, until it was over. Then I undressed completely and bathed in the cold brook water and had a quiet talk with myself.

It was clear that I had the first lap, possibly the hardest, behind me – crossing the valley of Aosta. I could not go over the Valpellines, so I must keep on a parallel course to the Great St. Bernard. The St. Bernard was bigger, farther, and more difficult, but offered more possibilities. Indeed, it had been considered in my plan. It was a good thing that I had not gone through the Valpellines; perhaps I should already have perished there. My little journey in a circle was the lesser evil and a warning. Thus did I give myself a good talking to, ate another meal, observed that my knapsack was less swollen, and lay down to sleep.

The next evening I bore more to the left, away from Valpelline, toward Mont Blanc, because the Great St. Bernard was between them. I wandered on, now by night, now by day; soon the days and nights were confused, and I did not know whether it was Sunday or Friday! My knapsack began to shrink. It was lighter on my shoulders but heavier on my heart. I began to observe a strict economy.

I did not keep so strictly to traveling at night. Night, the dark lady, made my eyelids heavy. I began almost to long to meet someone. Lo, one morning, a broad glade – a plateau – goats – a solitary cow. And not far away, a hut too!

A little girl stood before it, I saw from far off. She ran away and returned with a woman. I strode toward them. A lazy old dog lay sleeping in the sun. A conduit brought water from a mountain spring to a big barrel in front of the house, which had long been filled and was running over.

Now I could see the woman distinctly. She had her arm around the little girl, who was about twelve years old. I bent over the conduit and drank. Drank long and slowly, while we observed each other. Soon another woman came out.

I tried to approach, and she said, "Better be careful, that dog bites." Or so, rather, she hoped – for the dog lay there dozing and ignored me.

"Oh no, he won't – he's a good dog and doesn't bite nice people." And with that I went nearer and assumed the most harmless and meek expression I could.

The women smiled back at me, and one of them asked, "Where have you come from?"

"From very far," I sighed, "and it is a long story, hard to tell on an empty stomach."

One of them went into the house and brought me a half loaf of bread, which I greedily devoured, and I drank again, this time out of the barrel.

"You are not an Italian," said one of the women.

"No, I'm a Russian who has run away from a German prison camp, but the French won't believe it. So I have to try another way to get home. I have a wife at home, a fine woman like you, and three sweet children – the oldest is a girl, just the size of the little one there."

And I believed it myself, the story I was telling, and felt a great longing for my three alleged children and my wife, and my voice cracked and tears ran down my cheeks, and I was half ashamed, but I felt too that I was making an impression on them.

"Martha," said the one who had brought the bread, "ask him in, and I'll make coffee."

Soon I was sitting in a comfortable room over coffee, and I learned that a revolution had broken out in Russia, and that Martha spoke Croatian – she was a refugee from Fiume – and so we conversed in Russian; that is, she spoke Croatian, I Ukrainian, and it was homelike and friendly. She packed a knapsack full of whatever they had: cheese, bread, polenta, and even some canned goods. She described the vicinity to me exactly. I was between the Valpellines and the Great St. Bernard. So – thank God – my nose had led me right!

Martha set out with me and pointed out where, to the right, I must cross another mountain chain, to get into the St. Bernard Pass, which would lead me into Switzerland.

So we walked through the woods together for several hours, and then we lay down, and we both felt that we had known each other for years. We put our arms around each other and joked and laughed and kissed, as if we had been waiting for each other a long time. And without questions or answers, without priest or rabbi, we were married in that deep wood in the high mountains. And we were man and wife, and we laughed and wept for joy, and we went to sleep....

When I awoke, she was gone, my beloved. I was sad, but I knew that I was a human being again, a man.

And if life had ended then, if I had been captured, my flight would have been more than worth it! So full of life did I feel! So filled with that experience! I was not yet free, I was but halfway on my road – but life, laughing, weeping, irresistible life, had touched me with all its splendor, all its richness, all its intoxication.

36

A Promise That I Shall Always Keep

Four weeks I had been on the march. My experience with Martha, that wedding in the woods, filled the man in me with so much strength and confidence that that alone would have been a sufficient recompense for my flight.

I had long been out of the wooded regions; now I crossed a rocky ridge, now a green plateau, here and there the snow lay, and one day I saw a real marvel. Spread out before me lay a gay, many-colored carpet, a living carpet, that moved. It was made of green, yellow, brown, blue, red, and black dotted fluttering beings, side by side on the stones and grass, so that I had to step carefully to avoid treading on them. Butterflies! Butterflies of all sizes and colors had made a rendezvous here. I could hardly feast my eyes sufficiently on their splendid colors, and I do not know yet whether it was only a dream, or a butterfly assembly meeting there to exhibit their colors. A color festival, a butterfly international!

I was now climbing higher and higher into the mountains. Martha had told me exactly how to go to avoid the border patrols, the Bersaglieri. The nights were now so cold that I had to shelter myself from the sharp, whistling wind in caves. By day Mont Blanc looked very near through the thin mountain air. The saddle of the Great St. Bernard seemed near enough to touch, too. I rested and slept and ate my dwindling cheese and drank much spring water and went on and on, and often I thought that the mountains were marching too, moving just as fast as I was, and only beckoning to me to make a fool of me.

Until one morning I saw the gorge of the Great St. Bernard, just as my sweetheart had told me I should. I was on a wild jagged mountain ridge, whence I could see everything, Mont Blanc, the Great St. Bernard, and behind me the Valpellines.

But what was that? Watch out! Over my head, very low, eagles were circling! Gigantic beasts, like fat Christmas geese, were circling round me. I ran as fast as I could, but I could not run very fast, for my knapsack and my stomach were empty. The last bit of bread crust was gone, the last mouthful of cheese. Since early the morning before! I was horribly tired and hungry. So hungry that I began to chew grass and suck roots. But they tasted bitter, and I was afraid of being poisoned.

As soon as I found a spring I drank my fill, much more than my thirst demanded, and my water-filled stomach made me tired and gloomy. The eagles had left me. I had doubtless passed near an eyrie, and possibly they were afraid of me.

It was now noon, for the sun, about which the poets all sing so affectionately, hung in the sky over the center of the world and burned and scorched so malevolently and mercilessly that I would have cursed if I had had the strength!

Then suddenly I saw a hut! Lord God, yes, a real hut, a sign of human life! To the hut, quick, I thought – no, not really I – it was the hunger in me that now thought and felt for me: That is a hut, there are certainly men in it, men, border guards, Bersaglieri, they are waiting to catch you, to shoot you! But if you go to them of your own accord and give yourself up, they'll give you one meal before they send you into the Beyond. You must die in any case. But before you are dead, you will have the pleasure of chewing once more, once more your throat will feel the joy of swallowing! Lord God, yes, to have something more solid than water in my stomach again! Death, a thousand deaths – I am ready to meet a hundred thousand deaths for one meal.

Down to the hut! The prospect of food drew me, drove me, flung me down to the perilous hut. My tired legs flew, ran, slid, crawled as fast as I could make them. It was soon so steep that I had to cling to the side to keep from falling down the slope. The hut now vanished from sight, now reappeared. I had to take a zigzag course, I was in mountains! You can't just go through the air! The earth forces you, you little worm, forces you to obey her laws.

It was late in the afternoon, the hut looked clearer and larger, but the distance fooled me again! I did not give in. I slid and crawled and went on, but the sun was going his way too. Soon he began to disappear behind the trees. The ragged shadows of night thickened, darkened the air. Soon a few stars were visible.

I gathered my remaining strength. I almost ran. I must reach the hut! Another rock and another bend, another slope and another detour, on, on! It was already dark. There – a trodden path, a trail, a real road, a turn! It was black night, and I was standing outside the hut.

I felt no fear of the patrol. I went in....And there sat a monk, looking like Friedrich Kuehne as Domingo in *Don Carlos*. He was sitting on a wooden bench against the wall, beside a fire, and a goat rested between his knees. They both had the same gray-green eyes and looked at me with the same indifference. "*Mangiare* – food!" I shouted impolitely. "*Sì, sì, signore, un momento,*" and he got busy. In his intonations too, in his slightest movements, everything was like Kuehne as Domingo.

He brought me a tin bowl of milk and a piece of stale bread. It crunched between my teeth, that dry bread. Saliva deluged every bite, and I gobbled the milk. It all went greedily down my throat into my empty stomach. He filled the bowl with milk again, gave me another piece of bread. I did not look up. I bent over my food like a hungry dog and began to feel my strength returning and my nerves slowly calming down. My first desperate hunger was satisfied. I felt almost ashamed and looked up for the first time.

The monk was sitting with his goat again, staring straight ahead of him. In the fireplace a last, solitary stick of wood was burning. I looked at my Kuehne-monk and felt suspicious and afraid. He is no monk, I thought; he is a disguised mountain robber. He never looks me in the eye, he will not let me see his face. What are his intentions toward me? Surely he has weapons hidden here somewhere! So that was now the situation. I believed that I was in peril of my life! This was the fatal night!

Mistrustfully I asked him for a place to sleep. He showed me a sort of barn outside the hut, a hay pile. There I lay down. He was back in the hut with his goat, and I was alone outside.

"Outside" in a village is bigger than "outside" in a town. "Outside" in a field is bigger again than "outside" in a village. But here it was really sinister. Here it was so vast and so cold, and those big stars, how evilly they looked at you! How dangerously and how threateningly! In addition I was dead tired. But, I thought, that sneaking Kuehne is only waiting for me to go to sleep, then he'll come creeping out with a long sharp knife in his wide sleeve and cut my throat like a chicken's, and I'm finished, dead. Dead? Now, when I have my strength back, and possibly can cross the border in the morning? No, he won't come with a knife. That is too difficult and too dangerous for him. But come he will! He can sneak up behind me nicely with an ax, old Kuehne, and smash my skull with one unseen blow! Not with one blow, though! After all, I'm strong. No, he can't do it with one blow. I'll throw myself at him, I can wrestle, I'll get a half-nelson on him, squeeze his throat, and finish him off like a frog! I tensed my muscles, gathered my strength. Against all the rules, I will take him by the throat, yes – hold his throat between my hands and squeeze and squeeze with all my strength, until he hasn't a whimper left in him. Until his eyes start out of their sockets, till he turns red and blue, till he is stiff and motionless, till he is beautifully dead, dead as a doornail. Then, yes, then I'll bury him in the hay and fill up my knapsack again. He must have more bread, perhaps even goat cheese. I'll put it all in my pack, and go across there, across the saddle of the Great St. Bernard.

But now from behind the mountain something blood red was appearing! What could it be? A vast fire was rising behind the white snowy peaks. Was the whole world on fire? A round, flaming ball! The sun, the sun was rising! Day broke. My God, had I been dreaming all night of murder and murderers?

I sat up slowly. I had not even taken off my knapsack. Good morning, Sun, I mumbled, ashamed and apologetic; good morning, Alex, I said to myself. Good morning, Shaiko, I said genially – so as my father used to call me when he had something to praise me for. What a relief that I had murdered no one and no one had murdered me during the night! I must go see the monk. Perhaps he had something to eat. I could at least wake him, old Kuehne, the crafty Domingo.

I went into the hut. The door stood wide open, as it had been when I had entered and when I had left him last night. The old monk was sitting in the same place, with the goat between his knees – only now he looked tired.

He hasn't slept either, thought I. Of course not, I saw at once – he thought that I would try to kill him! Our two minds had had a long talk about murder through the night.

"*Buon giorno,*" I greeted him.

"*Buon giorno, signore, un po' di cibo?*" he asked, and without waiting for an answer he brought me milk in the same bowl and a piece of old polenta.

I asked him the way to the Valpelline. He pointed it out to me, and I knew that the direction I must take was the opposite one.

I had not been walking an hour when I saw cows grazing. Soon I saw a young lad, whom I approached. He was busy at work. A stream ran through an artificial channel. He had a sheet of metal with which he would block the current, which then ran diagonally off across the meadow and soaked the thirsty grass. Then he would wait a while, and then block the water off again a little farther on.

I gave him cigarettes, and we smoked. He was about twenty years old, emaciated, with sick-looking eyes, and wore his cap pulled down over his face. We smoked slowly and never looked at each other, as if we were old acquaintances.

For the last two weeks, since my wedding in the woods, except for yesterday's excursion to the hut, I had been going steadily up, climbing higher and higher in the mountains. *"A che distanza è la jrontiera Svizzera?"* I asked my peacefully smoking friend.

"Questa è la frontiera" and he made a brief gesture toward the snowy peak before us. Exactly as if I had asked him, "Where is Herr Schultz's house?" and he had pointed at the nearest house and said, "That's Schultz's house there."

It was so near that instantly there shot through my head: Run, run fast, in ten or fifteen minutes you'll be across! No, no, I answered myself, you have already had experience with distances in the mountains. Weren't you deceived only yesterday? Didn't you run for that hut from noon till late in the night, when you thought it was only half an hour away? The air at this altitude is thin, and things look nearer. Watch out!

While I was thinking all this, my new friend pulled his metal plate out of the water and put it in again farther on, to soak another part of the meadow; then he turned to me again and said quietly, as if continuing a conversation: "A whole company went through here yesterday. Do you see the little hut there?"

No, I really had not seen it. It was built right against a cliff, out of the same gray stone.

"That is the fifth and last guardhouse in the pass."

"In what pass?" I asked, shaking.

"Look," he pointed again to the snow-covered peak, "that is the Bernard, the border, and that is the fifth border guardhouse in the Bernard Pass. Here we are between the fourth and the fifth. The fourth guardhouse is a little way back of the hermitage you came from, and there on the right is the farm."

That too, although it was right in front of my nose, I had not seen.

"To the right in that last guardhouse live three *carabinieri*, who come by here every morning to drink milk at the hermitage."

While he was still speaking, I saw three befeathered soldiers in capes approaching; then they disappeared around a bend behind a rocky wall.

"There they come," he said, and I, as if we had agreed on it, slowly let my knapsack drop, went to the stream, pulled out the plate and thrust it in again. But I did not wait for the grass to get soaked, I pulled it out again and thrust it in steadily, as if I were chopping wood slowly, as if I wanted to make the hole deeper. Meanwhile, my friend had hidden my knapsack under a stone.

The *carabinieri* approached us, nearer and nearer. I could hear their voices. I did not look up, and worked quietly on, not hurrying. Now they were so near that I heard their footsteps in the loose scree, and expected every instant that one of them would lay his hand on my shoulder. No, they had gone on! I thrust the plate into the channel as hard as I could and left it there. And the water flowed slowly over the thirsty grass.

My friend picked up my knapsack and said, "Follow me," and led me not more than fifty paces down a slope to a barn that I also had not seen before. He took me into a loft, disappeared, and came back in a few minutes with a pitcher of cold water and a tray on which were a piece of hot polenta and a chunk of goat cheese, and told me to stay there all day and sleep. And he promised to wake me at night and to show me the way across.

That was the longest day of my life! I did not fall asleep until late in the afternoon, and at night, when the stars came, my friend came too and explained the road to me once again.

In half an hour I was near the last guardhouse – there was a light in it. I crawled around it in a curve. Then, over boulders and scattered stones, higher and higher. Suddenly I was in the snow – frozen, hard glacier snow, but still far from the saddle, where I must bear to the right. Soon I was on a blanket of white – it was midnight – winds whistled and hissed through the air, now cold, now warm. I trembled with loneliness. The stars were bright and evil, and many of them looked like little jagged moons. Here was the saddle now! Bear to the right! Now the way was downward and terribly steep!

Soon I was out of the snow field. Here was wet scree. I slipped, sat down on my behind, and the scree behind me slid with me. I threw myself on my stomach and rolled sideways off to the right. The scree shot down diagonally and struck, its fall rousing the echoes. The noise grew louder and louder, as if it were thundering. Good that I'm not falling and thundering with it, thought I. Soon I came to shrubs and the first trees. Daring to hope, I descended faster and faster.

After a few hours it began to grow light, night took her departure. Dimly I saw ghosts approaching. Of course not! They were people, men, I heard them talking. At ten paces' distance I stood still. They stopped too.

"*Ola, signore, a che distanza è la jrontiera Svizzera?*" I asked.

"*Questa è Svizzera!*" was the answer.

This was Switzerland! They were Swiss tourists.

I yelled with joy, laughed and cried and jumped and danced and told them disconnectedly about my flight from the Italian prison camp.

The quiet Swiss congratulated me, then they explained matter-of-factly that very few came over on this side because there was so much softened scree that often broke loose – there had been an avalanche only a few hours earlier. That was the damp mass on which my feet had slipped, and with which I began to slide; and from which I then rolled off to one side and left it to thunder down alone!

They told me that I had barely two hours' journey to reach the highroad; to the left it ran into France, to the right into the nearest Swiss town, Orsieres.

I sang every joyous song I knew and made up a few new ones, and danced and leaped to the tune of them all the way instead of walking. The nicest things a man can say, I said to myself. I felicitated myself and praised myself! I was only sorry that I could not embrace and kiss myself! Two souls lived in my breast. One accomplished the deed, the other praised me for it.

So I entered Orsières, turned in at the first little inn, and got completely drunk on coffee and bread and butter. I told the story of my escape to the old woman who waited on me. It made absolutely no impression on her, which did not trouble me in the least.

Soon I was at the little railway station. The people spoke French. I addressed strangers and told them the story of my escape. But few understood me.

Among them was a young woman – a schoolteacher from Basel. She spoke German and was the first to be much impressed. Soon a group had gathered around me in the quiet, sleepy station, and I told my story at the top of my voice. The teacher offered to buy me a ticket to Basel. Whereupon a short gentleman with mustache and a beard took me aside and said, in a strong French accent: "Don't go to Basel. They're crazy there and all violently pro-German. They'll send you back to war. Better come to Lausanne with me. From there you can go to Geneva, where you can stay until the war is over and you won't have to go bang-bang."

"Yes," I said, "but I haven't much money, and the lady is willing to buy me a ticket to Basel."

"I'll buy you a ticket to Geneva," and the short gentleman went to the ticket window. So two free Swiss citizens battled over my soul.

In Lausanne I had a good lunch with my benefactor, and the same afternoon I arrived in Geneva. There I spoke to people already at the station and, again, told them the story of my escape whether they wanted to hear it or not.

Suddenly a train from Serbia, carrying German and Austrian wounded who were being exchanged, rolled in. I was soon surrounded by a ring of soldiers, who lapped up my story. They went to the different carriages and repeated it – I was congratulated and shouted to from all sides. I was the man of the hour at every carriage window.

A Swiss gendarme came up, put his hand on my shoulder and brought me to the commandant.

"Who are you?"

"I am an Austrian soldier."

"What are you doing here?" Well, I had another chance to tell my story from beginning to end.

While the commandant was listening to me, someone called the Austrian consulate. A young official appeared, asked a few questions, and vouched for me to the authorities. He apologized to me for the absence of the consul, who had been unable to come in person, took me to a first-class hotel, and once again I told him the whole story of my escape.

He introduced me at the hotel as an Austrian officer (which I was not). I looked healthy enough, but terribly ragged and scratched. I was given a fine room with a bath, and the official told me that I was the guest of the Austrian consulate, so they would pay my expenses; and he went down to tell the story of my escape in the hotel.

I had hardly been left alone in my room before a pretty little maid appeared with towels. The minute she came in, I wanted to tell her about my escape, but she interrupted me and said, "Have you any handkerchiefs?"

"No, I haven't."

"Well then," a pair of impudent, smiling eyes informed me, "when you've had a bath and dinner downstairs, I'll bring you some handkerchiefs. Then you can tell me the whole wonderful story. Right now I'm in a hurry."

I bathed quickly, and with my rags and my beard and happy thoughts and a tremendous appetite, I went down to the dining room.

Ladies and gentlemen in evening dress were sitting at the tables; they already knew the story of my escape. The headwaiter came. My journey and my hunger looked out of my eyes and I ran my finger over the menu and said, "This side first!"

There was caviar and oysters and the best that the house afforded. To go with it, I ordered the most expensive champagne, Mumm Dry, two bottles – one for now and one to take to my room with me. Dead Franz Josef had at least been spared the cost of my meal. It was Karl who had to pay for it.

The waiter was radiant with enthusiasm. He had never before served so hungry a guest. The people at the other tables, stiff as they were, smiled over at me. But I was thinking of the promised handkerchiefs and hurried, took my bottle with me, and went up to my room.

I did not wait long. The cherry-eyed maid came in, slowly and shyly, bringing a small handkerchief. I filled two water glasses with champagne and began to tell about the war, my imprisonment, and Italy, and my escape.

She kept interrupting me to ask if Italy was not a beautiful country. Yes, that it truly was! And, God in heaven, how we flew into each other's hearts! The room had been dark for a long time, and all night we sang to each other the eternal song of love.

And when it was time to part in the morning, when she was ready to leave me, she only said, "Please, you foreigner, you must promise me something." And her eyes filled with tears over our parting.

"Yes, sweet cherry-eyes! I'll not only promise, I'll do it!" I thought she would want me to marry her, would want to come with me – I was prepared for anything and ready for anything – only she must not cry. The very thought filled me with shame and grief.

And she looked away and spoke slowly and haltingly, "You see, my foreign soldier, I'm an Italian girl and I have two brothers in the war. Don't shoot them, please!...Do you love me?" she asked suddenly.

I stammered something and took her into my arms.

"If you love me, you must promise me never to shoot at an Italian soldier, at an Italian man again!"

With shame in my heart and a choking in my throat, I gave cherry-eyes my promise and – so help me God! – I shall keep it to all eternity!

37

"Home, Home – There's Where a Welcome Waits You!"

The next day at the Austrian consul's – he was a young, confidence-inspiring gentleman with a well-kept blond beard – there was a reception. Elderly gentlemen, young protégés, professional tea drinkers of the female sex, raved and reveled over my story and praised my "patriotic deed."

I realized for the first time that patriotism had not been the motive for my escape. I had escaped out of a longing for freedom, but that was another bloated word. I had escaped out of a longing for the theater! Or out of sexual need and curiosity to see that one *could* escape. But above all, for the fun of it – just because it seemed so impossible. Certainly not for the reasons for which the assemblage was honoring me.

The same afternoon the consul took me to his private villa and told me that, according to the laws of war, the law of neutrality, I would have to be interned in Switzerland. He could not send me home, but my observations were of the utmost importance, and he would advise me to smuggle myself on board the train for the exchanged wounded that night, so that I could report at home on all that I had seen and heard in the prison camp, at work, and during my escape.

"Yes, sir," I said, with no attempt at diplomacy, "but for my part I'm through with this war, and I feel no desire to begin all over. I want to be free again and act!"

"And so you shall," said the diplomatic blond beard, "but here you will be interned, and thus become a prisoner again, and I'll give you a letter to take with you which will authorize you to retire from military service and be demobilized."

Good, thought I; anything rather than be a prisoner again!

The same evening I smuggled myself onto the train for exchanged wounded, and the next morning we were at the Austrian border town of Freiberg, in Vorarlberg. Home again!

There the exchanged wounded were unloaded. A reception had been arranged for them in the station restaurant. They had set off to music; they returned to their homes wrecks. Many were carried into the station dining room on stretchers, young fellows without legs, without hands, on makeshift crutches, many with a bandaged eye or black glasses, led by the lame. Committee aunts, charity ladies, beamed lying "welcomes" to them.

A shaky old gentleman wearing a pince-nez and an old-fashioned general's uniform, in which he looked like a cobbler dressed as a general for a masquerade – you could see by looking at him that he had been living on a pension in some hole in the country for the last thirty years – this comic-strip general took charge of the trainful of wrecks; his whole appearance was a good match for these poor fragments of men, the result produced by the diplomats and warmakers of our century.

He was stone-deaf besides, so that I was obliged to shout my arrival into his ear at the top of my voice. I also handed him the letter from the consul in Geneva in regard to my demobilization, and wanted to leave for home at once.

He read the letter, wagged his head disapprovingly over it, and said in a sickly sniveling voice, to which he could still give a military harshness which made it sound like an angry croak, "Since when have these civilians had the right to give orders to soldiers?"

He handed the letter to an idiotically smiling adjutant and ordered that I should be given a pass to my reserve battalion.

"Home, home – there's where a welcome waits you!"

In the station restaurant there was another banquet, thin soup with sweetish, clammy bread. A scanty meal, with plentiful speeches of greeting by the mayor, the general, and a priest.

So I traveled by way of Vienna to Austrian Silesia and my cadre.

On the train were soldiers weighed down by packs, and they talked about business. I soon learned that Vienna was hungry, and these soldiers did a smuggling business in food and so earned money. Since my pass specified no date on which I must report to my reserve battalion, I joined one of these groups and traveled through occupied territory to Lublin, where I was loaded with two knapsacks full of bacon, which I delivered in Vienna.

There in Vienna I went to the theaters and had auditions. In one little theater they were playing Goldoni's *Mirandolina* in verse, and, as the first comedian had just been taken ill, I was given the part and had to perform it that same evening. There was to be a rehearsal an hour before the performance, but none of the actors showed up. So when the performance began and I went on the stage and saw all those strange faces, I stumbled over my very first line. My Viennese colleagues laughed at me before the audience, the audience laughed with them – a darkness came over my eyes, it was all like a bad dream – I ran off and was glad to have a reserve battalion as a means of escape from my Viennese colleagues.

When I arrived at battalion headquarters I created a small sensation. The commanding colonel congratulated me personally and in the battalion orders. In short, I was the only soldier in our regiment, if not in the entire Austrian Army, who had escaped from an Italian prison camp.

The next day I had to appear before his adjutant, Captain Weigel, who wanted to talk to me about a decoration. Weigel told me that my breakneck flight over the Alps would certainly bring me the gold medal of honor for bravery. It was a good thing, too, he said, that my field commander, Captain Czerny, was with the reserve battalion, and I was to report to him at company headquarters the following morning, and that evening the colonel had invited me to the officers' mess, where, after dinner, I was to tell the story of my imprisonment and escape.

There I found comrades who had been with me in the officer candidates' detachment – now first and second lieutenants, with decorations – but some had already fallen, and others I had left behind in prison. After dinner, coffee and cognac were served and other liqueurs and beer, and I began my narrative. The alcohol I had drunk had stimulated me, and I talked steadily, without diplomacy or discretion, about our capture, our life in prison camp, the friction in the camp between different nationalities, and about the Czechs too!

Czerny coughed uneasily, drank quickly, and threw me angry glances. His little sharp eyes danced and stung as they had that day at the front. The attitude of the Czechs was known in the Army, but it was not mentioned. I permitted myself to mention it! I spoke openly. I withstood Czerny's angry, venomous looks. Just so had he looked when he had forced me, sick with fever, to straighten my arm into the position of "attention" and the abscess in my armpit had burst.

I told how the Czech officers, who, before our capture, had maintained an iron discipline and tormented us, began, *after* capture, at once to fraternize with the Italians! I had realized that the struggle of the Czech people was a righteous one – here, however, I had a personal account to settle with my superior officer, my tormentor, who had wished to humiliate me – indeed, to shoot me – over nothing and less than nothing! My sentences burst in his face, which was flushed with embarrassment and alcohol, every sentence a blow – bursting now as the abscess in my armpit had burst then!

Then I told about my escape; there was no vengeance in my voice now; I told my story humorously, and it was a great success. Everyone congratulated me, we sat on and on, drinking till morning.

At eleven o'clock I stood before Czerny and officially reported my escape, so that he could recommend me for a decoration.

The old torturer hardly heard me out before he let fly: "You – escaped from prison? You can tell that to your Jewish grandmother! You deserted, you slippery Jew, kept yourself in hiding, and now you want to be decorated for it too! You want to get a medal for it! A turd is what you'll get, as long as I'm captain!"

But this time I was not at all afraid, and I shouted back even louder: "Captain, that is not the truth! You have no right to abuse me and insult my people!"

"Hold your tongue, hold your tongue, you fresh barnstormer! Shut up or I'll shoot you down like a dog!" I cared nothing for his threats now, and I outshouted him so loudly that the civilians in the neighborhood came running. "Go on and shoot, Captain, go on and shoot!" And I was ready to jump at him if he made a move toward his holster.

But he didn't. He realized the seriousness of the situation. "You'd better think it over a long time, Captain, before you shoot!"

"Corporal of the day, take this criminal out of here! Take him out and lock him up till he turns blue!" his hysterical voice somersaulted.

And with the sympathy of the bystanders, I was led off to the guardhouse. "Home, home – there's where a welcome waits you!"

Now I realized that my escape had been a fine piece of stupidity! I had risked my life to get out of an "enemy country," only to be locked up for it "at home"! I roared with rage, got some writing paper and wrote a ten-page letter to the War Ministry. I wrote my anger out of me! I wrote with no attention to official formulas or to style, I wrote full of wrath and resentment.

I began: "To the Minister of War. Dear Sir:" – as if I were complaining to some elderly gentleman of my acquaintance about the injustice that was being done me! I wrote as though to a storekeeper who, instead of good wares, had given me shoddy; to a fishmonger who had swindled me with spoiled and stinking carp! I cried out against my country to my country!

I told about Czerny's behavior at the front, about the officers who had fraternized with the Italians after their capture, and who, before, had demanded the strictest discipline of us and tormented us. I told about life in the camp, my escape, my letter from the consul in Switzerland, the shaky general who took it away from me, and about Czerny's reception of me and his threats to shoot me. The last sentence ran: "All this, Mr. Minister, I write to you from prison, and I now ask you if, as a citizen, I have only a duty to die for my country, and no rights." I signed my full name and the address of my company and regiment.

The next day I was released, and I mailed my thick letter, addressed to the Minister of War, Vienna. I did not complain to anyone in my battalion. Czerny I saw no more of, for I was serving now in another company.

Life in the reserve battalion was entirely altered. It was now the winter of 1917. The food had become worse, the discipline greatly relaxed. The older reserve officers were tired; the young ones still proudly wore their decorations, which no longer impressed anyone. Rumors came drifting in from Russia of the fall of the Czar, revolution, separate peace. Our Ukrainians began to philosophize in their private conversations. We felt that Austria was tottering. We did not speak of it much – it was impossible to imagine a total collapse, but everyone believed that the war was lost. There was peril in the air, and the men simply wanted to get home. The war now seemed even more meaningless than it had in the beginning. They wanted to be home, to lead useful lives again. They wanted to go back to their jobs, to cultivate their land again, and sow and reap, sleep with their wives and raise children, sit in the inn with their neighbors on Sunday, drink vodka, smoke their pipes, and talk.

Besides, the population here was foreign to them and inimical, and then there were these brutal sergeants and these young squirts, hardly out of school, dressed up as cadets and lieutenants, and this eternal drudgery and drill and bad food.

The alienation between our Ukrainian regiment and the Austrian population of the district reached the point of hatred. The hungry soldiers disappeared from their quarters every night and stole what they could. The civilian population kept complaining to the commandant, patrols went the rounds at night inspecting the barracks, but it was all of no use. The men vanished from their beds in various ingenious ways. They put things on their mattresses and covered them up so skillfully that the patrols always thought the men were in bed asleep. They wanted to believe it too! Meanwhile the unfriendly civilians were robbed of their last potato, their last bushel of wheat, their last hens, and other things, which were then peddled in some nearby village. The men even sold their own coats, tent canvases, and shoes – just to get something to eat! I remember one night when I was on patrol duty and discovered a fire in a field not far from our village. When I arrived I found a group from my platoon standing there boiling something in a big bucket. They were not at all embarrassed. One of them stirred the bucket with a lath, and up floated two fat stolen geese, and they calmly invited us to eat with them, and there, at three o'clock in the morning, we had a wonderful breakfast: hot boiled goose and bread and beer.

When I went to report in the morning, the mayor of the village was already complaining to the captain that his two fattest geese had been stolen the night before. Yes, they were really nice and fat! I, however, as non-commissioned officer on duty, reported that I had inspected the barracks every hour and found everyone in his proper place. But I had seen suspicious civilians lurking about, I supposed they were natives, and I proceeded to give an accurate description of these thieves whom I had never seen.

My captain knew that I was lying, but was glad that I had at last given him an opportunity to call down this mayor of the neighboring village, who wanted to make his company of honorable soldiers responsible for every civilian vagabond and thief! In spite of all the friction in the Army itself between superiors and inferiors, there was yet a sort of solidarity against the "rabble of civilians."

The row came a few months later. I was ordered to report and was informed that I had been charged with a terrible crime. I had slandered Captain Czerny in an unofficial document addressed to the Ministry of War! I was shown a thick dossier, with my unofficial letter from jail addressed to the Ministry of War, which had now traveled the long official route from the Ministry of War to the division, from the division to the regiment, from the regiment to the battalion, from the battalion to my company. Every office had written an addition to it, and there it stood in black and white that as a result of my breach of discipline I was "politically untrustworthy," was not to be sent to the front, and would be summoned before a court-martial to be sentenced for my crime.

One day an order came for me to present myself before the court-martial in Maehrisch-Ostrau. There I went first to one of the officers of the court, a first lieutenant. He was a person of entirely unmilitary appearance, his uniform fitted him loosely, he had a melancholy expression and a quite unmilitary head of long gray hair. On his table was a calendar inscribed in large letters: "Man, fret not thyself, this too will pass!"

He told me that he had studied my dossier and it was his duty to inform me that I had the right to demand a sort of attorney for the defense. He was a lawyer in civilian life, and he spoke half officially, half privately, advising me.

"Your case," he said, "is not so bad. In the first place, you're an actor and have a certain right to have a temperament. In the second place, your escape from prison is a big thing in your favor, and if you provide yourself with counsel, he'll get you out of it!" He pointed to his motto on the table: "Man, fret not thyself, this too will pass!" and gave me a pleasant, intimate smile.

I thanked him for his advice and said: "I will not have an attorney! In the trenches I did my own shooting; I escaped from prison on my own; I shall be able to defend myself in my country on my own too."

"Very good," grinned the unmilitary military man, "just stick to that line when you speak, and I have no doubt of the outcome."

On the first day of the hearing I delivered a memorized speech with histrionic verve, giving a good place in it to the story of my escape. Judges and prosecutor listened tensely; I had a lot of fun out of it too – it was just like being on the stage! I felt that I was a leading man in real life!

When it was all over, I was sent back to my company. My speech started on its travels through the official channels, to be verified. After many weeks I was summoned again, and the same thing happened all over again.

Then our reserve battalion was sent back to its home town, Kolomea, in East Galicia.

East Galicia was now completely ruined by the war. Armies, had succeeded one another, the land was squeezed dry, the men were dead or in prison or crippled. The people were embittered, the Army without discipline. Everyone knew that the war was lost and that the end might come any day.

My eldest brother and his family were now living in Kolomea too. He had fled from our native village of Werbiwci before the Russians, and although the Austrians had long ago retaken it, he did not return there because his house and all his possessions had been destroyed. The Czarist Army had taught the Galician people the pogrom. Particularly in small towns and villages, they got the people drunk and plundered and destroyed Jewish homes. My brother, nevertheless, was homesick, and he asked me to go back with him to see whether he could establish himself there again. I got leave, and with my carbine we traveled to our birthplace, Werbiwci.

The road ran down a hill into the village, unpaved and full of ruts and holes, so that every wagon jolted and banged, and people always could recognize each wagon and its owner by the noise it made and would come slowly out of their huts, to call a greeting, to chat, and also to hear the latest news from town at the source. This was by way of being an old custom in the village of Werbiwci. But now, when the noise of our wagon announced our arrival to the village, not only did no one come out to meet us, but those who happened to be standing in their yards went silently back into their huts!

And when we drove up to the house, the house in which we were all born, which my father had built, the house was a corpse. It was like the sight of a being loved and near, lying dead and maimed before us! A ruin, with one wall standing and the windows in it all smashed. The thatched roof still leaned steeply against one wall, there was a confusion of shattered doors and benches, tables and pots, and all among them loose pages, torn from sacred books that my eldest brother had inherited from my father, who had inherited them from his father, and he from his. And a wild growth of weeds and nettles had already sprung up around everything.

No, no one came to meet us, and we sat as if paralyzed in our wagon before our desecrated home, where as children we had first seen the light of day. The house in which we had lisped our first words was now a maimed corpse!

Old Fedorkiw, our neighbor and our father's friend, came slowly and hesitantly toward us. First he gave our chestnut a friendly pat – the horse recognized him and politely whinnied an answer. Then he leaned on the wagon, put one foot on the front wheel, chewed thoughtfully at a straw, and simply helped us to be silent....Then he slowly raised his white head, wiped his weather-beaten cheeks and his kindly, moist eyes with the palm of his broad hand, and muttered angrily, as if in continuation of spoken thoughts, "That is how they thanked you – for your bread, for your salt, for your good hearts."

And chokingly, stammeringly, came my brother's words: "If they had at least burned it down! But no, they dragged it apart piece by piece, as if you were to tear the bones apart in a living body...."

Old Fedorkiw now took my brother's hand and said: "Oh, Schachne Eber, I say it is a disgrace, a disgrace to the village! And now they are ashamed too – and that is why they do not dare to greet you. But – let me tell you – it was a crazy night altogether. The Cossacks and a mob from other towns and villages came in drunk, drummed the village together, tied the innkeeper to his bed with ropes, then rolled every barrel, vodka and mead and beer, out onto the square and drank like animals. Even women and children got so drunk that they were sick for days. And, drunk like that, they simply carried everything off. Doors and walls, chests, tables, benches disappeared. When, days later, they sobered up, they were ashamed of their sin, and then, piece by piece, they brought everything back. For they understood and feared the accursedness of their deed."

His youngest son Nikola, my foster brother, who was serving in the same regiment as I and was on furlough too, now joined us. And we talked together, and they asked us into their house. As we crossed the yard we saw a pile of boards and beams lying there, and old Fedorkiw said: "My sons too, I am sorry to tell you, took part in it, but now they are collecting material and they want to help you to build again!"

Toward us now came the eldest son, Andry, who was growing gray-haired in his turn, and he said with embarrassed humor: "See here, Schachne Eber, we grew up together, we were always like Jacob and Esau, we betrayed each other and fought each other often enough, but we were brothers! But this was really too much. Yet what did you run away for, anyway?"

And as soon as we entered the sitting room he opened a bottle of vodka and poured us each a glass. Old Jusecha set on the table a big earthen pot of *piroggen* stuffed with *kasha* and potatoes and sour cream. And she was cooking hard-boiled eggs for my brother.

More and more neighbors came in. All sat around the big table and drank and smoked, and Andry said again, "See here, Schachne Eber, your ruined house is like a hole in the heart of the village. We are ready to help you build everything up again!"

Soon the room was full, and no one said anything more about what had happened – they were counting up how many boards and beams were on hand, and someone asked my brother if he would not like to have the new roof covered with tiles or shingles.

"No, no," said he, "I'd rather stick to thatch, the way my father built it."

And old Fedorkiw was glad and said, "I could have told you that. Schachne Eber is like a true believer, one of our own people. He doesn't want to imitate the landlord and the nobles and the townsfolk. He wants his roof to be just like his father's – God bless him! – and that is the way it should be."

The village elder, Vassili Bohacz, then said: "So Andry was right when he went to work and sowed Schachne Eber's field. He was sure that Schachne Eber would come back."

And Andry called out with a laugh: "Hi, you, brother out of the Holy Scriptures, I'd almost forgotten that – next fall you will have to help me sow my field and pay me back the seed. But it looks well this year, we shall have a good harvest!"

Then the others went home. My brother and I slept with Nikola and Andry in the barn and had another long talk about everything. The next morning we rode out into the field, and there stood the half-ripe grain like a huge, yellow-green brush, a joy to look at, and Andry said: "You can see there, the earth doesn't ask if it is giving bread for a Jew or for a Christian. It gives its gifts to whoever tills it."

Nikola and I laughed. "The two of them will soon be holding long pious conversations like our fathers," Nikola said.

"We're gray already," my brother joked, "it's time to begin."

Then we drove to Kolomea. Andry harnessed his two best horses to a big hay wagon. Nikola came with us, and we four men loaded my brother's goods and chattels on the two wagons, and, with his wife and children, my brother went back the same day to our native village of Werbiwci. "Home, home – there's where a welcome awaits you!"

38

A Man Is Not a Tree

It was the summer of 1918. Even before the collapse of the Austrian Army, soldiers began to go on "leave" and return either much later or not at all. Tired reserve officers, who likewise longed for home, were not so particular any more. As the Austrian "slovenliness" reached its height, a day came when the word went round, without creating any sensation: "It is over."

The men were drawn up in formation at the barracks once more, the colonel appeared, was going to make a speech, but seemed a little bewildered by the situation – and asked Captain Weigel, his adjutant, whom all the men of the battalion liked, to do it. Weigel made a few bitter jokes and sent the men home. It was like being at a funeral that suddenly turns funny. The only ones who looked pale and unhappy were the sergeants. They lost their long years of service, and they were also afraid of the men, whom they had tormented.

Anyone who could write now sat in the office and wrote passes. There was some attempt to stick to regulations, but the stamps lay around within reach, so that anyone could use them.

Slowly and with mixed feelings the men went their several ways. Part of the soldiers stayed on in the barracks, eating what was left in the storerooms and kitchens.

The subject upon which the greatest interest was concentrated was the battalion kitchen's dog, whose name was Czolowicze. Czolowicze means "man," and that was the name of a middle-sized dog of indeterminate breed who had gone to war with our battalion in 1914 and shared the fate of our troops.

"Man" had taken part in the snowy Carpathian campaign on his four paws, and later knew the burning sun of Italy, until one day he was shot in a front paw and lamed. In the end he hung around the kitchen and grew fat from good eating and little exercise, our "Man." Now and again an order would come through to shoot him – but the men always hid him and reported that he had been shot.

But now that everything was going to pieces and no one offered to take the dog with him, the men decided to give him the *coup de grace*, and thus spare him the slow death of a war cripple.

So what men remained assembled on Sunday morning: first they went to the fields and dug "Man" a grave, then they called him, and all accompanied him – a living creature – on his journey to eternal rest.

His best friend, the cook, was the only one who carried a rifle, and our four-footed comrade in arms seemed to understand it all and barked and howled the whole way. The cook made him sit down in the grave, took careful aim, and fired, and "Man" gave one more howl – it sounded like "Mama" in his dog language – and stood up once more on his hind paws, as tall as a real man, and fell over, and the body twitched a few times, and then the dog "Man," our comrade in arms, lay in his grave with closed eyes.

The grave was filled, and someone had brought a wooden tablet with an inscription: "Here lies 'Man,' dog of the Royal & Imperial Twenty-fourth Infantry Regiment. May the earth be light upon him."

The officers and men could by no means get home as fast as they wanted to, because Kolomea was now a stagnant railway junction. Trains from the east and the west met here. Routed armies and war prisoners clung to the cars like clusters of grapes. They stood in open cars, jammed full, and they sat on the roofs, pressed close together. Every day there were more dead soldiers to be buried, soldiers whose identity no one knew. The town overflowed with detachments of strange troops, who began plundering.

Soon we heard that forces under the command of a bandit general named Wrangel were starting pogroms in the vicinity. We organized a protective guard and maintained order in the town, which suddenly was without a government. The municipal council still functioned, Polish officials wanted to organize a Polish administration – but the majority of the population were Ukrainians and Jews.

Now it grew hot in Kolomea! Every day there were many meetings. Poles, Ukrainians, Jews, old and young politicians, talked and argued in the churches and synagogues, in the movie theaters – they all wanted the same things: work and bread! But work and bread were just what was not to be found in Kolomea!

Wild rumors of the Russian revolution and civil war reached us – we heard too that riots had broken out in Hungary and Germany. I went to the various meetings, was soon in a circle which wanted to make an alliance with Russia or Hungary, but it was all vague and indefinite.

The most successful of the orators was a young man in a black shirt who wore a full blond beard. He was an eternal student, who never finished studying, with long hair and a puckered-up, offended childish mouth. One day he spoke before the demobilized soldiers and the poor in an empty movie theater, which was narrow and overcrowded. It normally held only five or six hundred people, but now there were over two thousand in it.

He spoke with ardor and feeling, using many fine foreign words, and so carried the people with him that he could have made them do anything. He painted a sunny future and a beautiful world for us, and the high point of his speech was more or less as follows: "The time has arrived when the poor shall at last come out of their filthy back streets into the sun! The poor will now live in the good sections and the children of the poor eat white bread with butter. The rich have slept in their fine beds long enough! Now everything must be reversed."

The audience screamed and applauded rapturously, and a broad-shouldered porter, who was blind in one eye, shouted in a booming bass voice: "That's right, that's wonderful, what this noble man has just said! And now, you people, come on, let's move into our new houses! Why wait? First get the poor people into the fine houses! The rich can live in the back streets for a while, then we'll see what more's to be done!"

The noble orator with the well-kept beard turned white. He was frightened to death and began to soothe his audience: "No, no, no, that is not what I meant!"

The people were all shouting together; the chairman rang ceaselessly. Not a word could be understood in the uproar.

Finally the trembling, excited voice of the noble full beard was heard again. "Comrades! Friends!" he cried soothingly. "First there must be an organization, there must be directives! And tactics!"

And he shouted other strange words, which were swallowed up, for now the porter with the deep bass voice interrupted him again: "Where will we get them? They cost money too!"

Now another wild uproar.

"We haven't any money, and those who have won't hand it over!" Others shouted: "What are they exactly? Where can you buy them?"

"Buy!" screamed a woman hysterically. "You can't get flour or eggs or milk even *with* money!"

"Money isn't worth anything any more!" cried another voice, and at the same time someone yelled: "Who would sell what he has now – for bad money?"

The gathering was swaying back and forth like a ripe wheat field whipped by a stormy wind. I suddenly felt myself a part of the excitement, was carried along with it; suddenly I was up on a chair; I began shouting and yelling with the rest, and outshouted and outyelled them, and then words were pouring out of me. At first confusedly – some were still calling "Quiet!" People began to look at me. Soon I had the attention of the gathering, and I spoke about war, about prison, about Ludovico Merlo, about friendship, about those who had come home and those who had not come home, about "Man," the dog we had shot – and somewhere I recited Shylock's speech: "If you prick us, do we not bleed?…" I spoke about everything and about nothing, and I didn't know how to go on – but it hurt, and I spoke and cried and could not stop and thought about a conclusion, the end of an act, a curtain! And suddenly I cried, thinking of the pogroms: "And anyone who doesn't want his weak, suffering mother killed by Wrangel's bandits must get into the Protective Guard! And anyone who doesn't want his young sister dragged through the streets by the hair by murderers must get into the Protective Guard!"

A storm broke loose. Everyone shouted, and I was lifted into the air by the bystanders, and the meeting dispersed, and I was surrounded by faces I had never seen, and I was taken to a private house, to the home of Gisela Herrmann.

The drawing room was packed, among those present being the one-eyed porter. He was still raving about the full-bearded orator, whom he called a "bubble blower." In any case the transfer of the poor into the fashionable section had not taken place that day.

But now matters were quietly discussed in Gisela's house, and it was decided to send a deputation to the larger town of Stanislau, to find out what was being done there.

I went with the deputation, of which the broad-shouldered porter and Gisela were also members.

Gisela was a thin, careworn woman in her forties, but she looked older because she was always doing things for other people. She was a nurse. She never had any time for herself. She got up very early in the morning and was on the go all day. She was always overworked and worried constantly about the many sick people she took care of. Gisela had her own view of life and lived accordingly.

Now, traveling in our small compartment on the crawling, coughing train, she explained her point of view to me in her nervous, slightly stuttering manner of speech: "The m-m-main thing in life is responsibility. Take a m-m-match – is that useful? Should a man try, all by himself, to make a match? However many things he did, his life would be over before he had f-f-finished making it! Or a watch! A r-r-railroad! But all the people together make watches and railroads and matches, and everything we need! We depend upon one another and we m-m-must bear the responsibility for one another. Especially for weaker people and children! Ch-ch-children..." she stuttered excitedly. "Look, when a f-f-fool teacher hurts a child – there's a wound made that lasts all his life. When people of our own age hurt us, we get w-w-wounds too. So everyone is s-s-someone's teacher, and everyone is responsible for everyone. Until all live in accordance with that, there will be no b-b-better world! In the meantime I worry about children and animals. People laugh at me and call me c-c-cat-mother. But what am I to do, I can't sleep when I hear a hungry dog howling or a frozen cat m-m-mewing on a winter night. Yes, b-b-but, above all, children – just to look at children, your own or s-s-someone else's, it's all the same – makes you happy! Not to mention that one knows pretty well what grownups are – l-l-look at me! But a child can still become anything! Who knows, perhaps a sage, a s-s-s-scholar, make some new discovery – something that we can't even imagine! Just look into a child's eyes – they're full of s-s-secrets, children are! How stupid that one has to talk about it at all – how stupid!"

Arrived in Stanislau, we were amazed at how much more these people knew, when it was only three hours' journey from home. We had the addresses of various workers; soon we were in a private house, where people from the whole district had gathered, some from a great distance, even from Lemberg and Przemysl. Among them I recognized my old friend Shimele Ruskin, the baker – who still could neither read nor write but who was the soul of the meeting nevertheless. He saw to it that the people from different districts should first tell how things were going in their districts – later, the general decisions could be made.

A delegate from the Russian border reported that, on the other side, the estates of the landlords had first been divided among the poor peasants, then suddenly the bands of a General Wrangel and one Petjlura appeared and began blood baths, particularly among the Jewish population.

A delegate from Lemberg had even brought Berlin and Vienna newspapers which told of civil war in those places.

Another reported that there was a real revolution in Hungary and that we were right in the middle, between the Russian civil war and the uprisings in the west.

Right in the middle! And that if we did not make an alliance with the revolutionary forces in Russia or in Hungary, we in this section would be ground to bits between the Wrangel-Petjlura bands and the Poles who had just shaken off the Czarist yoke. Because both were already fighting for Galicia.

The prime thing was to let no soldier throw away his rifle – on the contrary, we must all arm ourselves, so that we should not be defenseless.

Many, many things we learned in those two days and two nights. But just what to do, no one knew. Only one thing was clear: we must hang on to our rifles, so that we could stand up for our bare lives; for the terror of the Wrangel-Petjlura bands was already notorious in the vicinity.

To me personally, something else was clear: that in this homeland, which I had left of my own free will so many years before – even were it orderly and peaceful, here I could not live! The home of my choice was the theater, the theater in

Berlin. And I must really go home! Had I not a calling, for the sake of which I had gone through an operation on my legs? For the sake of which I had escaped from imprisonment! I must go back to the theater, I must fight my way home!

When the conference was over, I went out into the street – it was Stanislau! Stanislau, where I had worked in the bakery as a little boy and been beaten, where we had lost our first strike, and where, homeless and jobless, I had wandered through winter nights, but where, too, I had had my first wife, Malka, in Zosina Wolja Alley.

While I thought of all these things, I found myself in the same neighborhood, and asked in the same houses for Malka. Yes, she was still there, she still lived in the same alley, in the old shoemaker Borella's house.

I loosened the heel of one of my boots with my bayonet and stepped into the shoemaker's to have it nailed on again. We were soon talking, and I asked him if I might speak to his wife.

"Of course, stranger. Malka!" he called into the small adjoining kitchen. "A soldier wants to speak to you."

And then she came, my first wife, who had always looked so smart with her three-story red hair-do. Was it really she? A small, plump, frowzy figure with neglected, uncombed hair, ashy gray now instead of red, came in. A pair of dull, sickly eyes blinked in her furrowed, flabby face. Old rags hung on a shapeless body with a small pot belly.

She did not recognize me. I asked if I might speak to her, and she followed me indifferently. We walked a few steps. Not far from the house was a bench under a chestnut tree, and she sank down on it with a tired sigh. My heart was pounding, and I could not open my mouth.

"Well, soldier," she said softly, as if she were talking to herself, "which shall it be? Dark, blond, fat, thin – and, first of all, how much do you want to spend?"

So she was still in the business! "Malka, don't you recognize me?"

"Don't try to be funny, soldier – I've known many, but not you."

"But I'm Saschka – Saschka who used to write letters to your Sonjutschka for you."

First she was silent, then she said thoughtfully, "Oh, Saschka," and she raised her sickly eyes and looked at me for the first time, wiped her hand on her apron and held it out to me. "Saschenka, of course, that's who you are. You used to write beautiful letters to my Sonjutschka. Yes, and you used to read to me from such fine books about fine people." And she eyed me with the half-quenched remnants of a coquettish look. "God, you were so little and puny. And now you're a big fellow, you've grown up into a real man!"

Then she was silent for a while, and, now all the proud mother, quite transformed, she went on: "But you ought to see Sonjutschka now. She's working at the Seyboldts' – rich people. She is quick and buxom, and so pretty that you can't look in her face, just like the sun! And she's big and full-breasted and innocent. A virtuous girl, thank God! Not like her sinful mother!" And she blew her nose on her apron. "Saschenka, perhaps – perhaps you two would marry? As sure as I live, you would make a wonderful couple! She has always asked me who used to write those beautiful letters for me – come on Sunday afternoon, she's free then, come and get to know each other, will you?"

"Yes, I'll try to come," I murmured.

"Listen," she said, aware of my embarrassment, "back when you had no work and I took you in, I used to think, I have Sonjutschka and you – two children – perhaps it will come true, and you will both be my children – be sure and come on Sunday afternoon!"

And I took leave, and promised again to come, and went – just as I had gone those many years ago – to disappoint her for the second time. So ended my third welcome home.

I hastily rejoined the deputation, and the same afternoon we were back in Kolomea.

Sitting alone with Gisela in a corner of a compartment, I told her about my three welcome homes: the first, when I encountered Czerny; the second when I went to the village with my brother; and now Malka's.

Gisele said: "You are really not at home in your own c-c-country any longer."

"No, no – in Werbiwci I am at home, there I feel my roots!"

"Oh, r-r-roots!" stuttered Gisela warmly. "A man is not a tree. A man moves around and grows into other s-s-surroundings. Where he works, where he creates, where he loves – there he s-s-strikes root! There he blooms, there he bears f-f-f-fruit – there he's at home. You must go back where you belong, where you are drawn. R-r-roots! No, no, no, a man is not a tree!"

Then we both remained silent until we had reached Kolomea.

39

Interrupted Rehearsals

In Kolomea a great change came now. Over the barracks, the county offices, and the town hall, Ukrainian flags flew. Suddenly there was a Ukrainian Government.

The commandant of the town was a fellow veteran from my regiment, Tymczuk. We were both in the officer candidates' detachment and used to give entertainments together. Tymczuk, who had a fine voice, used to sing Ukrainian folk songs and was something of an actor. We had always liked each other and were friends.

I went to him, and he offered to help me in every way. In his opinion there were only two things I could do: either enter the Ukrainian Army or hurry west, back to Berlin. I decided upon the second!

He went on speaking about the Ukrainian Government, about the liberation of his people, about Hetman Petjlura and General Wrangel. Those names were symbols for us both! He considered them the liberators of his people, I the murderers of mine! But as fellow veterans we spoke politely to each other, and he gave me a piece of paper with an official stamp and his signature – it was half a birth certificate, half a pass to leave Kolomea.

I next took leave of Gisela and her circle. The following day she took me to the station, and I listened gladly while she spoke – warm human being that she was, living only for others. Her last words in the waiting room sounded like a testament:

"Politics is a specialty, if you 1-1-like – a science. An economic science, for the problems of daily living. One has to study it, dedicate his whole 1-1-life to it, love it, as you love the theater. P-p-politics is weekdays, art is holidays. Politics looks after the body, art after the soul. What can you say in a meeting? Wh-wh-what can anyone think of in such excitement? But as an actor you have all the thoughts and the feelings that the p-poets and artists of all countries have ever thought and dreamed! Look at me: I have been in the s-s-socialist movement for twenty years – but I don't know the first thing about it – in reality I am only a nurse, a person who wants to h-h-help those who are still more helpless than myself. And in our world there is no one so poor that there isn't s-s-someone still poorer!"

"Gisela," said I, "I want to live not only for myself, I want to help too!"

"I b-b-believe that – and so you shall – but you can help in your way. L-l-look, if you become a good actor, you will help your people that way too. Because then people will say" – she teased me half in jest, half in earnest – "people will say: 'Look at that Hamlet, that Shylock, that M-m-mephisto – why, he comes from miserably poor Galician Jews.' And, believe me, after that people will think of your people with more respect, with more esteem. Isn't that a help? For that reason everyone m-m-must do what he can do best."

And then she went with me to the crowded train, and I squeezed my head out the window, and there was a puffing and a whistling, and two things rolled: the train into the west, and the tears down my cheeks.

We were overloaded with men returning home: Austrian and German officers and soldiers. We even had our own fireman and engineer.

We felt as though we were on an unseaworthy ship that has to cross the ocean; and in fact soon after Stanislau, halfway to Stryj, we were stopped by a Polish patrol, searched, and allowed to proceed only after several hours.

But outside Stryj we were stuck again. There was a battle on for the station. We rolled onto a siding, took shelter under the cars, and the next day there was a Ukrainian patrol in the station. But there was still firing in the vicinity, so we remained definitely stuck.

We could now go neither backward nor forward, and we decided to leave the train long enough to go into the town. Soon the Ukrainians were gone too – not a soldier was to be seen, but stray bullets whistled in all directions. For the battle seemed to be going on one or two kilometers from the station.

On the tracks stood derelict freight cars loaded with flour and sugar and fruit and petroleum. People from our train and from the town simply took what they could carry or drag; some rolled along barrels of petroleum, others dragged sacks of fruit, flour, or sugar. I decided to take a sack of flour on my shoulders, and hours later I came stumbling and sweating into the town.

In front of a house a woman with grown children was standing, and we soon agreed that, in return for the flour, I might live there until the train could go on. I was given a small room, and the same day – to the joy of the family – I baked bread. Stryj was as hungry as Kolomea. The household enjoyed the bread, and their neighbors envied them the wonderful luck that had come to them when I took up my quarters there.

In the town the next day I encountered the beautiful orator with the blond beard from Kolomea. He was wearing an expensive fur coat, and he told me that he too had got stuck here with a load of petroleum from Drohobycz, which he was to deliver in newly created Czechoslovakia. He was now dealing in petroleum instead of in revolutions.

"People take everything so seriously at meetings nowadays," he said. "Before the war you could say anything and promise anything, but now they want to have it right away.

Like that one-eyed porter in Kolomea, who wanted to move the poor streets right into the rich ones. No, no – it's much better to be in petroleum."

The Poles and Ukrainians continued to fight for the station, for Stryj, for Galicia – the men on their way home. And the Jews were in the middle. The Galician Jews, who had lived peacefully until now, suddenly sensed that they had lost the war along with Austria. The two armies, Polish and Ukrainian, had the same slogan: Down with the Jews!

After some weeks a regiment of Poles from Posen, outfitted with German equipment, appeared and overran the town. Our officers went to the commandant at the railway station and were given permission to start our train, and, with some short halts, we arrived in Vienna a week later.

Vienna presented the same picture – the same disorder, the same insecurity, only on a bigger scale. Demonstrations, meetings, shooting. The city was hungry. There was every evidence that Austria was in decay.

I went to a demobilization board, where soldiers from the front were given advice and assistance. There they explained to me that I was no longer an Austrian.

"But I fought four years for Austria," I answered.

"Yes," said the official, "I'm sorry, extremely sorry, it was a mistake."

"I have decorations, I escaped from prison!"

"I'm very sorry, you made a mistake!"

"And if I had died your hero's death?" I asked him.

"I'm very sorry, that would have been a mistake too."

"Well, thank God I at least didn't make that mistake," I shouted in his face and went to the brand new consulate of the Ukrainian Government.

They gave me a passport, but no financial assistance.

Then I saw placards: "Moissi, guest star at the Neue Wiener Buehne." I simply went there. Rehearsals had begun, and the great Moissi did not ask me if I was still an Austrian or a Pole, a Ukrainian or a Jew, he asked for neither identification papers nor passports – he greeted me warmly and affectionately, as a young brother who had survived the war. He introduced the manager of the theater to me, I was hired for the period of Moissi's engagement, and had something to eat again and a place to sleep and felt at home in the theater. As Speigelberg in *Die Raeuber* to Moissi's Franz Moor, I was mentioned by the Viennese critics. But my great experience there was something else entirely.

I saw a small, boyish, fragile girl play Ophelia in *Hamlet* for the first time. It was impossible to determine what was the dominant note of her appearance: a head of reddish-brown hair, wild, tousled, but with it a clear, high, arching forehead – the forehead of a thinker – which revealed a profound quiet. Then two large eyes, warm, dark brown, foreboding, questioning, and eloquent. Those eyes understand the most unspoken suggestions. Then a firm, small, semicircular mouth, like a half moon. A half-moon mouth; when it opens, puckering a little, there is no sound for a long time – your eyes hang on it in suspense, you listen intently. Then her eyes speak something – then comes a hesitant gesture of her hand, restrained, from the shoulder, then slowly from the half-moon mouth words are born. Darkly colored, ripe words! And the words are immutable, fixed! Then again there is a happy gleam, a light in those strangely ambiguous eyes, a light that is a blend of frivolity and seriousness, between hymn of praise and song of rejoicing. Like the thankful prayer of a pious soul after a recovery, after a miraculous experience. That little girl reminded me of Riffkele, my first love. But from an entirely different world! A world which was my goal, but in which she was already at home!

In the mad scene this child Ophelia comes softly and sweetly on stage, smiling to herself, and her great eyes are full of tears. In her left arm she holds, carefully as a child, a sheaf of bright wild flowers which she shyly gives away with her right hand. But in reality she has neither sheaf nor flowers – her empty hand, from the no-sheaf in her empty arm, gives away her no-flowers. But never in the world have there been flowers so bright and gay and fragrant! Spectators and actors are breathless in the presence of this sweet madness, of this poetic Shakespearean child, of this novice, Elisabeth Bergner.

When the engagement was over, I bought a ticket and returned to Berlin.

In the station I threw my arms around a pillar and kissed it, holding it in a long embrace. A fat Berlin beer-wagon driver looked down at me over his horses and said: "Man, it's girls you should kiss, not stones!"

"I promised myself that in 1914 when I went off!"

"Well, then, you must keep your word," he growled amiably.

In 1914! It was 1919 now!

I was soon in my old Café des Westens, found friends, went around auditioning, and soon had an offer from the Schauspielhaus in Munich. Hermine Koerner, the great actress, was organizing a company of her own there, and engaged me as leading character actor. We opened with Schiller's *Intrigue and Love* – I played Wurm. Earned eight hundred marks a month. On our first bi-monthly payday, I had four hundred marks in my pocket, four hundred marks earned on the stage!

I went to a restaurant and bought myself caviar and champagne, just as I had read in novels. Now I had a room of my own again, new friends, and every two weeks I played a different classic or modern leading part.

The years that the war had taken from me were not lost: I was stronger, more mature now, but not quieter! I could not be quiet. I cried out and shouted bloody murder together with the whole young generation who had come home. We found ourselves in a world that was fat and cowardly and wanted to be left in peace. We cried out our disillusionment, our despair, our protest in its face. Youth cried out in art. With stiff, stylized gestures, we in the theater cried out expressionistically against the older generation, against the old teachings, against the old traditions, against old customs, but especially against fathers! Hundreds of father-and-son dramas were produced. Reinhard Sorge's *The Beggar*, Toller's *The Transformation*, Hasenclever's *The Son*, Feuchtwanger's *Thomas Wendt*, George Kaiser's *Gas*, Bert Brecht's *Drums in the Night*. Hundreds of plays accused and cried out and raved, and I cried out and raved with them. I could make good use of my experiences in my work.

I threw myself into my work ravenously and never even noticed that I was living in a country that had lost a war and had bloodily repressed a revolution. My life had been spared, I had found my life. Every night I stood on the stage in another role. I was intoxicated with happiness.

I got to know new circles, new people, there was a gay young set in Schwabing, studio parties at a different place every night. There was Kati Kobus's *Simplizissimus*. The young generation that had returned home disillusioned was sowing its wild oats in sexual orgies.

And one day there was great excitement at the theater: the parts for *The Merchant of Venice* were assigned, and I was given Shylock! Four older character actors were fighting for the role! But I had Shylock in my contract. I had him in my contract, I had him under my belt, I had him in my heart, I had him at my fingertips! I trembled with excitement, I could not sleep. A dream, the longing of years, was to be fulfilled! The day of the first rehearsal came. I was shaking inside like an earthquake.

The director was a young, flaxen-haired, stupid man, a Herr Nebeltau from Bremen, the son of a rich father. He financed the company and was business manager. Before rehearsal he took me aside and said to me, word for word: "You understand, with this play we want to take a poke at the Jews!"

"Why?" said I, angrily.

"Why not?" and he looked at me suspiciously. "You aren't by any chance – "

"Yes, yes, yes, I am a Jew," I shouted in his face, so that he stumbled back and almost fell into the orchestra pit.

The four old character actors who were trying to get the part, one with a monocle, one in white gloves, suddenly woke up and laughed provocatively, delighted at the explosion. I hurried away, and the first rehearsal blew up.

Hermine Koerner, the artistic director of the theater, had me come to the office at once, and Herr Nebeltau was also present. Hermine Koerner was a great actress; I honored her, and my heart always thumped when I was in her presence. She knew it, and now she said, smiling and full of charm:

"Well, it was wonderful, the way you thought that up – of course you only made a scene for the sake of the superstition."

"Of course, Hermine," Herr Nebeltau bore her out.

"I do just the same thing before an important part, don't I, Otto?"

"Just exactly," Herr Nebeltau agreed, and they both laughed.

"When I like a part very much, there has to be a row at the first reading rehearsal and the first dress rehearsal."

"Yes, yes, reading and dress rehearsal," confirmed Herr Nebeltau, laughing, and I laughed too, without knowing what for.

"And of course what Herr Nebeltau said earlier today was said only as a joke, wasn't it, Otto?" she now asked the flaxen-blond directly.

"Yes, of course, Hermine," he agreed.

"How could you think such a thing of him!" she turned to me. "He is far too intelligent for that! So, children, shake hands! And tomorrow rehearsals will begin again. And I shall be present myself!"

And so it came to pass.

40

Shylock

At seventeen, I lay on the ground and became acquainted with Shylock in Karl Emil Franzus's novel. I lay there and wept over the injustice that was meted out to him. I was determined to put my whole life into gaining the ability one day to fling that injustice into the world's face. I was now twenty-nine, and again I lay on the ground, with the fulfillment of my task just before me.

For twelve years I had been absorbed in Shylock, and still I could not wholly understand him. I compared him with my father, I compared him with Shimshale from Milnitz, but could find no great resemblance. Perhaps he resembled Jungermann, the banker – but Jungermann I did not know so well.

The play itself I had often read and often seen, and it was always two plays: First, there is that gay, careless circle around the rich Antonio, whose heavily laden ships sail all the seas. There is the wild Gratiano, who chatters gaily and goes on audacious adventures. There is that elegant coxcomb Bassanio, who is set on marrying the richest girl in Belmont and borrows money any and everywhere to put up a fine front and swindle a marriage. There is the singing and dancing Lorenzo, who steals the girl along with her father's money. To the strains of sensuous and seductive music and under an eternally blue sky, there are balls and masquerades, all at the expense of Antonio, the rich man, the melancholic youth who is so glad to be amused by these boon companions. Later Portia's world comes in too, but it is still the same.

On the other side lives the Jew Shylock, in a narrow ghetto alley. He is a foreigner in the city, there are laws against him, he wears a yellow patch, the symbol that he has not the same rights before the law as the others. He lives alone, with no festivities, no society, no great expenditure; he lives his creed, his business, and for his little, delicate daughter Jessica, whom he loves more than all else, because she is all that is left to him of his beloved wife, his Lea. He loved her very much, his Lea, for since her death many, many years have passed and he has not married again. He lives with the memory of his beloved and the thought of his child.

Then, one day, the other world appears at his house, the world that despises him, spits on him, persecutes him. They come and want to borrow money from him! Instead of saying yes or no, he says both. He is pleased that his enemies need him, and he proposes a weighty, jesting contract: that, if his enemy, who only last Wednesday spat in his face, who had spurned him from his doorstep like a strange dog – that if this enemy cannot pay back the specified sum he wishes to borrow at the specified time and at the specified place – a jest – he will then have the right to cut a pound of flesh from his body, in whatever spot he may please! An utterly insane bond! An audacious, impudent bond! A grotesque bond, which can only be taken as a devilish joke.

So at least we understand the poet's intention. The play is a comedy, a merry game of love. The fun is in the fact that at first obstacles are put in the lovers' way – first they are threatened with great perils, first their life is made bitter and sour, in order that they may overcome the perils, the obstacles, by the sweat of their brows, so that, at the end, the song of love may sound even more sweetly, even more intimately, even more happily. Then everything becomes like a midsummer night's dream! Then everything is as you like it!

Therefore, in this gay game, in this comedy of Venice, a black figure is needed, to frighten the lovers, to threaten them, so that the denouement in Act V, beginning with the poetic "The moon shines bright: in such a night as this..." may be resolved in the giving of the rings and a happy going to bed! Yes! Shylock was only a black obstacle, planned by the poet, a black fool, a wicked fellow, to be made a goat of at last.

But, but, but...and here the world stops in wonder! If that was the plan, how does it happen that Shylock's defense becomes an accusation?

> *"If you prick us, do we not bleed?*
> *If you tickle us, do we not laugh?*
> *If you poison us, do we not die?*
> *And if you wrong us, shall we not revenge?"*

The answer must be a perfectly simple one. God and Shakespeare did not create beings of paper, they gave them flesh and blood! Even if the poet did not know Shylock and did not like him, the justice of his genius took the part of his black obstacle and, out of its prodigal and endless wealth, gave Shylock human greatness and spiritual strength and a great loneliness – things that turn Antonio's gay, singing, sponging, money-borrowing, girl-stealing, marriage-contriving circle into petty idlers and sneak thieves.

I now knew how Shylock, by the whim of his Creator, entered that circle. But I must also know what happens to him after the curtain goes down, when the play is over. What does our Shylock do when, swindled out of his rights by the trick about not shedding one drop of blood, when, a broken man, he leaves the courtroom, when he whispers his last words: "Send the deed after me, and I will sign it"? Will he sign it? Can he? Perhaps he can sign away all his property.

But can a Shylock also sign a deed by which he renounces his faith and accepts another? Can you change your faith, your point of view, as you change your shirt? Would my father have done that? Or Schimshale from Milnitz? No, no, no! They would rather have died a thousand deaths. Neither a believer nor a man of character can change his faith, his point of view! When a man is sixty years old, like Shylock, his view of life does not change. It remains the same until his life comes to an end! To that he clings, to that he holds, or he dies of emptiness and loneliness. Never can a Shylock change his faith, the man who sobbed out in the courtroom:

> *"Nay, take my life and all; pardon not that:*
> *You take my house when you do take the prop*
> *That doth sustain my house; you take my life*
> *When you do take the means whereby I live."*

For that, he is first mocked, and then the "noble" people divide his property among them before his face; and for that "mercy" he is to forsake his old faith besides, his only traditional and moral strength! No, no, no! *That* my Shylock will not do! A man of his intelligence and strength fights to the last breath with every weapon – especially with craft. I see it like this:

When Shylock, a broken man, leaves the unjust court of justice, it is already evening. He walks slowly at first. But when he sees that no one is following him, he hurries, rouses his friend Tubal and the other fellow believers who live with him in the ghetto, and complains to them of the new danger which threatens them. For, though they lived in the ghetto, though they were persecuted and oppressed, the All-Highest was not touched. And since Shylock owned no houses and land, only easily transportable goods, money and jewels, he puts it all in his bag and charters a boat that same night and runs away, and he makes a successful escape.

Then one day he arrives in Holland, in the rich city of Amsterdam, which is already full of refugees from the Spanish Inquisition. There he decides to wander still farther, into the East! He wanders for a long time and travels through the lands of the Hungarians and the Rumanians, the Poles and the Russians. He wanders through those countries until one day in East Galicia, in the Ukraine, he finds a wise old wonder rabbi, the wisest in all the country round. To him he goes to bemoan his sorrow and to ask for counsel.

The lean old man is tall and ancient, he has a long yellow-white beard, and bushy brows shadow his knowing eyes. And his fame has spread far over the earth, and it is unbecoming to talk about his age – the thought of the years he has lived makes men tremble.

He sits there in his high ancestral chair, like an incarnation of human dignity. He smiles at our Shylock hospitably. The old man's goodness and understanding trust unlock Shylock's tongue and his heart, and he begins to tell his story. He tells of his father's house, his youth, his schooling, his wanderings, until he had met Lea. How he loved her, his Lea, and how she had given him Jessica and died, and how he had lived with her memory, embodied in his daughter, and how then his own child had betrayed him, and how in his old age he had had to take up the wanderer's staff again. He tells everything; he talks for many days and many nights, until his heart grows warm and light. Meanwhile the sage encourages him with questions and hears him attentively.

And when he has finished speaking, friendly comprehension and trust smile at him from the old man's face, and the old man speaks softly and warmly: "It is well, my son, that you have come to us, for after such sorry experiences a man must change his habitation, because that changes his luck as well. It is well that you have come to us. Here we live among a friendly people, and here we may not only engage in business, we can follow trades too and till the soil. And that does us good, and we live according to our old laws. Had you asked a wise man in the lands from which you have come, he would likewise have advised you to come here, for it is written: '*Meschane mokim, meschane mazl* [Change your dwelling and you change your luck].' Now," the old man sighs with a smile, "the Eternal be praised – you are here!"

And Shylock feels wholly eased, but he is embarrassed by gratitude, and the old man goes on: "And now I wish to give you some advice: that is, you must marry again, you are still vigorous, and I know that the Lord will bless you with children."

"Rabbi," Shylock almost stutters, "I wanted to ask your counsel about that very thing!"

"Yes, my son," nods the sage, "take a daughter of the people, a healthy girl, a tradesman's child," and both men now smile understandingly, and Shylock rises and takes his leave respectfully, a thankful and redeemed man.

Then Shylock married the daughter of a carpenter there in the Ukraine, and the Lord made his marriage fruitful and blessed it with children. The children grew up on that black and juicy earth and tilled it, and they sowed and harvested and saw the four seasons come and go and heard no more that light, seductive music under the eternally blue skies of the South. Their Hebrew melodies were mingled with the long-drawn-out, melancholy songs of the Slavs, and they grew up, the children, broad-shouldered, industrious, and inquisitive....

Then many, many generations went by, and one or another of their descendants would often feel a longing for the West again and would set forth on his wanderings. There they chose new professions; many became actors and found their original ancestor, Shylock, in Shakespeare again. They had heard the story of his sorrows from their parents and grandparents and recognized him in their kindred hearts. And they acted that ancestor tragically and one-sidedly, fortified by the genius of Shakespeare, which had given a black, negative figure so much strength, so much life, such a sense of justice, such human dignity. They acted him against the evil society that spits on him and persecutes him, and for the positive qualities that his Creator had bestowed on him.

And thus must he be acted, until all artificial distinctions fall from us, and man recognizes his brother in his fellow man and loves him, his neighbor, as himself, and does not do to him what he would not want done to himself.

With these feelings I played the part I had longed to play, Shylock, and my tremulous dream was fulfilled. It was not yet as I wanted it to be – but with the years it will grow better.

* * *

Timeline

1893 Born in Werbowitz, Austro-Hungarian Galicia
1906 Runs away from home; works as journeyman baker
1909 Comes to Berlin via Vienna in pursuit of acting career
1911 Enters the Max Reinhardt drama school in Berlin
1912 Undergoes high-risk operation to straighten legs
1914 Marries Martha Guttmann
Drafted into Austro-Hungarian army for WWI
1915 Birth of son Gerhard (later "Gad") Granach
1916 Sent to Italian front; captured and interned in war prison
1917 Escapes from prison camp over the Alps into Switzerland; assigned to reserve batallion until war's end
1919 Returns to Berlin to resume career
1920 First portrays Shylock in *The Merchant of Venice*. End of memoir period. In 56 stage and 25 film roles from 1920–33
1921 Role in F. W. Murnau's silent horror classic *Nosferatu*
1931 Role in G.W. Pabst's *Kameradschaft*. First visit to US
1933 Flees Germany for Switzerland as Gestapo pursues him
1934 Performs in Yiddish theater companies in Poland
1935 Seeks refuge in Russia; works in film and theater in Kiev
1936 Son escapes Nazi Germany for Palestine with his assistance
1937 Caught in Stalin's purges and imprisoned in Russia; Lion Feuchtwanger intervenes for his release
1938 Emigrates to the US; resides first in New York City then Santa Monica, California, starting Hollywood career
1939 Role in MGM's *Ninotchka* with Greta Garbo
1943 Roles in *For Whom the Bell Tolls* with Ingrid Bergman and Gary Cooper, and in Fritz Lang's *Hangmen Also Die!*
1944 Roles in *The Hitler Gang* and *The Seventh Cross*; appears in a total of 20 Hollywood films from 1939–44
1945 On Broadway in *A Bell for Adano*; suffers appendicitis attack during its run; dies in New York hospital from post-surgery embolism on March 13th; memoir published 6 weeks later

A NOTE ON THE TRANSLATOR

Alexander Granach's memoir was translated from the German by Willard Ropes Trask, who undertook rendering such influential works as the memoirs of Giacomo Casanova – a notable twelve volumes worth – and works by Pushkin, Thomas Mann, José Ortega y Gasset, Émile Zola, and Johann Wolfgang von Goethe, as well as compiling a translation of Joan of Arc in her own words. Trask was Ford Madox Ford's personal secretary, an independent scholar, and a recipient of the National Book Award.

Further Readings & Resources

Akademie der Künste. 1971. *Alexander Granach und das Jiddische Theater des Ostens.* Berlin: Akademie der Künste.

Granach, Alexander; Angelika Wittlich & Hilde Recher (eds.). 2008. *Du Mein Liebes Stück Heimat: Briefe an Lotte Lieven aus dem Exil.* Ausburg: Ölbaum Verlag.

Granach, Gad. 2009. *Where Is Home? Stories from the Life of a German-Jewish Émigré.* Trans. David E. Lane. Los Angeles: Atara Press.

Hay, Julius. 1975. *Born 1900: Memoirs.* Trans. & abridged by J.A. Underwood. La Salle, IL: Open Court Press.

Klein, Albert & Raya Kruk. 1994. *Alexander Granach: Fast verwehte Spuren.* Berlin: Edition Hentrich.

Lewis, Herbert S. 2010. "Introduction" to *From the Shtetl to the Stage: The Odyssey of a Wandering Actor.* (Retitled edition of Alexander Granach's memoir, *There Goes an Actor.*). New Brunswick: Transaction Publishers.

Patterson, Michael. 1981. *The Revolution in German Theatre, 1900–1933.* London: Routledge.

Schmidt, Michael. 1999. "The Shtetl's Curiosity and Style: Alexander Granach's Autobiographical Novel Da geht ein Mensch." In Anne Fuchs & Florian Krobb (eds.) *Ghetto Writing: Traditional and Eastern Jewry in German-Jewish Literature from Heine to Hilsenrath.* Columbia, SC: Camden House.

Shahar, Galili. 2004. "The Jewish Actor and the Theatre of Modernism in Germany." Theatre Research International 29: 1–16.

Willett, John. 1988. *The Theatre of the Weimar Republic.* New York: Holmes & Meier.

Wittlich, Angelika (director). 2012. *Alexander Granach: Da geht ein Mensch* (documentary film). Munich: Zorro Film.

Zer-Zion, Shelly. 2010. "The Shaping of the Ostjude: Alexander Granach and Shimon Finkel in Berlin." In Jeanette R. Malkin & Freddie Rokem (eds.) *Jews and the Making of Modern German Theatre.* Iowa City: University of Iowa Press.

GAD GRANACH
Where Is Home?
Stories from the Life of
a German-Jewish Émigré

atarapress.com
In paperback and ebook editions

"A charismatic witness to the Berlin of the 1930s, Israel during its kibbutz years, and present-day Jerusalem."
– Der Taggespiegel

"Did you come here out of personal conviction or are you from Germany?" was a question German Jews were asked when they arrived in Palestine in 1933. Few came out of conviction. A majority of the 60,000 German Jews who took refuge in the then-British mandate came because they had no other option. Palestine was not the land of their dreams, but rather a place of asylum where one would have to start life anew. Doctors became bus drivers, lawyers raised chickens, and artists worked as waiters. For the young, however, immigration to Palestine was a great adventure, the beginning of a new life free from old conventions, and sometimes the beginning as well of a life or death battle.

Gad Granach still went by Gerhard when he arrived at Haifa Harbor in 1936 at the age of twenty-one. The son of a famous actor, he encountered a land of neither milk nor honey, and lived through five major wars and a number of smaller ones, wishing all the while that God would "choose" another people and leave the Jews in peace.

"Granach is highly entertaining and thought provoking. A supreme raconteur." – Sueddeutsche Zeitung

"An absolute must-read!" – Radio Bayern

atara press

www.ingramcontent.com/pod-product-compliance
Lightning Source LLC
Chambersburg PA
CBHW021133230426
43667CB00005B/104